Papua [New Guinea]
a travel survival kit

Papua New Guinea — a travel survival kit

Published by:
Lonely Planet Publications
PO Box 88, South Yarra
Victoria 3141, Australia

Printed by:
Colorcraft, Hong Kong

Typeset by:
Lonely Planet Productions

Illustrations by:
Peter Campbell

Photographs by:
Tony Wheeler

Designed by:
Pru Borthwick & Mary Miklos

First Published:
April 1979

Published in Papua New Guinea by:
Robert Brown & Associates
PO Box 3395, Port Moresby

National Library of Australia
Cataloguing in Publications data
Wheeler, Anthony Ian
Papua New Guinea, a travel survival kit.

ISBN 0 908086 05 9
ISBN 0 908084 6 7

1. Papua New Guinea — Description and travel —
Guide-books. I. Title.

919.5

DISTRIBUTION

Ask your local bookshop to order Lonely Planet guides from one of the distributors listed below. If you have any trouble write to us directly in Australia — we'll rush copies to you as fast as the mail can carry them.

Canada — Dominie Press, 55 Nugget Avenue, Unit J, Agincourt, Ontario — **Hong Kong** — Hong Kong University Press, 94 Bonham Road, Hong Kong — **India** — New Book Depot, Connaught Place, New Delhi — UBS Distributors, 5 Ansari Road, New Delhi — Karachi Stationery Mart, 46 Janpath, New Delhi — **Japan** — Intercontinental Marketing Corporation, IPO Box 5056, Tokyo 100-31 — **Korea** — Pan Korea Book Corporation, PO Box 101, Kwangwhamun, Seoul — **Malaysia** — see Singapore — **Nepal** — see India — **Netherlands** — Nilsonn & Lamm bv, Pampuslaan 212, Weesp, Postbus 195 — **New Zealand** — Caveman Press, Box 1458, Dunedin — **Papua New Guinea** — Robert Brown & Associates, Box 3395, Port Moresby — **Philippines** — see Singapore — **Singapore** — Apa Productions, Suite 1021, International Plaza, Anson Road, Singapore 2 — **Thailand** — Chalermnit Bookshop, 1-2 Erawan Arcade, Bangkok — **UK** — Roger Lascelles, 16 Holland Park Gardens, London W14 8DY — **USA** — some titles are available from: Bookpeople, 2940 Seventh Street, Berkeley, CA 94710 — if they haven't got the books you want write to us for details

This is only one of the Lonely Planet guide book series. Other books include: *South-East Asia on a Shoestring* — the most popular guide to the region. *Kathmandu & the Kingdom of Nepal* — the "best, little modern guide to Nepal" according to an influential American travel magazine. *Africa on the Cheap* — is there any guide to Africa like it? *New Zealand — a travel survival kit* — complete information on the "land of the long white cloud". *Across Asia on the Cheap*

— currently the third edition of the "complete guide to the overland trip". *Australia — a travel survival kit* — the first low-cost guidebook to down-under. *Hong Kong & Macau* — the low down on the Chinese city-state and its Portuguese neighbour. *Trekking in the Himalayas* — everything you need to know to explore the highest mountains on earth. Even *Europe — a traveller's survival kit* although that one is only available in Australasia. Plus lots more on the way.

Lonely Planet

A few short years ago Maureen and I made a lengthy overland trip and turned the info we'd gathered into the first edition of *Across Asia on the Cheap*. Since then we've kept on moving and managed to gather an enthusiastic band of fellow travellers around us to produce the Lonely Planet travel guide series.

We're still a very small organisation but we're very proud of our guide books — because what we publish comes from people who've been there and found out for themselves. Not from glossy travel brochures.

Tony

SOME THANK-YOUs

In particular to Air Niguini — who flew me here, there and everywhere in between with great efficiency; to Trans-Niugini Tours — who drove me all around the Highlands; to Melanesian Tours — who sent me up and down the Sepik and even introduced me to crocodile wrestling (ultra-flyweight class!); to the PNG Tourist Office — who even produced a Pidgin English letter of introduction for me. Also to the many people who were so helpful and kind — I'm sure I've lost some names so my apologies in advance: David Frodin, Ruediger Kurth, Bill Kitchen, Daniel O'Toole, Myra Hauben (thanks for the loan of your motorcycle), Fred Batten, Judy & Cam Bennet, Brian Parkinson, Kevin & Karen Kay, Brian Bennet, Stephen Durie, Ray Hargreaves, the police at Konos in New Ireland (I got stranded there one night and stayed at the police station), Tara Monaghan, the brothers-Bates, Peter Barter, Tony Meehan, Bernie Gash, Jeff Liversidge and everybody else I met on the way through.

AND A REQUEST

Guide books are only kept up to date by feedback — it's also one of the nicest things about producing them, the amazing letters they generate. So if you've got anything to feedback please do — comments, suggestions, criticisms, abuse, changes or improvements are all gratefully accepted. The best letters score free copies of the next edition. See you on the road.

Contents

continued ➞

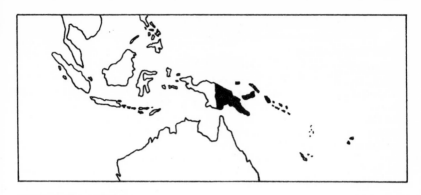

Introduction

Papua New Guinea is truly the "last unknown" — it was virtually the last inhabited place on earth to be explored by Europeans and even today some parts of the country have only made the vaguest contact with the west. It's also a last unknown for travellers and tourists. Yet it can be a fascinating and rewarding experience and not at all difficult to visit, although it takes a little ingenuity to avoid some of Papua New Guinea's steep prices. But where else in the world can you riverboat down a waterway famed for its dynamic art and its equally dynamic crocodiles? Climb a smoking volcano and in the same afternoon dive on what a keen scuba diver told me was the best reef he'd seen anywhere in the world? A Highland sing-sing can be a sight you'll never forget, a flight into one of PNG's precarious "third level" airstrips is likely to be a fright you'll never forget. It's an amazing country and one that, as of yet, is barely touched by the modern tourist trade.

A Visit to Papua New Guinea

You're visiting a country with a tourist trade in its infancy so you'll have to put up with a few associated expenses and problems along the way. To get the most out of PNG I think you have to approach it in one of two ways — which I call "tight" and "loose". By "tight" I mean having everything arranged and sorted out beforehand. PNG is not a country where you can simply arrive and expect it all to happen — and waiting around can be frustrating and very expensive. So get a package deal which whisks you from place to place with the minimum of fuss and with everything packed in as tightly as possible.

On the other hand it is possible to do PNG "loose" — if you're the sort of very experienced shoestringer who can find places to stay in villages, doesn't mind hanging around in a port waiting for that elusive boat to come by, and can sit patiently waiting for things to happen. And can be sufficiently inured to hardships to put up with the discomforts of cheap travel PNG-style.

Facts about the Country

WHAT'S IN A NAME?

Few countries can have as confusing a name as Papua New Guinea — or as long a one. When the first Portuguese explorers came along they named it "Ilhas dos Papuas" — Island of the Fuzzy-Hairs — from the Malay word Papuwah. Later Dutch explorers called it "New Guinea", because they thought it was like Guinea in Africa. Then, towards the end of the last century, the country was divided up between the Dutch, the Germans and the British. The Dutch half became "Dutch New Guinea", the German quarter "German New Guinea" and the British quarter "British New Guinea". When Australia took it over from the British in 1905, it was re-named the "Territory of Papua".

At the start of WW I the Australians captured the German part. After the war it was assigned to Australia as a League of Nations Trust Territory. Therefore, Australia ran the two parts as separate colonies — or more correctly, a separate colony and a Mandated Trust Territory. After WW II the two were combined and administered as the "Territory of Papua and New Guinea", sometimes written as Papua-New Guinea or Papua/New Guinea. Finally, with independence, the country became simply "Papua New Guinea". A search for a less cumbersome name for the country turned up "Nuigini" which, although it sounds like a pidgin derivation of New Guinea, actually means "a stand of coconuts". As yet this much handier name has only been applied to the national airline.

Meanwhile, across the border the Dutch half of the island went on as "Dutch New Guinea" right up into the '60s when Indonesia started its push to take it over. In a last ditch attempt to keep it out of Indonesian hands, the Dutch renamed it "West Papua", but it was too late. In 1962 the Indonesians took over and renamed it "Irian Barat", West Irian, then later changed the name to "Irian Jaya", New Irian.

POSITION

Papua New Guinea lies barely south of the equator, to the north of Australia. It is the last of the string of islands dribbling down from South-East Asia into the Pacific and really forms a transition zone between the two areas. After PNG you're into the Pacific proper — expanses of ocean dotted by tiny islands. Although the island which PNG is part of is known as New Guinea, the country only makes up part of it. The western half of New Guinea is the Indonesian province of Irian Jaya. Additionally there are a collection of smaller islands around the main land mass. To the north, Manus, New Ireland and New Britain are all provinces of PNG, while the eastern islands in Milne Bay and the North Solomons group also belong. To the south of PNG the Torres Straits Islands are part of the Australian state of Queensland. Some of these tiny islands are a mere stone's throw from the PNG coast.

HISTORY

The island of New Guinea has a history of real European contact little more than a century old, although it was known to the European colonial powers for much longer than that. Its own history dates back to far earlier times. The first people arrived in New Guinea probably 30,000 years ago — at that time it was possibly part of a continuous land mass stretching down from Asia to Australia. Some of these first New Guineans must have continued south where, when the rising sea level separated Australia and New Guinea, they became the Australian aboriginals.

The people of New Guinea have been described as "imperfectly mixed". They are amazingly varied, from the dark Buka people, said to have the blackest skins in the world, to the lighter, more Polynesian people of the south Papuan coast. After a spell in Papua New Guinea you'll soon learn to recognise the shorter, often bearded, Highland men and many other distinct groups of people. Diversity of languages goes along with this diversity of racial characteristics. The same rugged terrain that kept their physical features from mixing also kept their languages and cultures separated. It has been estimated that there are over 700 languages spoken in New Guinea.

The first definite sighting of the island by Europeans took place in 1512 when two Portuguese explorers sailed by. The first landing was also Portuguese, Jorge de Meneses landed on the Vogelkop Peninsula, the "dragon's head" at the north-west corner of the island. He named it "Ilhas dos Papuas" and got his name in the history books as the discoverer of New Guinea. In the following centuries various Europeans sailed by, around and through the main island and its smaller associated islands, but the spreading tentacles of European colonialism had quite sufficient and far richer prizes to grapple with. New Guinea was a big, daunting place, it had no visible wealth to exploit, but it most definitely did have some rather unfriendly inhabitants. It was left pretty much alone.

Only the Dutch made any move to assert European authority over the island and that was mainly to keep other countries from getting a toe-hold on the eastern end of their fabulously profitable Dutch East Indies empire (Indonesia today). They put their claim in by a round-about method. Indonesian and Malay traders had for some time carried on a limited trade with coastal tribes — for valuable items like Bird of Paradise feathers. So the Dutch simply announced that they recognised the Sultan of Tidor's sovereignty over New Guinea. Since in turn, they held power over the island of Tidor, New Guinea was therefore indirectly theirs — without expending any personal effort. That neat little ploy, first put into action in 1660, was sufficient for over 100 years, but during the last century firmer action became necessary.

The British East India Company had a look at parts of Western New Guinea back in 1793 and even made a tentative claim of the island, but in 1824 Britain and the Netherlands agreed that Holland's claim to the western half should stand. In 1828 the Dutch made an official statement of their claim to sovereignity and backed it up by establishing a token settlement on the Vogelkop. Nothing much happened for 50 or so years after that, although the coastline was gradually charted and Australia, now evolving from a penal colony towards independence, started to make noises about those foreigners claiming bits of land which were rightfully theirs.

A whole series of British "claims" followed, every time some British ship sailed by somebody would hop ashore, run the flag up the nearest tree and claim the whole place on behalf of good Queen Vic. The good queen's government would then repudiate the claim and the next captain to sail by could do the whole stunt again. in 1883 the Queensland premier sent his Thursday Island police magistrate up to lay claim — at that time the British population consisted of a handful of missionaries and a solitary trader. That claim was also given the same treatment, but next year Britain finally got around to doing something about their unwanted would-be possession.

There was still very little happening over on the Dutch side of the island, but on the north coast of the eastern half a third colonial power was taking a definite interest — Germany. When Britain announced, in September 1884, that they intended to lay claim to a chunk of New Guinea, the Germans quickly raised the flag on the north coast. A highly arbitrary line was then drawn between German and British New Guinea, at that time no European had ventured inland from the coast and it was nearly 50 years later, by which time the Germans had long departed, that it was discovered that the line went straight through the most densely populated part of the island.

A crashed Japanese WW II aircraft makes a modern playground

New Guinea was now divided into three sections — a Dutch half to keep everybody else away from the Dutch East Indies, a British quarter to keep the Germans (and anybody else) away from Australia, and a German quarter because it looked like it could be a damn good investment. They were soon proved wrong, for the next 15 years the mosquitoes were the only things to profit from the German New Guinea Kompagnie's presence on the north coast. In 1899 the Germans threw in the towel, shifted to the happier climes of the Bismarck Archipelago islands off the coast and quickly started to take those fat profits they'd wanted all along.

Over in the Dutch half nothing was happening at all and the British were trying to bring law and order to their bit. In 1888 Sir William MacGregor became the administrator of British New Guinea and set out to explore his possession and set up a native police force to spread the benefits of British Government. He instituted the policy of "government by patrol" which continued right through the Australian period. In 1906 British New Guinea became Papua and administration was taken over by newly independent Australia. From 1907 Papua was the personal baby of Sir Hubert Murray who administered it until his death in 1940.

Almost as soon as WW I broke out in Europe, New Guinea went through a major upheaval. Australian troops quickly overran the German Headquarters at Rabaul in New Britain and for the next seven years German New Guinea was run by the Australian military. In 1920 the League of Nations officially handed it over to Australia as a mandated territory. It stayed that way right up until WW II and this split government caused more than a little confusion for the Australians. In the south they had Papua, a place where they had to put money in to keep it operating and where the major purpose was to act as a buffer to an unfriendly state which was no longer there. In the north they had New Guinea, run by Germany as a nice little money spinner and continued in much the same role under the Australians. The discovery of gold at Wau and Bulolo, in the New Guinea half, only compounded the difficulties since the northern half became even more economically powerful in comparison to the south.

Then WW II arrived and all the northern islands and most of the north coast quickly fell to the Japanese. Soon Australia only held Port Moresby as the Japanese steam-rollered their way south. The Japanese advance was fast but short and by September 1942, with the Pacific War less than a year old and Port Moresby within sight, they had run out of steam and started their long, slow, drawn-out retreat. It took until 1945 to regain all the mainland from the Japanese and the islands — New Ireland, New Britain, Bougainville — were not recovered until the final surrender after the atom bombing of Hiroshima and Nagasaki.

There was no intention to go back to the pre-war separate administration and in any case Port Moresby was the only major town still intact after the war, so the colony now became the Territory of Papua and New Guinea. The territory entered a new period of major economic development with a large influx of expatriates, mainly Australians. When it peaked in 1971 the

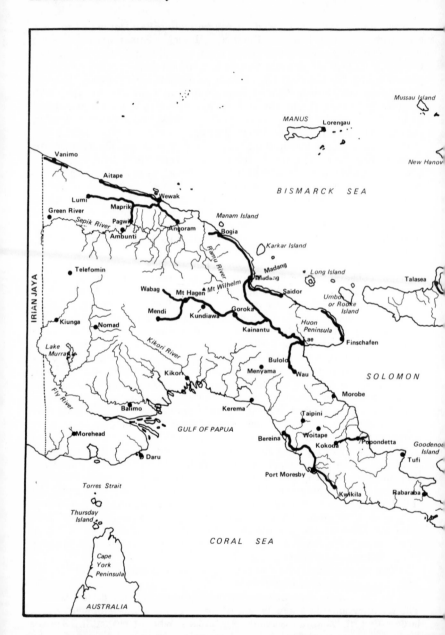

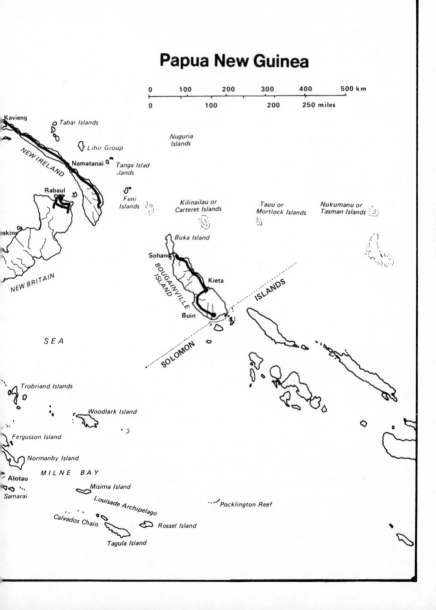

Papua New Guinea

| 0 | 100 | 200 | 300 | 400 | 500 km |

| 0 | 100 | 200 | 250 miles |

Kavieng

Tabar Islands

NEW IRELAND

Lihir Group

Nuguria
Islands

Namatanai

Tanga Islad
slands

Rabaul

Feni
Islands

Kilinailau or
Carteret Islands

Tauu or
Mortlock Islands

Nukumanu or
Tasman Islands

iskins

NEW BRITAIN

Buka Island

Sohano

BOUGAINVILLE
ISLAND

Kieta

ISLANDS

SEA

Buin

SOLOMON

Trobriand Islands

Woodlark Island

Fergusson Island

Normanby Island

MILNE BAY

Alotau

Misima Island

Samarai

Louisade Archipelago

Pocklington Reef

Calvados Chain

Rossel Island

Tagula Island

expatriate population had expanded from the 1940 total of about 6000 to over 50,000. Since then it has fallen to closer to 30,000 and is still, gradually, declining. The postwar world had an entirely different attitude towards colonialism and Australia was soon pressured to prepare Papua and New Guinea for independence. A visiting UN mission in 1962 stressed that if the people weren't pushing for independence themselves then it was Australia's responsibility to do the pushing. The previous Australian policy of gradually spreading literacy and education was supplemented by a concentrated effort to produce a small, educated elite to take over the reins of government.

Meanwhile things were not going nearly so smoothly in the Dutch half of the island. Indonesian resistance to Dutch rule had been simmering, or occasionally flaring up, almost from the moment the Dutch arrived. During WW II the Japanese released the political prisoners held by the Dutch and used them to form the nucleus of a puppet government. When the war ended Sukarno, leader of the pre-war resistance to Dutch rule, immediately declared Indonesia independent and the British forces who arrived in Indonesia to round up the Japanese troops met with stiff Indonesian resistance. Britain quickly got out of that sticky mess, but the Dutch were not so sensible. For the next few years the Dutch East Indies were racked by everything from minor guerilla warfare to all out battles. Eventually Dutch military superiority got the upper hand, but politically the Indonesians outmaneouvred them and in 1949 the Republic of Indonesia came into existence.

Dutch New Guinea was the final stumbling block to a Dutch-Indonesian agreement. It was part of the Dutch East Indies therefore it should be part of Indonesia went the Indonesian argument. The Dutch were determined to hold on to it as a small piece of face saving, so right through the '50s it continued as a Dutch colony, while the Dutch searched desperately for something to do with it. Obviously a political union with Papua New Guinea would have been the most sensible thing, but at that time independence on the Australian half was something for the end of the century and equally obviously the problem of confronting Indonesia would be an Australian problem, not a Dutch one if the colonies were amalgamated.

The Dutch decided on a quick push to independence; in the late '50s they embarked on a crash programme to develop an educated elite and an economic base — a policy that pre-dated by some years similar moves by Australia. The Dutch started to pour money into their colony, an expensive move that soon had to be followed by Australia also.

Unfortunately for the Dutch, things were not going too well in Indonesia. The economy there was falling apart, Sukarno's government was proving to be notoriously unstable and his answer to these serious internal problems was simple — look for an outside enemy to distract attention. Holland proved an ideal enemy and the effort to "regain" Dutch New Guinea became a national cause. Eventually it was Sukarno's own impotence that led to the Dutch departure. As Sukarno started to flirt more and more with Russia, the Americans became more and more desperate and eventually opted for their long running policy of bolstering up corruption and inefficiency wherever it looks like falling on its face. The Dutch were soon politically out-maneouvred at the UN once again and in 1963 the Indonesians took over.

Indonesia's economic collapse was rapidly accelerating by this time and it was in no shape to continue the massive investment projects the Dutch had initiated. By the time Sukarno fell from power in 1965, Irian Barat (west hot land), as it was renamed, had turned into a nice little asset stripping situation with shiploads of Dutch equipment being exported and local businesses and plantations collapsing right and left. It's interesting to note that similar activity took place in Portuguese Timor after the Indonesians took over there in 1976. Relations with Australia were none too good, perhaps helped by Sukarno's habit of referring to Papua New Guinea as Irian Timor (East Irian) and Australia as Irian Utara (South Irian).

After Sukarno's departure relations rapidly improved, the Indonesian half was renamed Irian Jaya (New Irian) and Australians and Indonesians co-operated on accurately mapping the border between the two halves. Part of the Dutch hand-over agreement was that the people should, after a time, have the right to vote on staying with Indonesia or opting for independence. In 1969 this "Act of Free Choice" took place. The "choice" was somewhat restricted by Indonesia's new President Suharto stating that "There will be an act of self-determination, of free choice, in West Irian but if they vote against Indonesia or betray or harm the Indonesian people, this would be treason . . . . ." When the 1000 "representative" voters made the act of free choice there was not a treasonable voice to be heard.

In Papua and New Guinea the path to independence was fairly rapid through the '60s. In '64 a House of Assembly with 64 members was formed, 44 open elected members, 10 appointed and 10 elected Australians. In '68 the house was expanded to 94 members and in '72 to 100. Internal self government came into effect in '73, followed in late '75 by full independence. PNG still has a very low rate of literacy and there are many parts of the country only just emerging from the stone age, where contact with government officials is still infrequent and bewildering. Under these conditions it is hardly surprising that democratic government is in some ways more form than substance. It is quite probable that the first many people knew of a central government was when they were told to vote for their parliamentary representative!

Additionally, a country divided by a large number of mutually incomprehensible languages, where tribal antipathy is a long established way of life, would hardly seem to be a firm base for democracy. Yet somehow it has held together and appears to be working remarkably well. Due credit for this must be given to the continuing large Australian presence and the accompanying Australian cash flow, but PNG is also fortunate to have a

Prime Minister, Michael Somare, who has proved to be a remarkably astute politician and able to compromise between a diversity of peoples that no Australian or British parliamentarian could dream of in his worst nightmares.

Apart from having big brother Australia close to hand, Papua New Guinea is also fortunate to have a remarkably strong economy by third world standards. One of its biggest problems continues to come from across the border in Irian Jaya. The long smouldering resistance movement flared up dramatically in 1978 and time and again Papua New Guinea finds itself walking the political tightrope between good relations with a powerful neighbour and an obvious sympathy for the racially related Irian Jaya rebels. In late '78 the leader of the Irian Jaya resistance was arrested in Papua New Guinea, charged with being an illegal immigrant and put into custody for two months, a short term answer to Indonesia's demand for instant extradition. This problem apart, PNG's future is bound to be complicated by the normal run of developing nation difficulties — economic growth and political stability topping the list.

Cargo Cults

The recurrent outbreaks of "cargo cultism" in New Guinea are a magnetic attraction for assorted academics. Essentially cargo cults are attempts to explain the wealth of the whites. The arrival of the first Europeans in New Guinea must have had much the same impact as a flying saucer touching down would have upon us. Indeed, like something from the film *Close Encounters of the Third Kind*, local history is divided up into the days "pre-contact" and "post-contact". To many people the strange ways and mysterious powers of the Europeans was something that could only be described by supernatural means.

Cult leaders theorised that the Europeans had acquired their machines and wealth from some spirit world and that there was no reason they too could not acquire similar "cargo". Some went further and insisted that the Europeans had intercepted cargo that was really intended for the New Guineans, sent to them by their ancestors in the spirit world. One cultist even suggested that the whites had torn the first page out of all their bibles — the page that revealed that God was actually a Papuan.

If the right rituals were followed, said the cult leaders, the goods would be redirected to their rightful owners. Accordingly, docks were prepared, or even crude "airstrips" were laid out, for when the cargo arrived. Other leaders felt that if they mimicked European ways they would soon have European goods — "offices" were established in which people passed bits of paper back and forth. But when people started to kill their pigs and destroy their gardens, as a prerequisite for the better days to come, the government took a firm stand. Arresting cult leaders simply reconfirmed the belief that an attempt was being made to keep goods rightfully belonging to the New Guineans, so a number of cultists were taken down to Australia to see with their own eyes that the goods did not simply arrive from the spirit world.

The first recorded cargo cult outbreak was noted in British New Guinea in 1893. A similar occurrence in Dutch New Guinea dates back to 1867.

Cargo cult outbreaks have occurred sporadically ever since. One of the largest took place in the Gulf area just after WW I, it was known as the "Vailala Madness" and was considerably spurred on by the arrival of the first airplane in the region — as predicted by one of the cult leaders. The cults took another upswing after WW II when the people witnessed even more stunning examples of western wealth. Seeing that black American troops also had access to the goods had a particularly strong impact. A more recent example was the Lyndon Johnson affair on the island of New Hanover (see the section on New Ireland). No doubt there will be new occurrences to keep academics happy for some time yet.

EXPLORATION

Exploration was one of the most interesting phases of the early development of PNG. This was almost the last place to be discovered by Europeans and the explorers were only too happy to put their daring deeds down on paper. Gavin Souter's book *The Last Unknown* is one of the best descriptions of these travels. At first, exploration consisted of short trips in from the coast, often by parties of early mission workers. Later the major rivers were used to travel further into the forbidding inland region. The next phase was trips up river on one side, over the central mountains and down a suitable river to the other coast — crossing the tangled central mountains often proved to be the killer in these attempts.

It is interesting to note that more than one early explorer commented on how the curiosity and even awe with which they were met on a first trip turned to outright antagonism on a second. It's more than likely that a lot of this was due to the extreme trigger-happiness of some visitors. The final death count from the exploration of New Guinea undoubtedly showed that the head-hunters had more to fear of the white explorers than vice versa.

From the time of the Australian takeover of British New Guinea, government-by-patrol was the key to both exploration and control. Patrol officers were not only the first Europeans into previously "uncontacted" areas but were also responsible for making the government's presence felt on a more or less regular basis. The last great phase of exploration took place in the '30s and was notable for the first organised use of support aircraft. This last period included the discovery of the important Highlands region. By '39 even the final unknown area, up towards the Dutch New Guinea border, had been at least cursorily explored. Since the war there have been more exploratory patrols, but in general the country is now completely mapped.

People

Undoubtedly one of the most interesting of PNG's diverse racial groups is the "expat" tribe. They come in various nationalities including, illogically, Papua New Guineans, but their most visible characteristic is, usually, a white skin and their amazingly varied outlook on life in general and their position in it particularly. Someone once said to come to PNG you've got to be a missionary, a mercenary or a misfit. Sometimes you seem to be talking to all three types at once. The bible thumpers seem to thump bibles harder than anywhere else, the "in it for what it's worth" brigade seem to be in it deeper than anywhere else, the "my world is falling apart" gang can be seen propping up the bar taking solace in the bottle. You can even meet planters from remote plantations who, far from not knowing that Independence has arrived, probably didn't even hear about WW I, you almost feel they regret they can't use the whip these days! I should add that I also met some of the nicest people going in PNG — but there certainly are a large proportion who are just a touch "strange".

GEOGRAPHY

Papua New Guinea's remote and wild character is very closely tied to its dramatic geography. The place is a mass of superlatives — the mountains tower, the rivers torrent, the ravines plunge — name a geographical cliche and PNG has it. These spectacular features have much to do with the country's diverse people and its current position. Travel in PNG is difficult — when a mighty mountain range or a wide river separates you from your neighbouring tribe you're unlikely to get to know them very well. Nor, in modern days, will communications be easy.

The central spine of PNG is a high range of mountains with peaks over 4000 metres. It's unlikely that a permanent road across this daunting natural barrier will be completed until the end of this century although temporary tracks were attempted during WW II. Meanwhile travel between the south and north coasts of PNG still means flying, or a lengthy, circuitous boat trip — unless you care to walk that is.

Great rivers flow from the mountains down to the sea. The Fly and the Sepik Rivers are the two largest — the Sepik flowing into the sea in the north, the Fly in the south. Both are navigable far up from their mouths and both are among the world's mightiest rivers in terms of annual waterflow.

In places the central mountains descend right to the sea in a series of diminishing foothills, while in other regions broad expanses of mangrove swamps fringe the coast — gradually extending as more and more material is carried down to the coast by the muddy rivers. In the western Gulf region there is an endless expanse of flat grassland — sparsely populated, annually flooded and teeming with wildlife.

Papua New Guinea is in the Pacific volcano belt but, apart from a few exceptions along the north coast such as Mt Lamington, near Popondetta, which erupted unexpectedly and disastrously in 1951, the live volcanoes are not on the main land mass. There are a number of volcanic islands scattered off the north coast and in Milne Bay plus, of course, the active region on the north coast of East New Britain.

One of the most interesting features of the geography of Papua New Guinea is the central Highland valleys. As the early explorers pushed further and further in from the coast the general conclusion was reached that the central spine of mountains was a tangled, virtually uninhabited mass and only along the coast would any great population be found. Then in the '30s the Highland valleys were stumbled upon. That empty badland turned out to be the most fertile and heavily populated area of the country. Population estimates for the country were immediately adjusted sharply upwards. The best known valleys are around Goroka and Mt Hagen, but there are other more remote places right across into Irian Jaya.

PNG is also more than adequately endowed with striking coral reefs making it something of a paradise for scuba divers. There are reefs around much of the mainland coast and, more particularly, amongst the islands of the Bismarck Sea and Milne Bay areas. The major offshore islands — New Ireland, New Britain and Bougainville — are almost as mountainous as the mainland with many peaks rising to over 2000 metres.

Birds of Paradise & other fauna and flora

Of the 43 known species of the exotic and colourful Birds of Paradise, 38 are found in Papua New Guinea. The other five are found on nearby islands or parts of northern Australia. The existence of these spectacular creatures was one of the first reports to trickle back to Europe from New Guinea. The Dutch explorer Linschoten (1563-1611) reported that they were:

> . . . . . *called Paradice-birdes, for ye beauty of their feathers which passe all other birds; these birds are never seen alive, but being dead they fall on the Island; they flie, as it is said alwaies into the Sunne, and keep themselves continually in the ayre, without lighting on the earth, for they have neither feet nor wings, but only head and body and the most part tayle.*

This rather improbable notion came from the habit of Malay Bird of Paradise hunters cutting off the wings and feet. The first Bird of Paradise skins brought back to Europe were indeed for "the most part tayle" and the birds were named *Paradiseaea apoda*, the "a poda" meaning "without feet". In actual fact they have feet and wings much like any other bird but it is that magnificent tail which attracts attention.

The Bird of Paradise is probably the most ostentatiously plumed creation in the air. Their feathers are long and dramatically coloured and they are put to use in spectacular mating dances. The male Bird of Paradise is the playboy of the bird-world, a true believer in the "find 'em and forget 'em" philosophy. In comparison to his plumage, most females are dowdy and after mating are immediately discarded by the male who takes no part in the hatching or rearing of the young.

During their mating season male birds take up positions on "display trees", a number of male birds collect on the branches of the selected tree and go through a highly energetic dance routine — displaying their feathers, leaping up and down, clapping their wings together behind their back and calling out raucously. The females watch this extravagant display and when sufficiently impressed, offer themselves to the most inspired dancer. It's a fantastic sight, most likely to be seen in the early dawn hours between May and December.

Unfortunately for the Bird of Paradise, his feathers are just as beautiful to man as to the female of the species. Their feathers have long been part of an important man's decoration and the slaughter of birds accelerated with the arrival of Europeans and shotguns. Today there is an absolute ban on the export of Bird of Paradise feathers and they may be hunted only by traditional means. Despite this, the continuing importance of the feathers as a sign of traditional wealth, together with the reduction in the area of rain forest, puts a heavy strain on the birds' safety. Fortunately, since it is only the male bird which is hunted, the breeding females continue without effect.

Of course the Bird of Paradise is not the only bird life in Papua New Guinea. Altogether there are estimated to be 650 species, only 100 less than in all of North America. Among the other birds there is the huge beaked hornbill, many varieties of cockatoos and parrots, the impressive Harpy eagle and three types of cassowaries. This large, flightless, ostrich-like bird has glossy black feathers and a horny ridge on its head. They are another important wealth-symbol and many villages have a cassowary pen. They are generally killed soon after they reach full size for their powerful feet can tear a man apart with one lethal kick and fully grown ones often have a nasty temper.

In comparison to this prolific bird life the animal life in PNG is very sparse. Most are Marsupials, which carry their young in pouches. Many live in trees — like the slow moving cuscus, or the varieties of tree kangaroos. There are many reptiles, ranging from tiny lizards to huge salt water croco-diles plus a large variety of snakes — some huge pythons and some deadly poisonous varieties like the large taipan. Insect life is also very numerous — particularly mosquitoes, you may feel inclined to say! The PNG butterflies are especially colourful and attractive.

Most of Papua New Guinea is covered in a dense blanket of rain forest — an exuberant tangle of vines, creepers, plants and trees. At times everything seems to be layers thick, to see a tree growing by itself is a rare sight. PNG is

notable for its amazing variety of orchids, more than in any other country
in the world. There are many orchid fanciers in PNG and growing orchids is
a very popular hobby.

CLIMATE

Papua New Guinea's climate can generally be described as hot and wet year
round, but there are a number of dramatic exceptions to that hard and fast
rule. Officially there's a wet and a dry season, but in practice, in most
places, the wet just means it is more likely to rain, the dry that it's less
likely. The exception is Port Moresby where the dry is definitely dry — the
configuration of the mountains around Moresby account for this two season
characteristic. The wetter time of the year is from December to March, the
drier time May to October. During the two transition months (April and
November) it can't make up its mind which way to go and tends to be
unpleasantly still and sticky.

Two places in PNG further confuse the pattern by being drier in the
"wet" and wetter in the "dry". They are Lae and Wewak and again the
cause is the peculiar configuration of the mountains surrounding them.

Rainfall, generally heavy, varies enormously. In dry, often dusty, Port
Moresby the annual fall is about 1000 mm (40 inches) and, like places in
Northern Australia, the rain tends to come short and sharp and is then followed by long dry months. Other places can vary from a little over 2000 mm
(80 inches) in Rabaul or Goroka, to over 4500 mm (180 inches!) in Lae. In
extreme rainfall areas such as West New Britain or on the Gulf of Papua,
west of Port Moresby, the annual rainfall can average 6000 mm or more per
year — a drenching 20 foot of annual rainfall.

Temperatures on the coast are reasonably stable year round — hovering
around 25°C to 30°C (70°F to 80°F) but the humidity and winds can vary
widely and one day feels quite differently to another. As you move inland,
and up, the temperatures drop fairly dramatically. In the Highlands the day-
time temperatures often climb to the high 20°Cs but at night in Mt Hagen
open fires are the order of the day in the hotels. During the dry season,
when there is little cloud cover to contain the heat, Highland mornings can
be very chilly. If you keep moving up into the mountains you'll find it
colder still. Although snow is rare it's certainly not impossible on the tops
of the highest summits and ice will often form on cold nights.

Central District & Port Moresby:	Dry, dusty and windy from May to October.
Lae & Morobe:	In Lae it's hot and humid from November to February, wetter but cooler from May to October with the heaviest rain in June, July and August. In Wau and Bulolo it is the exact opposite.
Highlands:	In most of the Highlands the rain comes from November to April but is generally

not unpleasant. May to October is cooler and drier. In the Southern Highlands the wet lasts a bit longer at both ends and it is more likely to rain at any time year round.

Madang: Rainy, often thunderstorms, from November to May.

Sepik: October and November are the wettest months.

Gulf & Western: The Gulf region is very wet year round — reaching a crescendo between May and October. Inland in Western can also be very wet.

Northern: October to May wet season with heaviest rain at the beginning and end of the season.

Manus: November to April wet season.

New Ireland: November to April wet season in most of the country, inverted on a small part of the south coast.

New Britain: November to April on the north side is the wet season (including Rabaul), while on the south side of the island the rain comes May to October and comes much heavier.

North Solomons: January to April is wet but cooler, November and December are pretty hot.

Milne Bay: Unpredictable year round — two possible wet seasons and periods of high wind. February-March and September-October are likely to be the best months.

THE ECONOMY

The Papua New Guinean economy is based on three major elements. First there is the annual Australian grant: this was only about half a million kina in the first year after WW II but it grew steadily and rapidly through the '50s and '60s and, although the percentage rate of growth may have slowed in the '70s, the figures are now very large indeed — in each of the last three years it has been around A$200 million. A very recent, but very important, support for the PNG economy has been the huge Bougainville copper mine. Copper exports are of similar size to the Australian grant and there are other copper mining projects under way. Third leg of the economy is coffee, long a developing industry it sprung into prominence with the dramatic worldwide zoom in coffee prices in the mid-'70s. Coffee exports shot up to over

K100 million a year but now are falling back as coffee prices drop.

Copra (the dried coconut kernels which are processed into vegetable oils) and other coconut products were the backbone of the economy for many years, but have slipped far behind the other big Cs — copper and coffee. Copra is bedeviled by extremely variable prices on the world commodity markets. In contrast, cocoa's big problem has been local diseases but, like coffee, it has been aided by rocketing price rises over the last few years. Rubber production has grown slowly but steadily, timber is starting to develop as the huge timber resources are utilised, tea has not been the great success once expected (though Highland tea is quite nice), and the enormous potential of fishing around the New Guinea coast is just starting to be used — canned fish is still a major import though. Oil has been looked for over many years and at great expense, but never found in anything like economic quantities.

Imports include almost all manufactured goods and many basic foodstuffs, not a few of which could conceivably be produced locally. Papua New Guinea is remarkably lucky by third world standards to have a fairly well adjusted trade balance. By comparison with some of its Asian neighbours, wages, which have a touch of the Australian contact about them, are fairly high.

Of course, a large proportion of the population still lives partially or completely outside of the cash economy — a subsistence way of life where what they grow is what they eat. Like some other countries which on a per-capita income basis look very badly off, PNG is actually very short of squalor, some people may suffer from bad nutrition but nobody starves, and beggars are something that simply do not exist.

POPULATION
The population of Papua New Guinea is estimated to be about three million, over a third of which is concentrated in the Highland provinces. Some authorities divide the people of PNG into "Papuans", predominantly descended from the original arrivals when the island was connected to the Asian land mass, and Melanesians, who are more related to the peoples of the Pacific. Additionally, some people, particularly in outlying islands, are closer to being pure Polynesian or Micronesian. The dividing line between these definitions is a very hazy one. PNG still has a considerable expat population, although it has fallen considerably from its 1971 peak of around 50,000 to a current figure closer to 30,000. There is also a smaller minority of Chinese who, as in most Asian countries, control a large number of shops and similar local businesses. Many of them arrived during the German days and Rabaul has always had the strongest Chinese influence. Their numbers too have declined over the last 10 or 20 years. At Independence many long term Australian and Chinese residents were eligible for citizenship of PNG but only on the condition that they renounced their original citizenship.

Facts for the Visitor

GETTING TO PAPUA NEW GUINEA

From almost every angle the only way into Papua New Guinea is to fly — passenger shipping services these days are few and far between and the only people likely to arrive in PNG by sea will be yachties or those on cruise ships. Prior to Independence connections with PNG were naturally mainly from Australia. The expatriate population was predominantly Australian and the flights were operated by Australian airlines — at first Qantas (when PNG was an "international" destination) and later by Ansett or TAA (when it became a "domestic" route).

Since Independence Air Niugini has become the national "flag carrier" operating connections to Australia and other countries. Since PNG is once again an international route, Australian connections are also made by Qantas. But the expatriate population mix is changing — many Australians are leaving and their replacements come from New Zealand, America, Britain and other European countries or from Asian neighbours. Other air links are being formed.

From/to Australia

Air Niugini's 707 flies four times a week between Sydney and Port Moresby — on two occasions it goes via Brisbane. The direct flight takes 3 hours 40 minutes, via Brisbane it takes 5 hours. Qantas makes three flights a week, one of which is via Brisbane. One way economy fare Sydney-Port Moresby is A$203.

Air Niugini have a second link to Australia, the short 1 hour 25 minutes flight to Cairns in North Queensland. This sector is operated by the little F-28 jets and at A$83 it's absolutely the cheapest way to fly out of Australia. Air Niugini fares can be discounted 25% to student card holders.

From/to Indonesia

The Indonesian link is one of the most interesting ways to flight hop through Asia. Eventually Air Niugini hope to have a direct link between Port Moresby and Bali or Jakarta which will make PNG a very attractive stepping stone between the US and Indonesia if their Port Moresby-Honolulu route also opens up.

Meanwhile the "back door" route into Indonesia involves a series of flights and airlines. From Port Moresby you fly to Wewak, either direct (K90) or with a variety of optional stops on the way (Port Moresby-Lae-Madang-Wewak for K102, for example). Every Tuesday there's an Air Niugini flight from Wewak to Jayapura in Irian Jaya for K38. From there frequent flights will whisk you away to Bali or Java with Garuda or Merpati, the two main Indonesian airlines.

You'll usually go via Ujung Pandang in Sulawesi so it's easy to include the fascinating Toraja land area of central Sulawesi in your travels. Flying this way you can travel Sydney-Port Moresby-Wewak-Jayapura-Ujung Pandang-Bali for approximately A$640, or a bit cheaper with Merpati rather than Garuda. In contrast Sydney-Bali costs A$359 one way and adding on Bali-Ujung Pandang-Bali would bring it up to A$449.

If economy were all important you could fly Cairns-Port Moresby, take a ship along the northern PNG coast or travel by road from Lae up into the Highlands then fly down to Wewak, after that obligatory flight to Jayapura you could again ship from there to Ujung Pandang and then to Surabaya. You'd save yourself a lot of dollars in fares but spend many weeks travelling! See my other book, *South-East Asia on a Shoestring* for more details.

To/from other Asian Countries & New Zealand
One day Air Niugini may have more flights to its Asian neighbours. At the moment they fly once weekly to Manila for K340 (backed up by Philippine Airlines), once weekly to Hong Kong for K415 (Cathay Pacific have the reciprocal rights) and once weekly to Kagoshima in Japan for K501. There should soon be a connection to Auckland in New Zealand.

To/from Europe
Although you can fly down to Australia and then out to Europe the most direct route is known locally as the Hong Kong connection. The routine is to take Air Niugini's flight to Hong Kong then 24 hours later fly British Airways to London. The off peak excursion fare is K930 return (£700 approximately) and you're allowed one stop-over. The 24 hours in Hong Kong is an aircraft change, not a stop-over. Coming from the UK the Hong Kong stop is only seven hours.

To/from North America
Air Niugini has plans for a direct Hawaii-Papua New Guinea link but meanwhile there is no direct connection. You've got a choice of flying Port Moresby-Manila then connecting with Northwest Orient, Pan Am or Philippine Airlines or heading south to Sydney and flying with Qantas or Pan Am. Those are the most direct routes and cost K698 to Honolulu, K787 to San Francisco or Los Angeles.

Some Americans resident in Papua New Guinea have also tried out the Pacific roundabout route, see below.

The Pacific Link
You can considerably undercut the official IATA fare between the US and Papua New Guinea if you're willing to make a whole series of stops along the way and take a whole series of airlines. It takes careful plar..ing as many of these flights operate only once or twice a week. Some of the possible connections are Honolulu-Marshal Island-Nauru-Honiara (Solomons)-Port Moresby or Hololulu-Guam-Nauru or Honolulu-Caroline-Nauru or Honolulu-Nandi-Honiara. The tiny (and very rich) island-state of Nauru is the focal

point for a lot of these routes. It costs A$60 to fly Nauru-Honiara with Air Nauru on Mondays or Saturdays. Honiara-Port Moresby costs K122 with Air Niugini. Guam and the Marshall Islands are US dependencies and flights between there and Honolulu are treated like US domestic routes with nice low fares. The catch is they don't officially exist according to IATA logic and a travel agent can't write you a out a single ticket with all the connections included! Plus from PNG it works out cheaper to buy the last leg ticket when you get there rather than in Moresby since the IATA exchange rates work against you. So you can have some fun juggling the figures but for starters you can hop across the Pacific through Guam for about K460 (say US$670) whereas the honest IATA fare is about K700 (say US$1000).

Departing Papua New Guinea
There is a K2 airport tax for all overseas departures.

GETTING AROUND PAPUA NEW GUINEA

Air Niugini
Air Niugini may be one of the world's youngest airlines but it has a history and background of experience which would put many much better known names to shame. Papua New Guinea could well lay claim to being one of the real pioneers of modern civil aviation. There can hardly be a country anywhere in the world that has been more dependent on flying for its development. Even today, when a sketchy road network is finally creeping across the country, an enormous proportion of PNG's travel is still made in the air.

Aviation, after a couple of false starts and some extravagant ideas of exploring the country by Zeppelin airships, arrived in PNG in 1922. In that year the first flight was made from Port Moresby in a small seaplane and it was later used, with other seaplanes, to explore parts of the Gulf and Western Provinces. A few other pioneering flights followed but it was the development of the Wau and Bulolo goldfields which really launched aviation in New Guinea. Cecil John Levien, one of the pioneers on these goldfields, soon realised that they would never be successfully exploited so long as getting men and supplies up from the coast involved a long hard slog through difficult terrain peopled by unfriendly tribes. After a number of unsuccessful attempts to interest Australian operators in servicing the goldfields, Levien pushed through a proposal that his own Guinea Gold company should set up an air service, which they named Guinea Airways.

Their able pilot, "Pard" Mustar, had to do far more than just fly their first DH-37 biplane. First an airstrip had to be constructed at the port of Lae — which he managed to arrange by getting his friend, a local jail officer, to set his prisoners to work on it. Then Mustar had to walk up from Salamua to Wau to supervise the airstrip construction there. Finally he had to travel back to Rabaul, where the DH-37 had been shipped in pieces and assembled, and fly it to Lae — 650 km, much of it over sea or unexplored jungle, in a single engined aircraft of less than total reliability. In April 1927 Mustar took off on his first flight to Wau — and couldn't find it! He returned to Lae, took more directions and advice and tried again with an equal lack of success. Finally, on his third attempt and with an experienced miner on board, he made the first of many 50 minute flights to Wau.

For the next couple of years passengers and freight were shuttled back and forth — it cost £33 to fly up to Wau, only £10 to fly back. By comparison it costs only $18 today. Guinea Airways were not the only aviation pioneers on this run but they were certainly the most successful. Ray Parer had commenced operations with a DH-4 at much the same time but lack of finance always held his Bulolo Goldfields Aeroplane Service back. There were a number of other carriers who tried with less, or no, success to emulate Guinea Airways.

Mustar quickly realised the need for more capacity and reliability and before the end of 1927 had gone to Germany to buy a Junkers W-34 at the then astronomical cost of £8000. It may have been expensive but at the time it was the very latest thing in cargo aircraft and could lift over a ton. A second W-34 soon followed and with these aircraft Guinea Airways operated a service which proved the real possibilities of air transport just as convincingly as the much better publicised flights of Lindbergh or Kingsford-Smith. Wau became the busiest airfield in the world and more airfreight was lifted annually in New Guinea than in all the rest of the world put together!

Mustar left New Guinea but in 1929 was called back to accomplish a scheme which to many people at the time must have seemed like something out of the realms of science fiction. He had to find a way of flying, in pieces, gold dredges weighing 3000 tons into the goldfields! Mustar's response was another Junkers, the G-31, a three-engined all-metal monster which cost £30,000 and could lift three tons. In the early '30s a fleet of these aircraft carried not just gold equipment but also workers and even the first horses ever to be transported by air.

Through the '30s more and more aircraft and operators came into New Guinea. In 1931 regular services started between the goldfields and Port Moresby on the south coast. Holden's Air Transport Services developed but were later taken over by Guinea Airways. Longer lasting was the air service started by the island traders, W R Carpenter & Co. In 1937 they absorbed Pacific Aerial Transport (originally formed by goldfields pioneer Ray Parer) and became Mandated Airlines Ltd (MAL). In 1938 they started the first airmail service between PNG and Australia. The fierce competition had dramatically forced down the airfreight rates; Guinea Airways had even expanded south into Australia and operated a successful service between Adelaide and Darwin via Alice Springs using the ultra-modern twin-engined Lockhead Electra. During this same period pioneer missionaries had been proving that the airplane could be put to spiritual as well secular use. Possibly the first aerial mapping anywhere in the world was conducted in PNG in 1935. Aircraft also saw important use supplying the oil prospecting parties of the '30s and the exploration trips which opened up the final hidden parts of the country. One of the most spectacular forays was made by the wealthy American Richard Archbold who during his late-'30s expeditions used a Catalina amphibian and discovered the Grand Valley of the Baliem in Dutch New Guinea.

The arrival of the war in 1942 abruptly ended civil aviation. The bulk of the aircraft were caught on the ground by the first devastating Japanese raids on Lae, Salamua and Bulolo. The aircraft that survived made a final desperate series of flights to evacuate civilians away from the advancing Japanese. When the war ended aviation in PNG was a whole new picture. In 1944 Qantas had taken over W R Carpenter's Australia-PNG connections and got their first toehold in the country. Guinea Airways were unable to obtain a license to operate in PNG from the post-war Labor government and Qantas were now the dominant airline. Using DC3s and then DC4s they started regular passenger services between Australia and PNG. There was also a short flirtation with Short Solent flying boats in the early '50s. In 1960 the Australian government decided that Qantas should be purely an international airline and PNG services were handed over to Ansett-ANA and Trans-Australia Airlines since PNG counted as a part of Australia at that time. During the '50s Qantas had built up a quite incredible fleet of aircraft for internal use. They operated everything from Beaver and Otter STOL aircraft, through DH83 and DH84 biplanes to Catalina and Sandringham flying boats. PNG was looked upon as a very useful training ground for pilots who would later fly on Qantas' international network. The airline set up by W R Carpenter before the war for internal services, MAL, was the main opposition to Qantas and swallowed up smaller competitors such as Gibbes Sepik Airways before it was in turn engulfed by Ansett-ANA.

TAA and Ansett operated turbo-prop Lockhead Electras and later Boeing 727s between Australia and PNG. Internally they supplemented their DC3 workhorses with Fokker Friendships in 1967. In 1973, with the start of self government, PNG immediately decided to have their own internal airline. Air Niugini was formed on 1 November 1973 and took over the DC3s and F27s for domestic use. Later a Boeing 707 was added to operate international connections and the PNG government bought out the TAA and Qantas share of Air Niugini leaving only Ansett as an external shareholder. Today Air Niugini, a very young airline with a very long pedigree, operates one Boeing 707, two Fokker F28 jets and 12 Fokker F27 turboprops. They fly international connections to Australia, the Solomon Islands, Indonesia, the Philippines, Hong Kong and Japan with routes to New Zealand, the USA and further ports in Indonesia in the offing. Their extensive internal network is indicated with some of the relevant air fares on the next page.

In general there is no real "season" for visiting PNG although each region has its own best and worst times. Travel can be more difficult on flights into and out of the country and around PNG during the Australian school holidays when many expat children come to stay with their parents — May, August and particularly over Christmas are the danger times.

Air Niugini give a 25% reduction from normal domestic fares for people on inclusive tours. Students are also eligible for a 25% discount.

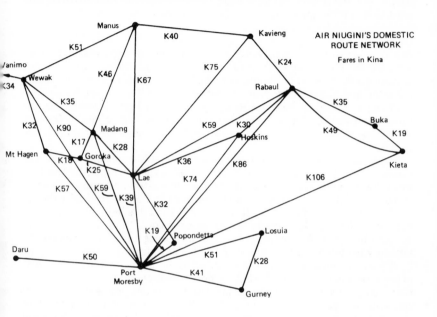

AIR NIUGINI'S DOMESTIC ROUTE NETWORK

Fares in Kina

Third-Level Flying

With Papua New Guinea's long history of aviation you should really try to make at least one third-level or charter flight while you're in the country. Particularly if it's up in the hills where flying can be a real experience. The "third-level" tag means they are three down in the airline importance scale. The first-level carrier operates internationally, the second-level makes the major domestic connections. The third-level operates between all the tiny airstrips, towns, villages — of which PNG has plenty. There are no less than 417 licensed airfields in PNG — about 100 are owned and maintained by the government, the larger 18 are suitable for use by F27s, while the rest are for smaller aircraft only.

The major third-level carrier is Talair, headquartered in Goroka. It operates no less than 60 aircraft and flies to 132 airstrips around the country with light aircraft, STOL aircraft like Twin Otters and Pilatus Porters and twin engined commuter lines on some of the more important routes. Other smaller airlines include Douglas Airways, Bougair, Chee-Air, Co-Air and the missionary air services.

Considering the terrain, the airstrips and the weather the safety record in PNG is very good. Most of the pilots are young Australians or New Zealanders intent on building up their command experience before heading home to a major airline. Experience it certainly is. They're not paid a fortune, but after a few years of scooting around the mountains in PNG anything else must seem a little tame.

Drive Yourself

It is possible to hire cars in most main centres but due to the sketchy road network in PNG you can't really drive "around" the country. Driving around would have to be a process of hiring a car in each new town. There are often additional charges for use outside city limits. The two major rent-a-car organisations in PNG are Budget with cars in Port Moresby, Lae and Rabaul and Nationwide-Avis who have cars in those places plus in Goroka, Mt Hagen, Wewak and Kieta. There are also some smaller local car hire companies.

Car rental costs in PNG are not cheap — the roads are mainly unsealed so the cars have a hard life and you can hardly expect costs to be too low. From Nationwide-Avis a Datsun 120Y with unlimited kms costs K25 a day in Port Moresby, K32 in Kieta, a Gemini K29 in Rabaul. In Lae a Datsun 120Y costs K13 a day plus 13t a km, in Wewak it's K25 plus 15t a km beyond 75 km. In Goroka and Mt Hagen a Datsun 180B is the cheapest car you can hire — K15 a day plus 15t a km. With Budget costs and cars are the same in each town — a Galant costs K11.50 a day plus 12t a km.

It's worth bearing in mind at all times when driving in PNG the tourist office's recommendation of what to do if involved in an accident. Don't stop. Keep driving. Report the accident to the nearest police station. Tribal concepts of "payback" and the motor age have not exactly gone together too well. Insurance coverage may be compulsory but most of the local citizenry prefer to take it out on the driver of the offending vehicle personally. There have been quite a few occasions of a driver who has been involved in a fatal accident being murdered by the relatives of the victim — often while in police custody/protection. Of course this is much less likely to happen to a foreigner than a local person but, nevertheless, involvement in a serious accident often means "pack up and leave the country" for an expatriate.

Head Offices:

Nationwide-Avis:	PO Box 3533, Port Moresby
	tel: 25 8258 office, 25 8259 airport
Budget:	Gateway Hotel, Jacksons Airport
	tel: 25 4514 or 25 4269

PMVs

The *Public Motor Vehicle* is both the secret of cheap travel in PNG and the most visible and successful example of local enterprise. Ten years ago the PMV probably didn't exist, now they seem indispensable. A PMV is a vehicle (it could be a mini-bus, a truck with wooden benches or just a small, plain, bare pick-up truck) which picks up and drops off people anywhere along its route. Some of them run regular, bus-like services; others just start here and go there via any route that takes the driver's fancy. You can more or less take it as read that anything with lots of people in it is a PMV — stick your hand out and it will stop, shout out where you want to go and if the PMV is going that way, you're on.

There are fairly standard fares for most routes. Around town the PMV fare will be the same as the local bus service — if there is one. Over longer distances there will be a generally recognised figure — ask your fellow passengers if you want to be certain of the cost. You always pay at the end of the trip.

You'll hear a lot while you're in PNG about safety, or the lack of it, in PMVs. Ignore most of this advice, you'll find that the people who are most hysterical about the dangers of riding on PMVs are the people who've never set foot in one. If the vehicle looks in pretty good shape, and the driver does too, you'll most likely have no worries. PMV travel is generally rather uncomfortable (it's definitely a form of transport for the hardy only) but apart from cheapness it has one other big advantage — if you want to meet the local people, ride to the market with the marketeers, then it's on the PMVs that you'll find them.

Shipping
There is not a lot of regular passenger carrying shipping around PNG — exceptions are between Lae and Madang or between Lae and Rabaul. Nevertheless, if you are an easy going, unscheduled sort of traveller you'll find it relatively easy to pick up ships in all sorts of places and get to ports and islands way off the beaten track. It's just a matter of sitting back and waiting until something comes by and then negotiating a fare — which will usually be extremely low as the curiosity of having you aboard generally helps to pay your passage.

TOUR OPERATORS
Papua New Guinea has two major tour operators. Both operate tours throughout the country — Melanesian are based in Madang and operate the Sepik Explorer houseboats on the Sepik. Trans-Niugini Tours, with their office in Mt Hagen, operate a variety of tours in the Highlands area and have recently taken over the Ramada Lodge at Minj in the Highlands and the Karawari Lodge on the Karawari River off the Sepik. They are also involved with the operation of the Bensbach Wildlife Lodge in Western Province close to the Irian Jaya border. Your travel agent can provide full details of their inclusive tours of Papua New Guinea, or you can write to them directly:

Melanesian Tourist Services
PO Box 707
Madang

Trans Niugini Tours
PO Box 3396
Port Moresby

ACTIVITIES

Apart from the standard "look at the scenery" style occupations, PNG has a number of areas of special appeal to the visitor. One is, of course, its prolific artistic activity, but others are more energetic — such as skin diving or mountain climbing.

Walking & Climbing

Considering how similar much of the country is to Nepal — vast areas of rugged, mountainous terrain where the only way to get from A to B is to fly or walk — it is surprising that walking has not caught on the same way trekking has in the Himalayas. I think it's an activity that could grow enormously. The best known of the walking tracks in Papua New Guinea is definitely the Kokoda Trail (see Port Moresby & Central Provinces section) which became famous in WW II. There are other lesser known but even more interesting walks — such as the walk from Woitape to Taipini (Port Moresby & Central again) or from Wau to Salamua (Lae & Morobe). The latter can be a hard struggle as the path is little used, as is the Bulldog Trail from Wau south. There are many others although quite a few require somebody with local knowledge along.

PNG's mountains don't reach Himalayan heights but many of them make interesting walking and climbing. Mt Wilhelm, at 4510 metres the highest in the country, makes an interesting two day climb (see the Highlands). Others include Mt Victoria and Mt Giluwe. The Mt Lamington volcano in Northern Province is a popular climb as are the many volcanoes in East New Britain. The small Matupit cone overlooking Rabaul harbour is probably the most popular climb in the country — it only takes half an hour.

Scuba Diving

Diving, whether with scuba gear or just snorkelling, is a great activity in PNG. There are plenty of excellent places to dive and lots to see. The coast of PNG is liberally dotted with reefs and for those who like diving on wrecks the reefs are liberally dotted with sunken ships — either as a result of the reefs or of WW II. Madang, Rabaul and around Port Moresby are three of the most popular diving places. Contact Bob Halstead, Tropical Diving Adventures, PO Box 1644, Boroko, for information on diving trips from Port Moresby.

War Wreckage

At the end of WW II the country was littered from end to end with the wreckage of Allied and Japanese aircraft, ships and army equipment. Much of it was shipped out immediately by bands of scrap dealers, but there is still much to be seen. There is a national register of aircraft wreckage and from time to time aircraft missing since WW II are still stumbled upon. In *The Hot Land*, John Ryan tells of some of these recently located aircraft and writes of some which are still being searched for. War-buffs can have a fine time poking around the debris in PNG.

Birds, Fish, Shells, Butterflies & Orchids
All fascinating subjects for some visitors. PNG has a huge variety of often spectacularly plumed birds including most of the Birds of Paradise in the world. Fish — there are plenty of them all round the coast to please the skin diver or fisherman. Papua New Guinea has an amazing variety of shells — see the section on New Guinea Shells in Rabaul, New Britain. The country is also a paradise for butterfly enthusiasts with many rare species and a vast number which are simply beautiful and colourful. Finally there are orchids, again PNG has more than its fair share and the expat population includes a surprisingly large number of orchid fanciers.

ACCOMMODATION
You can make two unfortunate generalisations about accommodation in PNG: there's not enough of it and what there is costs too much. Particularly in Port Moresby, and to a lesser extent in other towns, there is a shortage of rooms and you would be well advised to make bookings before you arrive. If you're travelling around the country by yourself, not on a tour, it's quite easy to book ahead using the excellent phone system. Remember there is no mail delivery in PNG and any booking by mail must be sent to a post office box number.

The accommodation picture is worse at the bottom end of the ladder. PNG would be an ideal country for the backpacker in many ways, since it's a place which repays effort. Unfortunately, from the shoestring traveller's point of view it is often rather disastrous. There is virtually no youth hostel style accommodation, in a couple of places (Lae and Rabaul) there are relatively cheap student-hostel places although in comparison to Asian neighbours even this is pricey. In some other towns there are mission run establishments which are quite cheap, but these often have very limited space. In a couple of places (Madang and Port Moresby) there are CWA (Country Women's Association) cottages which are reasonably cheap. In many towns there is absolutely nothing at all — Kieta in Bougainville and Wewak are two examples of fair sized towns with a complete blank in the low-priced accommodation bracket.

When you move up into a higher price bracket the picture is not so bad. Much of the accommodation is motel style and of quite recent construction. Prices are generally a little to a lot higher than similar standard motels in Australia, singles in the K15 to K25 bracket, doubles from, say, K20. Many of PNG's older hotels are delightfully Somerset Maughamish, right down to the ceiling fans lazily swirling around.

If you're really roughing it, well off the beaten track, look for the "haus kiap" — these are houses kept in every village for the use of the patrol officers. Since Independence, government-by-patrol has gone into decline, and there are not so may haus kiaps around, and many of them are slowly falling apart — in any case they're often little more than a roof over your head. You will often find mission workers or expats willing to offer you a place to stay but do not expect this as a matter of course. Some people may be only too pleased to see your face, but equally there will be many who have no interest in you at all! Remember that mission workers and people working with aid agencies are often very poorly paid, if you do meet someone who offers to put you up, make sure you pay your way. Teachers can often arrange to stay in schools.

FOOD

You don't come to Papua New Guinea for fine or exotic food although, on the other hand, you should manage to eat quite OK. You probably won't have much opportunity to try local food — which to a western palate is no loss since high starch content/low protein was long the order of the day in PNG. In much of the low-lying swamp country the staple food was, and still is, sago, a bland, starchy extract from the pith of the sago palm. It is thought that the population of the Highlands started to increase rapidly about 350 years ago with the introduction of the sweet potato (kau kau). Due to the limited animal life in PNG, protein deficiency has always been a problem although in the last century the introduction of more vegetables, domestic animals and better fishing has dramatically improved the local diet.

In all the big towns you'll be able to eat comparatively well in hotels or restaurants. At these places you'll find good quality Australian-style food at prices similar or a little higher than in restaurants in Australia. There are a few notable places — the classy *Moresby Dekanai* in Moresby, the excellent Chinese food at the *Lantern Lodge* in Goroka or at the Chinese restaurants in the old Chinatown area of Rabaul.

If you want to economise a little there are a couple of ways to do it. One is the clubs. Almost every town has a club, at one time they were havens of white-colonialism, but today they are fully integrated; despite this the falling expat population has thrown many of them on hard times and they are generally only too happy to sign in "out of town" visitors. In most of the clubs you'll find you can get excellent and economical "counter meals". To the non-Australians out there that means a meal which you order "at the counter". Something like steak, salad and french fries — at about K3 and often even less. Many of the hotels also have counter meals at lunchtime, but one of the drawbacks of PNG's hotels is that in the evening there is very often no alternative to their usually fairly expensive restaurants.

For the shoestring traveller, backpackers and so on, PNG can be a rather miserable experience. Because there are so few local food outlets, finding anything apart from the western-tourist oriented places can be difficult. It makes you long for the excellent and amazingly cheap food of South-East Asia. The closest thing to local eating is the Haus Kai, greasy spoon style take-aways where you'll find meat pies and fish & chips just like in Australia — except lower in quality and higher in price. Of course there are exceptions — some PNG take-aways serve quite edible, even reasonably priced, food.

There are a few other escapes. One is the Burns Philp and Steamships department stores which generally have snack bars where you can get a fairly decent sandwich or other light meal at fairly reasonable cost. Many of the cheaper places to stay either have communal cooking facilities available (CWAs in particular) or are self-contained with kitchen equipment in the rooms (Salvation Army flats). In these cases you can economise by fixing your own food, buying fresh vegetables in the market. Any way you cut it, you'll find the price of eating is a lot lower in Indonesia than in PNG though.

Eating Out
Two perhaps useful pieces of advice in coping with the Melanesian way of doing things: if the delay from ordering food until it arrives seems extraordinarily long, it's worth discreetly enquiring if your order has got from the table to the kitchen. Sometimes it gets forgotten on the way. When your bill comes it's wise to add it up again.

Beer
The Australian beer culture has been accepted a little too wholeheartedly in PNG. Until 1963, Papua New Guineans were strictly forbidden to consume alcohol, it was for whites only. As the country moved towards self-government it soon became obvious that there could not be two laws, one for the locals, one for the expats. Thus, despite some anguished Australian cries that nobody would be safe on the streets, the pubs were opened to all. Naturally nothing so disastrous happened but the effect of beer on PNG has certainly not been a happy one.

Perhaps it's a connection to that same feast or famine mentality of the pig kill where one went hungry much of the year then at a pig feast killed all your pigs and ate them in one non-stop orgy of over-consumption. Whatever the reason, some Papua New Guineans have a propensity to keep on drinking until they are either broke or flat on the floor. Drinking is definitely a joyless affair, conducted in depressing, open-air public bars where it's a simple matter of sink another and another and another until they're all gone.

Various means of fighting the drink problem have been tried — advertising of beer is forbidden, heavy taxes have been slapped on it, the drinking hours restricted, the bars were closed on Fridays (pay nights), but none of these measures seems to have had much of an effect. The two breweries, South Pacific and San Miguel are doing OK out of it — nice beer, but it's a shame it has such a large influence on PNG life.

Betel Nut
All through Asia people chew the nut of the Areca palm known as betel nut or, in Pidgin, Buai. It's a mild intoxicant but unlikely to attract western drug fans. For starters the betel nut is far too acidic to chew by itself — betel nut users generally chew it with lime obtained from crushed seashells and with the leaves or vine of the pepper plant in order to neutralise the acidity. Prolonged usage leads to your mouth becoming stained bright red and your teeth going black; if you keep on the acid of the nut will eat away your gums and is thought to cause mouth cancer.

PAPERWORK & OTHER INFORMATION

Visas
A passport and visa are required for visitors to PNG — no photos are necessary, no charge is made and a stay of up to three months is permitted. Since they seem to give you what you ask for, ask for too much time rather than too little and have to face the problem of extending your visa. Officially you may be asked to show your inward and outward ticketing, that you have sufficient funds and that you have made some sort of accommodation arrangements when applying for your visa. In practice that is unlikely to happen, although you may have to show your outward ticket on arrival. In countries where there is no PNG consular office apply to the nearest Australian office.

Two warnings on PNG offices and visas: in Australia try to get your visa from the Sydney Consulate-General, not from the High Commission in Canberra which can be painfully slow and unhelpful. In Sydney they're business-like and efficient. In Indonesia the PNG Embassy is in Jakarta; Jayapura in Irian Jaya may be the usual entry point from Indonesia to Papua New Guinea and may be only a few minutes flying time from the PNG border, but it has no consular representation. It's a long way back to Jakarta to get a visa! Make sure when you get that visa that it will still be valid when you arrive in Papua New Guinea.

PNG offices abroad are:

AUSTRALIA:

PNG High Commission
PO Box 572, Manuka, Canberra
ACT 2603

PNG Consulate-General, PNG House
225/233 Clarence Street, Sydney
(PO Box 4201 GPO, Sydney 2000)

PNG Consulate, Estate House
127 Creek Street, Brisbane
(GPO Box 220)

NEW ZEALAND: PNG High Commission
                                PO Box 9746, Wellington

FIJI: PNG High Commission
                                Ratu Sukana House, Govt Building
                                PO Box 2447, Suva

INDONESIA: PNG Embassy
                                Jaya Building, Halan Thamran No 12
                                Jakarta

JAPAN: PNG Embassy
                                Mita Kokusal Building
                                4-28 Mita 1-Chome
                                Minato-Ky, Tokyo

USA: PNG Embassy
                                1776 Massachusetts Ave
                                Washington, DC 20036

                                PNG Permanent Mission to the UN
                                801 Second Avenue
                                New York, NY 10017

Other addresses:

Air Niugini   PNG Office of Tourism
PO Box 7185   PO Box 773
Boroko, Papua New Guinea   Port Moresby, Papua New Guinea
(tel: 25 9000)   (tel: 25 4200)

Health

Papua New Guinea's only serious health risk is Malaria — it virtually wiped out the early German attempts at colonising the north coast and it's still a danger today in the more jungled and wet areas. Prevention is a simple weekly dose of the anti-malarial drug but there are some malarial strains thought to be developing a resistance to the drugs most frequently prescribed. Tell your doctor you're going to Papua New Guinea and he may have some new tricks up his sleeve.

Smallpox and cholera vaccinations are not required unless you need them for re-entering your own country (you don't for Australia) but I think as much protection as you can get is always a wise idea.

Otherwise health risks are no worse, or better, than any other tropical country. Simple cuts and scratches can very easily get infected so care should be taken to keep them clean and dry. On my first visit to PNG a simple little graze on my ankle took a dose of penicillin to heal it up when I eventually got home. Food, at least in the main cities, is hardly likely to cause you any hardships and water is generally drinkable. A personal insect repellant is a wise thing to carry, both for your own comfort and as a further precaution against malarial mosquitoes in those areas where they are on the prowl.

Money

The unit of currency in Papua New Guinea is the kina (pronounced "keener") which is divided into 100 toea (pronounced "toy-ah"). Both are the names of traditional shell money and this connection to traditional forms of wealth is emphasised on the notes too. It's not just chance that the K20 note, largest denomination note in Papua New Guinea, has that most valuable of village animals, the pig, illustrated on it.

kina coin

At the time of Independence the kina was on a par with the Australian dollar and many expatriates took great pains to ensure that their future salaries should be set in dollars rather than kina. A major mistake since the kina has zoomed ahead in value since 1975. It is generally held that the kina has now become rather overvalued and is due for a fall soon — a high value kina has done wonders in keeping the PNG inflation rate down to manageable levels but has made the country uncomfortably expensive for the outsider. Devaluation could make it much more attractive.

At last count the exchange rates were:

1 kina	= A$1.27	A$1	= K0.79
	= US$1.47	US$1	= K0.68
	= £0.75	£1	= K1.34
	= NZ$1.37	NZ$1	= K0.73
	= HK$7.14	HK$1	= K0.14
	= S$3.23	S$1	= K0.31
	= Dm2.70	Dm1	= K0.37

Most international currency traveller's cheques are acceptable in PNG. Banks can be found in all the big towns, but off the beaten track you may have trouble finding a place to change money. Don't run short.

Although the country has been shifted on to a cash economy to a very great extent, traditional forms of wealth are still very important, particularly in the Highlands where displays of affluence are very important. A wad of banknotes can never have the same impact as kina shells, cassowaries or pigs. Kina shells are large half-moons cut from the gold lip pearl shell — they are worn as personal embellishments, particularly for ceremonial occasions in the Highlands. The kina coin, there is no one kina note, has a large hole in the centre, probably with the idea that it too could be worn round the neck. In the Highlands another traditional display of wealth is the *aumak*, a chain of tiny bamboo rods worn around the neck. Each

Highland man with aumak

rod indicates that the wearer has lent out ten or so kina shells. A long row of these little lengths of bamboo is a subtle indication of great wealth.

You can do one thing to stop the cost of travel in PNG being even higher — don't tip, it isn't necessary.

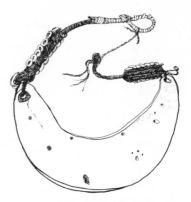

kina shell

Costs

Expats living in PNG complain about the costs a lot, particularly food, so I did a little supermarket survey in Kieta (Bougainville), Port Moresby and back in Melbourne. My imaginary shopping list included cornflakes, a can of soft drink, sugar, rice, butter, soap powder, cans of soup, fruit, vegetables, crackers, yoghurt and a packet of tissues. In Australia the price translated as K7.04, in Kieta (where I suspect prices may be slightly subsidised by the mining company?) K9.93 (41% higher) and in Moresby K10.50 (49% higher). Quite a steep jump. The item to item markup varied considerably — the tissues and cornflakes (big, lightweight boxes which are expensive to ship?) were nearly twice as expensive, cans were only 5% to 15% more expensive. I didn't compare meat or vegetable prices — much of which also comes from Australia since local production is insufficient or the goods in demand simply won't grow in the tropics. It's disappointing how limited the range of fruit and vegetables is in PNG though. Of course these price comparisons are rather ridiculous — the old story about trying to live one life style in a totally different environment. It's always expensive, you've got to fit in a little.

One place where the price differential operates the other way is cars. It makes a lot of sense for Australians working in PNG for a year or two to buy a new car and take it back on their return. Since PNG does not have the ridiculously high Australian import duties the new prices can be a lot lower. Qantas fly cars back to Sydney on their weekly 747 Kombi service — K450 for small cars, K550 for medium size, K650 for big ones. Second hand cars also appear cheaper, though it's hard to say since they tend to wear out very quickly (poor service, rough roads, lots of rust inducing rain) and many are differently equipped than the Australian editions. If you intend taking a car back to Oz make sure it meets the Australian Design Regulations.

Other costs — well fuel is much the same price as in Australia, accommodation is expensive and hard to find. Almost without exception expats have that colonial luxury of someone to clean up behind them, wash the dishes, do the laundry and ironing. Life isn't all hard in PNG.

Postal Services

PNG has no mail delivery service so if you're writing to people within the country you must write to a PO Box or to their place of work. There's a poste restante service at most post offices. Underline the surname and print it clearly if you want it to arrive safely. Even then you may have to just hope; on my last trip, of five letters sent to me I only got one — all had been mailed with plenty of time in hand. Mail going out of PNG is generally quite fast and efficient — count on about four days to Australia.

Postage rates are:

letters within PNG	7t
aerograms	15t
airmail letters to:	
Australia	15t
New Zealand, some Asian countries	20t
Other Asian countries	25t
Europe, North America	35t

Telephones

The phone system in PNG, although limited to the main centres, is extremely good — another example where the infrastructure seems totally out of line with the overall economy. You can direct dial between all the main centres, there are not even any area codes to worry about. You can also direct dial Australia even from public phones — try that the other way around! Simply dial 3 then the Australian area code and number. Calls to Australia cost about K1.60 a minute.

Pay phones are like Australian STD ones — 10t for local calls, keep feeding in coins each time the light shines for long distance ones. Your money is refunded if the call fails or if you've inserted more coins than you have used on long distance calls. Unfortunately pay phones can be hard to find in some places. In Port Moresby centre the post office has just two phones and there is always a queue to use them.

Time

The time throughout Papua New Guinea is the same as Australian Eastern Standard Time — 9 to 10 hours ahead of GMT. Situated so close to the equator, day and night are almost equal in length — the sun rises about 6 am and sets at about 6 pm. Don't confuse PNG offical time with PNG's unofficial time, Melanesian time. Melanesian time is always tomorrow — there is no rush, no hurry, no hassle — just as long as you roll with it, rather than fight against it! Lee Kuan Yew, the energetic leader of Singapore once said you could divide south Asia into the "intense" and the "non-intense". The Chinese, Japanese and Koreans are in the intense camp and the Papua New Guineans would be well to the relaxed end of the non-intense group. Although you should never expect things to happen on time, it's as well to remember that even though the bus is half an hour late on 99 times out of 100, on the 100th time it will be half an hour early.

Opening Hours

Most offices are open from 7.45 or 8 am to 4 pm. Shops generally stay open later, especially on Friday nights. They're also open Saturday mornings — trade stores and snack bars are likely to open more liberal hours. Banks are open 9 am to 2 pm, Monday to Thursday and until 5 pm on Friday. At Port Moresby airport there's a bank counter which opens for the arrival of all international flights — but not necessarily for departures. Post offices open at 9 am and are also open on Saturday mornings.

Safety

You are most unlikely to get an arrow in the back or have your head hunted for in modern PNG. "Payback" squabbles, which at times develop into something akin to tribal warfare, are very much a locals-only activity. So long as you didn't try to get between the opposing sides, should you happen to be at the wrong place at the wrong time, you'd be left alone. Where visitors and expats do, occasionally, have a little difficulty is in PNG's towns. PNG is not like Australia, England or many parts of Asia where you can happily wander the streets at any time of the day or night and know you're perfectly safe. On the other hand, nor is it like many parts of the US where you expect to be mugged at any second. Nevertheless a little circumspection is worthwhile, there are places in the cities where it is not wise to wander alone at night. Particularly if it's a big drinking night. Black-white relations in PNG are remarkably good and the unpleasant events that sometimes take place in formerly white-dominated African countries are virtually unimaginable in PNG.

Papers

It's often said that one of the best ways to understand a place is to read the papers — from cover to cover, classified ads and all. PNG's only daily (well week-daily) is the Port Moresby *Post Courier* — a part of the Melbourne Herald empire. It's a tabloid size paper, but a more serious minded one than that format usually indicates.

The readers' letters usually provides the most local colour and the paper gets an amazing number of them. There's always at least one letter complaining about or praising the PMVs, the rudeness of some segment of the population, or the rough deal some public figure is currently getting. Not quite as regular, but almost, are the scandalised letters from missionaries who appear to be in constant fear of Sodom & Gomorrah turning up in PNG. In mid-'78 the arrival of *Jesus Christ Superstar* was labelled "sheer blasphemy" by one keen bible quoter, obviously anxious to prove that the old-style, bible thumping, hell and brimstone traditions live on. But best of all is the readers' problem page which comes up once a week — no western women's page sob-sister ever had to provide advice on the sort of situation which seem everyday in PNG — like how many pigs in the bride price?

In really remote parts of PNG a newspaper, no matter how old, is worth more than its newstand price — for use as roll-your-own cigarette papers. It has become so widely accepted that newspaper makes the best cigarette paper that you can now buy machine produced newspaper rolled cigarettes in PNG.

The Rise & Fall of the Phantom

The sad saga of the mighty Phantom temporarily put the PNG newspaper business under the world spotlight in 1977. If the people of PNG have a national hero it would have to be the Phantom — you know, the "ghost who walks", the guy in the tight-fitting one piece suit who lives in the Skull Cave of Bangalla and runs around righting wrong and never marrying Diana? The hero of countless comic strips has some special appeal in PNG — perhaps, some say, because he is unfailingly even-handed and honest and has the same strong, mysterious aura that the first white men to arrive in PNG had — a sort of father figure in other words. There's even a hint of cargo cult in that strange cave of his, packed full of valuable items he got, God knows where.

The Phantom's rise to national fame came when *Wantok* started operations in 1972 — the church financed, national, Pidgin English paper started running the Phantom comic strip translated into Pidgin. Soon his fame spread throughout the country and copies of *Wantok* were zealously hoarded until someone able to read came by and provided a public reading. The government put the Phantom to work for them — promoting the virtues of toothbrushes or, as in the poster opposite, the nutritional wonders of the peanut: "If you eat plenty of peanuts you'll grow up strong, just like (olsem) the Phantom". Posters were no sooner pinned up in villages than they were swiped for home decorations.

But disaster lurked near to hand, the *Post-Courier* also ran the Phantom and in 1977 decided enough was enough, they held the exclusive rights and the Pidgin Phantom must go. Their strip was in English, and ran well ahead of the *Wantok* version, but international copyright laws proved stronger than the hero of the Skull Cave. A flurry of international protests were carried as far as the Australian Foreign Minister who decided it was not really important enough to justify his taking action. The Pidgin Phantom still lives in one small way, *Wantok* collected his Pidgin adventures into one big comic book which is an excellent and painless way to study the language. After all who could start a love letter better than Diana writing to the Phantom — "Lewa bilong mi, longtaim tumas mi no bin lukim yu. Wataim bai me lukim yu gen? Mi krai long yu. Mi Diana."

What to Bring?

Too little rather than too much is always the best advice for travel wherever you go. Papua New Guinea's generally warm climate also makes things easier — even in the cool Highlands, a sweater is all you'll ever need for the evenings. The only time you'll need a coat in PNG is if you go mountain climbing. It does reach freezing on top of Mt Wilhelm.

That apart it's lightweight clothing, T-shirts, swimming gear, you will need. Natural fibres, cotton in particular, will be most comfortable in the sticky, coastal humidity. Long sleeved shirts are not necessary except on the most formal occasions — coat and tie virtually never. Men will find Australian style "dress" shorts are wearable almost on any occasion but women would be advised to wear dresses rather than shorts.

Unlike other Asian countries, Papua New Guinea is not a good place to buy clothes so don't come expecting to get more gear on the way. On the other hand all those day-to-day western commodities which can be difficult to find in some Asian countries — toothpaste, toilet paper, etc — are easy to obtain in the major towns.

A folding umbrella can be extremely useful for those unexpected wet seasons. A mask and snorkel is definitely worth having for a little diving. A handful of teabags or instant coffee sachets and packets of sugar are useful for the places where there is an electric kettle but nothing else. My secrets for successfully getting the gear from place to place include using a shoulder bag rather than a suitcase; lots of small plastic bags or stuff bags to keep things apart; and a Balinese sarong which can be a dressing gown, a beach blanket, a bed sheet and, of course, a sarong.

Camera & Film

Papua New Guinea is very photogenic — you can easily run through a lot of film, particularly if you happen on some event like a big Highland sing-sing. The recommendation to "bring more film than you'll need and then some more again" is worth heeding. Film is easily available in the major towns but it is fairly expensive, even by pricey Australian standards.

Protect your film as much as possible from the humidity and heat. Allow for the high intensity of the tropical sun when making your settings but also remember that on many occasions you'll need to make fairly long exposures. Even on bright sunny days it can be surprisingly dim down in the jungle. I found a flash very useful in Papua New Guinea, particularly for shots inside the Sepik Haus Tambarans. Photographing the brilliantly painted fronts of the Maprik style Haus Tambarans is one of the more difficult technical feats because the forward lean of the front means they are always in shadow. Around noon (and hoping for a lot of reflected light) is the best bet.

You'll find the local people are generally very happy to be photographed, even going out of their way to pose for you, particularly at sing-sings. Of course it never hurts to ask before snapping. Remember dark skin will probably take a longer exposure for clear results. You'll rarely be asked to pay for photographing somebody, but a telephoto lens is very useful for shots in those sort of places where you want to be as unobtrusive as possible.

ARTIFACTS
Papua New Guinea's arts and handicrafts have been recognised as the most vital in the Pacific. The art is amazingly varied for the same reason as there are so many languages — lack of contact between different villages and groups of people. Particularly on the Sepik, where art is so important and so energetic, you'll find villages only a few km apart will have styles which are totally distinct. At the Chambri Lakes, for example, the people in Aibom express themselves purely through clay pots — which no other Sepik village makes. Only minutes away at Chambri it's masks and spears, of a very distinctive and easily recognised style, that the people specialise in.

The Sepik is easily the best known area of PNG for artifacts; in fact there's a temptation to think of all PNG art in terms of the Sepik when actually there is far more to be found. The strength of Sepik art is largely due to its spiritual significance. Every Sepik village had to have its Haus Tambaran, the men's spirit house. In this men-only club were stored the carvings that represented the various spirits. Since carvings had to be replaced fairly frequently it was a living and continuous craft. Today much of the spiritual significance may be lost, although certain ancient pieces are still zealously protected, but the craft continues — for the benefit of collectors and tourists.

Elsewhere the pattern may not be so instantly recognisable as on the Sepik, but the crafts are there. You'll find pottery in many areas, ritual Hohoa boards in the Gulf region, island carvings and shell money, or more recently introduced crafts like the pleasantly coarse weavings in the Highlands.

Like everything else in PNG, artifacts are not cheap — particularly if you compare them to the more sophisticated (but less dynamic) carvings in Indonesia or the Philippines. The price inflation of carvings is also rather astonishing — I've seen prices 600 to 800% higher in artifacts shops in PNG than at source. In fact many prices in shops within Papua New Guinea are considerably higher than overseas! There are a couple of reasons for this (apart from plain, straightforward profit). First of all the channels from the carver to the shops are lengthy and imperfect — long "buying trips" have to be undertaken for artifact dealers to obtain their stock-in-trade. Secondly many PNG artifacts are extremely unwieldy or very fragile — there's not a lot of thought given to meeting airline weight allowances! Thank God. So transport can be difficult and many items are really only purchasable by museums which can handle major shipping problems. Transporting a Sepik garamut drum or orator's stool would just about require a crane.

Arts and handicrafts anywhere in the world, and in PNG in particular, face two great dangers — lack of interest or too much interest. When the religous or spiritual reasons for an art form have died out — through changes in culture or circumstances — the art can die too unless there is a new reason for it. Such as demand from collectors. But it's a two-edged sword for too much demand can prompt careless, sloppy or lazy work. So if you like a piece, buy it — you'll be doing something to keep the craft alive. But be discerning — better one more expensive, carefully made item than half a dozen shoddy ones. You'll like it better in the long run too.

The descriptions that follow are just a few of the enormous varieties of styles and types of artifacts you may see in Papua New Guinea, there is far more than this actually available. If you want to get a pre-taste of New Guinea art in Australia I suggest you visit New Guinea Primitive Arts, 6th floor, 428 George St, Sydney. Alternatively there are some excellent books you can read.

Pottery
The village of Aibom, near the Chambri Lakes, specialises in pottery — virtually the only place on the Sepik to do so. Aibom pots are noted for their relief faces which are coloured with lime. They are made by the coil method and are very cheap on the Sepik, but become rapidly more expensive as you move further away because, like other PNG pottery, they are very fragile. Other interesting pots can be found at Yabob and Bilbil villages near Madang, at Zunim near the Highlands Highway from Lae, and from the Porebada people in the Central Province. The Amphlett Islanders in Milne Bay also make very fine and very fragile pottery. No pottery is glazed in PNG and it also often poorly fired so it all suffers from extreme fragility.

Weapons
The Chambri Lake carvers produce decorative spears remarkably similar to their masks. Perhaps with tourists in mind they take apart so they are relatively easy to transport. Bows and arrows are available from a number of places including the Highlands and Bougainville Island. Shields are also popular artifacts as they often have a decorative and spiritual role just as im-

portant as their function as protection for a warrior. In the Highlands the ceremonial Hagen Axes are similarly half-tool, half-ritual. Here you will also see the lethal cassowary claw-tipped Huli Picks or on the Sepik the equally nasty bone daggers.

Spirit Boards, Story Boards & Cult Hooks
In the Gulf Province the shield like Hohao or Gope boards are said to contain the spirits of powerful heroes or to act as guardians of the village. Before hunting trips or war expeditions the spirits contained in the boards were called upon to advise and support the warriors. At Kambot on the Keram River, a tributary of the Sepik, story boards are a modern interpretation of the fragile bark carvings they used to make. The boards illustrate, in raised relief, incidents of village life and are one of my favourite examples of New Guinea art. Cult hooks — small ones are Yipwons while larger ones are Kamanggabi — are carved as hunting charms and carried by their owners in a bag to ensure success on the hunt, the small ones anyway. Food hooks are used to hang bilums of food from the roof to keep it away from the rats but also have a spiritual significance.

Bilums
Bilums are the original string bags and are made in many parts of the country. They are enormously strong and expand to amazing sizes — they are used for everything from transporting or storing food to carrying a baby in. Good bilums can be rather expensive, particularly in the towns. They are time consuming to make since the entire length of string is fed through every loop. Beware of modern bilums made of plastic or nylon cord instead of the natural fibres.

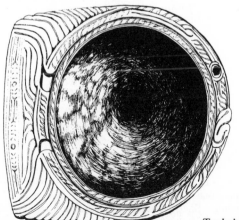

Trobriand bowl

Bowls
The Trobriand Islanders are prolific carvers of everything from stylised figures to decorated lime gourds, but my favourites are the beautifully carved bowls. They are generally carved from dark wood and laboriously polished with a pig's tusk. The rims are patterned, often to represent a fish or turtle. The Tami Islanders near Lae are also renowned for

their carved bowls. Further offshore the Siassi Islanders carve deep, elliptical bowls which are stained black and patterned with incised designs coloured with lime. In Milne Bay the Woodlark Islanders carve bowls somewhat similar to those from the Trobriands.

Musical Instruments

Drums are the main musical instruments in PNG — either the large garamut drums found on the Sepik and made by hollowing out a tree trunk or the smaller Kundu style drum — hour glass shaped and with a tympanum formed of lizard or snake skin. Trobriand drums are somewhat similar. Other instruments include the sacred flutes which are always found in male-female pairs and are generally reserved for initiation rites; the bull roarers which are spun round on a length of cord; the pottery whistles of the Highlands and the small, but eerie sounding Jews harps also found in the Highlands.

Kundu drum

Other Odds & Ends

Buka baskets, from Bougainville in the North Solomons, are said to be the finest baskets in the Pacific. They are very expensive. Similar but coarser baskets are found in the Southern Highlands. Figures of various types are carved on the Murik Lakes, the Yuat River and in the Trobriand Islands. The Trobriand Islanders also carve very fine walking sticks and some delightful little stools and tables. Tapa cloth, made from tree bark, is beaten and decorated in the Northern Province. Shell jewellery can be found at many coastal towns, particularly Madang and Rabaul.

Chambri mask

Masks

Masks in Papua New Guinea are more often intended as decoration than as something to be worn. They are found particularly along the Sepik River but also in other parts of the country. The Chambri masks from the villages on the Chambri Lakes are the most modernistic of the Sepik masks masks — instantly recognisable by their elongated design and glossy black finish with incised patterns in brown and white, colours which are unique to Chambri. They make nice gifts because they are smaller than the general run of Sepik masks, easily transportable since they are solid without projecting teeth, horns or other features, and they are very cheap. Small Chambri masks at the village or in Wewak are only one or two kina.

At Korogo, on the Sepik, the masks are made of wood then decorated with clay in which shells, hair and pigs' teeth are embedded. Other distinctive Sepik mask styles are found at Kamindabit and Tambanum. Maks from the Murik Lakes have an almost African look about them. At Maprik the yam masks are woven from cane or rattan. Masks are also carved at Kiwai Island, near Daru on the southern, Papuan, coast.

PIDGIN ENGLISH — TOK PISIN

A recent survey calculated that there were 717 languages in Papua New Guinea, 45% of all the languages in the world. With this amazing basis for mutual incomprehension it's not surprising that there has long been a search for a common linking language. During the early days of British New Guinea and then Australian Papua, the local language of the Moresby coastal area, Motu, was slightly modified to become "Police Motu", and spread through Papua by the native constabulary. It is still quite widely spoken in the southern, Papuan, part of PNG. You can easily pick up a Motu phrase book in Port Moresby.

Meanwhile in the northern, German half, of what is today PNG, the German planters were facing exactly the same communication difficulties. The solution here was Pisin, a local word that became corrupted into Pidgin — a term used today to define a trade language, a sort of mid-way meeting point between two languages. Pidgin English is a blend of mainly English words and Melanesian grammar forms. Since it first came into use around Rabaul, during the German days, the Melanesian words used in Pidgin are mainly from the languages of East New Britain. There are, however, a number of words indicating other foreign influences. Milk, for example, is "susu" as in Indonesia. In PNG, "susu" can also mean breasts.

Pidgin has been damned and condemned by everybody from the UN down. It's been called "baby talk". "broken English", "demeaning" and much worse. There have been a number of attempts to discourage its use and push for English to be the national linking language. All have failed and Pidgin continues to spread, supplanting Motu as the lingua franca as more and more Pidgin speakers come to Port Moresby. Of course Pidgin is far from an ideal language, mainly because it is extremely clumsy. There are only about 1300 words in Pidgin and they have to describe things that it takes about 6000 English words to do. This results in some very round-about and wordy descriptions. An absurd example of this is the word for cow. There is no separate word for bull or cow, they're described collectively as a "bulmakau" (bull-and-a-cow). "Meri" is the word for woman or female so a cow is described as a female-bull-and-a-cow or a "bulmakau meri".

I hope that also indicates what a hell of a lot of fun Pidgin can be. Many words or phrases make perfect sense if you just read them out slowly and thoughtfully. I saw a sign outside a cinema in Madang announcing that the film showing was a "piksa bilong bigpela man/meri tasol". That is it was a "picture for big-fellow men and women only", in other words it was for adults only. Or who was that uniformed Englishman at the independence day celebrations — why none other than the "nambawan pikinini bilong Misis Kwin", that is to say the "eldest child of the Queen's" — er Prince Charles! A public library? — why that's a "Haus buk bilong ol man/meri".

Like any language it takes a lot of study to really come to terms with it but you can be communicating on at least a basic level in Pidgin with remarkable speed. Invest in a pidgin phrase book, they're easily obtainable in PNG — a good one to look for is *The Book of Pidgin English (Buk Bilong Tok Pisin)* by John J Murphy, which has an interesting explanation of the language, phrases and pitfalls and an English-Pidgin and Pidgin-English dictionary. About K2.50 or K3.

There are quite a few Pidgin words and phrases that have crept into everyday English in PNG. You can always recognise somebody who has spent some time in PNG by the way they say "tru" instead of "really", "that's right" or "you don't say". Nobody leaves PNG when their work is completed, they "go pinis". It's never dinner time, always "kai" (food) time, which is followed not by dessert but by "sweet kai". You'll also be told "maski" which means "don't bother". If something is totally unimportant or doesn't matter at all, then it's "samting nating" (something-nothing). And a private problem, your own affair, is "samting bilong yu". Nobody gets fired in PNG, they're "raused" from "rausim" or "thrown out" — that one dates right back to German days.

If your Pidgin is not perfect, it is very wise to append "yu save or nogat?" (you understand or not?) to any sentence. "Save" is pronounced "savvy". Note that P and F are virtually interchangeable in Pidgin.

Some useful words:

yes	yes
no	nogat
thank you	tenkyu

greetings

good morning	gud moning
good afternoon	gud apinun
good night	gud nait
see you	lukim yu

commands & questions

put it there	putim long hap
show me	soim me
stop here	stop long hia
is it far?	em i long wai?
near, close by	klostu
a very long way	long way tumas
I would like to buy.....	
	mi laik baim...
where is the....?	
	we stap wanpela.....?
how much does that cost?	
	em i kostim hamas?
I want something to eat	
	mi laikim sampela kaikai
that is mine	em bilong mi
be careful	lukautim gut
go away! (forcefully)	rause!

communications

what is your name?	
	kolim nem bilong yu
where are you from?	
	yu bilong wanem ples?
I don't understand	mi no save
I don't understand Pidgin	
	mi no save tok Pisin
speak slowly	tok easy

useful words

a little	liklik
plenty	planti

big	bigpela
aircraft	balus
airport	ples balus
bathroom	rum was was
bedroom	rum slip
toilet	liklik haus
child	pikinini
decorations, uniform	bilas
forbidden	tambu
man/woman	man/meri
hospital	haus sick
police station	haus polis
letter, book, ticket	pass
(anything with writing on it)	
luggage	kargo
newspaper	niuspepa
photo	piksa
towel	lap lap bilong was was
countryman or friend	wantok*
friend	pren

*wantok literally means "one-talk", somebody who speaks the same language — the "ples tok", language of the place.

food

food	kai
restaurant	haus kai
menu	pass bilong kaikai
tea/coffee	ti/kopi
eggs	kiau
sugar	suga
meat	abus
unripe coconut	kulau
water	wara
drink	dring
breakfast	kaikai bilong moning
lunch	kaikai bilong belo
dinner	kaikai bilong apinun

pronouns

		they	oli
I/you	mi/yu	we/you	mipela/yupela
he/she/it	i	everyone	ol (or ol man/meri)

verbs & tenses

Tenses are all the same except you append pinis (finish) to make it past tense: "mi kaikai pinis" means "I have eaten". Two common verbs:

bring, give or take	kisim
fasten, shut or lock	fasim

INSTRUCTIONS FOR THE OPERATION OF THE EMERGENCY LOCATOR BEACON.
Remove Rubber Plug, Insert Finger & Push The Rubber Toggle Switch Downwards.

SAPOS BALUS I BUGARAP, YU MAS WORKIM DISPELA OL SAMTING.
Rausim Lik Lik Gumi, Putim Finga Bilong Yu Long Hole Na Suim Switch Oli
Karamapim Long Gumi Igo Daun.

Workim Ol Dispela Samting Taim Balus I Bugarap.

---

what to do if your "balus" (plane) should "bugarup"

Finally some Pidgin confusion. My brother is my "brata" and my sister is my "sista" but Maureen's brother is her "sista" and her sister is her "brata". In other words your "brata" is always the same sex, your "sista" always the opposite. "Kilim" just means to hit (but hard), to kill somebody (or something) you have to "kilim i dai". Careful of the sexual phrases — "pusim" means to copulate with, not to push! And while you can "ple tenis" (play tennis), "ple" is also a euphemism for intercourse. A man's trunk or suitcase may be a "bokis", but a women's "bokis" is her vagina. And a "blak bokis" is not a black suitcase but a flying fox or bat! You'll love the standard reply to "how far is it?" — "longwe liklik". It doesn't actually mean a long way and not a long way, it translates more like "not too near, not too far"

Village Courts

I heard the curious case, from one of the participants, of a European taking another European to court for compensation in a local village court. The offender, one of those lascivious New Zealanders, had been involved in a little activity with another westerner's local wife. The aggrieved gentleman decided to summon his wife and her lover to court and claim compensation. The proceedings all took place in Pidgin, the husband made his statement and since the guilty Kiwi didn't speak much Pidgin at that time he simply agreed with what the woman said. All three were then sent outside while the judge deliberated. Summoned back to the court, he was told that, if it was all right by him, he would be fined K50 compensation to the husband plus K10 court costs. The unfaithful wife was then given a very stern talking to (the whole point of the exercise) for in a case like this it is obviously always the woman's fault. Not only does she cheat on her husband but she also leads some otherwise innocent man into a sinful act. She too was required to hand over K50 to her husband as compensation and pay court costs. Justice at the village level.

BOOKS & BOOKSHOPS

There are plenty of books about Papua New Guinea — all that wild country, amazing tribes, fantastic culture, last frontier stuff has attracted countless writers and photographers. It was also one of the last great areas for European exploration, developed its own sub-category of literature known as the "patrol officers' memoirs", had a dramatic role in WW II and since the war there has been the intriguing developments leading to independence. The books that follow are just a small selection of the many that have been written. But first where to find them:

Bookshops

Within Papua New Guinea you probably won't find a great selection of books on the country, except in Port Moresby. The place to go there is the New Guinea Book Depot, there are two branches and the one on Waigani Drive is definitely the superior one. They will always have the latest releases on PNG and some interesting and often unusual older books. The Post Newsagency in Port Moresby also has quite a good selection but elsewhere in the country bookshops are mainly magazines and paperbacks only. One thing not to miss is a look in a Christian bookshops which can be found in almost every major town — plenty of useful little books proving Darwin is all wrong and the world really was created in seven days.

In Australia you can find some books on the country in almost any bookshop but the Henry Lawson bookshop in Sydney specialises in books on New Guinea and the Pacific and is a good place to try for current books.

History & Exploration

Gavin Souter's intriguing book on the exploration and development of New Guinea, *The Last Unknown* (Angus & Robertson, Sydney, 1963), is the book to read if you read nothing else on PNG. The descriptions of the early explorers, some of whom were more than a little strange, is positively enthralling. It barely touches on WW II and stops well before the '60s rush to independence but is a highly enjoyable read and available in paperback.

Parliament of a Thousand Tribes by Osmar White (Heinemann, Melbourne, 1965) was released in an updated Wren paperback in 1972. It covers WW II and the post-war years better then the previous book although it also suffers from not covering the rapidly changing years of the '70s.

Some of the early explorers' own accounts are highly colourful but long out of print. Captain Moresby's *Discoveries and Surveys in New Guinea and the d'Entrecasteaux Islands: A Cruise of HMS Basilisk* was published way back in 1876. The fiery and controversial Italian explorer Luigi D'Albertis had his book, *New Guinea: What I Did and What I Saw* published in 1880. A recent reassessment of this interesting character is *Rape of the Fly* by John Goode (Nelson, Melbourne, 1977).

Probably the most interesting of all the early explorers' stories would have to be Captain J A Lawson's *Wanderings in the Interior of New Guinea* which was published in 1875. Not since his epic visit has Mt Hercules (over a thousand metres higher than Everest) been seen again — or the New Guinea tiger, the waterfalls larger than Niagara or even the giant daisies or huge scorpions.

The patrol officers' memoirs category came into its prime between the wars and some of the books written then, when patrol officers were not only explorers but also the force of government, are classics of their kind. Books like *Across New Guinea from the Fly to the Sepik* (I F Champion, 1932) covering his agonisingly difficult traverse of central New Guinea. Or *The Land that Time Forgot* (Mick Leahy and Mick Crane, 1937) on their discovery of the Highlands, or *Papuan Wonderland* (Jack Hides, 1936).

There are also some much more recent reminiscences of those exciting days on patrol. J K McCarthy's *Patrol into Yesterday* (Cheshire, Melbourne, 1963) is another book I'd highly recommend for exciting reading. "My New Guinea Years", as he subtitled it, covered first contact with the erratic and violent Kukukuku people, the successful escape from Rabaul in WW II and other high adventure. Colin Simpson, the well known Australian travel writer, spent quite a lot of time in Papua New Guinea during the '50s and wrote three books on the land, its people and the explorers, many of whom he met. Parts of all three books were combined into *Plumes and Arrows* (Angus & Robertson, Sydney, 1962) which was available in paperback.

Because PNG's European-contact history is so recent it has been well documented in photographs. You'll find a lot of interesting pictures in *A Pictorial History of New Guinea* by Noel Gash and June Whittaker (Jacaranda, Brisbane, 1975).

World War II

The war, with its enormous impact on the country, naturally prompted some interesting books. For a very readable account of the decisive fighting on the Kokoda Trail, culminating in the bitter struggle to recapture Buna and Gona from the Japanese, look for *Bloody Buna* by Lida Mayo. Originally published by Doubleday, New York in 1974 it is also available in a cheap paperback. Although the author is an American it is not altogether complimentary to MacArthur or the US forces.

The amazing courage of the coastwatchers, who relayed information from behind the Japanese lines, knowing that capture would mean unpleasant death, is also well documented. Look for Eric Feldt's *The Coast Watchers* (Oxford University Press, 1946 and Lloyd O'Neil, Melbourne, 1975). A more recent study is Walter Lord's *Lonely Vigil — The Coastwatchers of the*

Solomons (Viking Press, New York, 1978). Peter Ryan's *Fear Drive My Feet* (Angus & Robertson, Sydney, 1959) recounts some nerve-racking adventures behind the Japanese lines around Lae.

Some people find poking around the rotting relics from the war is an interesting exercise — *Rust in Peace* by Bruce Adams (Antipodean Publishers, Sydney, 1975) tells you where to look, not only in Papua New Guinea but also in other parts of the Pacific. *Battleground South Pacific* (photos Bruce Adams, text Robert Howlett, Reeds, Sydney, 1970) also has much interesting material on the war in Papua New Guinea.

People
If you're in Rabaul you'll no doubt develop an interest in Queen Emma's highly colourful life which is described in *Queen Emma* by R W Robson (Pacific Publications, Sydney, 1965). A recent novel, based around her life, is *Queen Emma of the South Seas* by Geoffrey Dutton (Macmillan, Melbourne, 1976).

Much more recent, but perhaps equally colourful a character, Bobby Gibbes role in post-war PNG aviation is described in *Sepik Pilot* by James Sinclair (Lansdowne, Melbourne, 1971). Flying in Papua New Guinea in the '50s was clearly one hell of a business! James Sinclair is also the author of *History of Aviation in Papua New Guinea*.

Wildlife
Papua New Guinea's exotic and colourful birdlife, in particular the Birds of Paradise, has inspired many equally colourful books. Biggest and most coffee table of the lot would have to be *The Birds of Paradise and Bower Birds* by William Cooper and Joseph Forshaw (William Collins, Sydney, 1977) — at about $100 a copy definitely for the serious ornithologist only! A little more down to earth, in price at least, are two books you can find in Port Moresby. *Birds in Papua New Guinea* by Brian Coates (Robert Brown & Associates, Port Moresby, 1977) and *Wildlife in Papua New Guinea* by Eric Lindgrom (Robert Brown & Associates, Port Moresby or Golden Press, Sydney, 1975) provides an interesting introduction with plenty of excellent photographs.

Culture & Anthropology
New Guinea has been a treasure house for anthropologists and from Malinowski to Margaret Mead they've made their names here. They're still flocking in today. Malinowski's books are covered in the Trobriand Islands section in Milne Bay Province — they're weighty, academic books yet very readable. Margaret Mead's *Growing Up in New Guinea* was first published in 1942, but is still available in a paperback Penguin. She conducted her studies for that book on Manus Island and returned there after the war to investigate the dramatic changes that had taken place — partly prompted by the enormous impact the huge wartime American base had on the Manus people. Her second Manus book was *New Lives for Old* (Morrow, New

York, 1956).

The High Valley by Kenneth H Read (George Allen & Unwin, London, 1966) is a very readable account of the time the author spent with a Highlands village in the early post-war years when the impact of European culture was only just reaching the valley around present-day Goroka. *Gardens of War — Life and Death in the New Guinea Stone Age* by Robert Gardner and Karl G Heider (Random House, New York, 1968 — also in a Penguin large format paperback) describes the ritual warfare of New Guinea tribes, dramatically illustrated with many photographs. Fierce inter-village fighting was still the order of the day in the remote parts of Irian Jaya which the authors visited in the '60s.

Cargo cults have also come in for a lot of study, they're a fascinating example of the collision between primitive beliefs and modern technology. The classic book on these cults is *Road Belong Cargo* by Peter Lawrence (Melbourne University Press, 1964) but there have been a number of earlier books such as F E Williams' 1934 study, *The Vailala Madness in Retrospect* (Kegan Paul, London) or P Worsley's 1957 book *The Trumpet Shall Sound: A Study of Cargo Cults in Melanesia* (Macgibbon & Kee, London).

Curiously there is a gap for a good overall book on New Guinea arts — what is available tends to be lightweight with little more than pretty pictures or a heavy academic study from German or American museums. You may be able to get a copy of *Crafts of Papua New Guinea* in Papua New Guinea, it's just a magazine style production with colour photographs of a variety of styles accompanied by a one paragraph description, but it's better than nothing.

General Description

The frequently updated *Papua New Guinea Handbook* (Pacific Publications, Sydney, latest edition 1978) has lots of facts, figures, tables and fairly dry information. Ann Mallard's *A Traveller's Guide to New Guinea* (Jacaranda, Brisbane, 1969) is now long out of print and out of date but was an excellent overall guide to the country — one to look for in libraries.

One of the most interesting of the "wow look at these pictures" books is the *The World's Wild Places — New Guinea*, one of the glossy Time-Life series. This one is by Roy Mackay with photographs by Eric Lindgrom and covers the spectacular terrain and wildlife very well.

A more general visitor's view of the country can be found in *New Guinea* by Milton and Joan Mann (Kodansha International, Tokyo, 1972) one of the Japanese "This Beautiful World" series — lots of interesting photographs and a readable description of a short visit to PNG.

Odds & Ends

A couple of PNG residents raved about *The Hot Land* by John Ryan (Macmillan, Melbourne, 1970) while I was in the country. It's a journalist's account and therefore a lot of the contemporary reporting is already out of date, but I found the material on discovering long lost aircraft wreckage, the bits of local history, the drawn out business of marking the border to Dutch (later Indonesian) New Guinea, and the story of the Buka baby farm, all quite fascinating.

The Crocodile, by Vincent Eri, was the first published novel by a Papuan (Jacaranda, Brisbane, 1970 — available in a Penguin paperback). It provides an interesting look at the contact between Europeans and locals from the rarely seen, other side of the fence. Ian Downs, an Australian businessman from the Highlands (where he was earlier a pioneering patrol officer) who was deeply involved in the early steps towards self-government, publicised his views in a novel titled *The Stolen Land* (Jacaranda, Brisbane, 1970 and in a Wren paperback).

Port Moresby — Yesterday and Today by Ian Stuart (Pacific Publications, Sydney, 1970) is an interesting account of the history and development of the country's capital city. There are a number of guides to understanding Pidgin, *The Book of Pidgin English (Buk Bilong Tok Pisin)* by John J Murphy (Smith & Paterson, Brisbane, 1973) has been revised many times since it's first publication in 1943 and seems to have stood the test of time. *Introduction to New Guinea Pidgin* (Jacaranda, Brisbane) is an alternative guide to Pidgin English. If you'd like a little Motu, the predominant language in the Papuan part of PNG, then look for *Say it in Motu* (Pacific Publications, Sydney) by Percy Chatterton.

Tourism & the Cost of Visiting PNG

No way around it, PNG is expensive. There are a number of reasons for this sad state of affairs. One is geographical and physical — PNG is incredibly mountainous and rugged and it includes many offshore islands. There are few roads so much transport is by air and consequently expensive. Another factor is historical — PNG has shot from the stone age to the jet age in an incredibly short period of time, in many places the two ages continue to operate side by side. This transition has only been achieved with a lot of outside help and it has often been expensive help.

Many everyday, by western standards, commodities are imported in PNG. Even a lot of basic foodstuffs are shipped in since there has not yet been the effort or inclination to grow them locally. Finally there's the Melanesain outlook on life — that easy going attitude may be a great antidote to the stresses and strains of modern living but it certainly does not make for modern efficiency. Things tend to happen slowly and often carelessly.

How does all this tie in to tourism? Well, since it is inevitably expensive to be a tourist in PNG, some people try to make a virtue out of that expense. In many Asian countries it has become very popular to pontificate about the importance of "quality" tourists. I think it's one thing to search for those "quality" tourists by offering superior, albeit expensive, standards and quite another to search for them simply because your shoddy standards also happen to be expensive. Unfortunately shoddy is the ideal word to apply to some places in PNG and even in those that are really quite OK, value-for-money is a tag you'll have little cause to use. In general higher standards and more reasonable prices are something PNG could dearly do with.

Port Moresby & Central

Area: 29,940 sqare km
Population: 221,360

The Central Province consists of the narrow coastal strip along the south coast between the Gulf of Papua and the Milne Bay Province, plus the southern part of the central mountain range. Port Moresby, the capital of Papua New Guinea, is situated about half way along the coastal strip. Due to the "rain shadow" that effects the Port Moresby area it is much drier than the rest of PNG — which generally ranges from wet to extremely wet. The dry, brown, northern Australian look of "Moresby" soon fades into the usual lush green as you move away from the capital.

HISTORY

It was 1873 when Captain John Moresby, investigating the south coast of the mysterious island of New Guinea, sailed into the harbour of Port Moresby and named it after his father. He spent several days trading with the villagers at Hanuabada, the stilt village which still stands near modern Port Moresby. It was only a year later when the London Missionary Society established its first outpost here and they were soon followed by traders and blackbirders. For a time the export of forced "kanaka" labour by the un-scrupulous blackbirders was as important a trade as the beche de mer and pearl shell of the more conventional traders.

The island remained largely unexplored and totally "unclaimed" as Britain had quite enough colonial problems to tend to without adding New Guinea to them. Finally, with much pressure from the Queensland colonists, and not a little trepidation about the intentions of the Germans in the north of the island, British New Guinea was formally claimed and Port Moresby became the capital. The remarkable administration of Sir William McGregor commenced — during his period of control not only did he establish the gov-ernment in Moresby and the national police force, but also personally ex-plored large tracts of the rugged island.

After the federation of Australia in 1901, the colony was handed over in 1906. In 1907 Sir Hubert Murray took over administration of Papua, as it had been renamed, and ran it until the day he died, at the age of 78, in 1940. He was out "on patrol" at Samarai in the Milne Bay district when he died. Port Moresby had been overshadowed through much of the inter-war period by events in New Guinea, the northern half of Australia's end of the island, where the discovery of gold at Wau and Bulolo plus the productive plantations on the offshore islands had given it much greater economic importance.

With WW II the spotlight shifted back to Port Moresby as the Japanese pressed towards it around the end of the island and down the Kokoda Trail. They were unable to capture Moresby which remained in Allied hands throughout the war. After the war, Papua and New Guinea were administered as one territory and since the northern New Guinea towns were little more than rubble it was naturally Port Moresby which became the administrative HQ — a position it has held ever since, becoming the capital of the country with Independence. There has been pressure to move the capital elsewhere — Lae with its central location and excellent communications to the important Highlands is the usual suggestion. Port Moresby's isolation, the only major town in the southern half of the country and without road connections to any other important town, is its main drawback. Nevertheless it is now firmly established as the capital and largest city in the country.

GEOGRAPHY
Central Province consists of a narrow coastal strip rising rapidly inland to the 4000 metre heights of the Owen Stanley Range. Port Moresby is in the centre of the driest area of the whole country and this dry region extends about 100 km along the coast on either side. Beyond this low-rainfall strip it soon reverts to the normal damp PNG climate.

PEOPLE
The people of the Central Province are in some ways more closely related to the Polynesians of the Pacific Islands than to the darker skinned people further inland. Around Moresby the people are Motu and during the early years of English and then Australian contact their language was adopted by the admistration and spread throughout the territory in the form of "Police Motu". Its position as the lingua franca of PNG has now been usurped by the spread of Pidgin.

The Motu people were great sailors and before the arrival of Europeans the high point of the year was the annual Hiri trading voyages. Villages constructed gigantic *lakatois* made by lashing canoes together and rigging up a mast with the strange crab-claw shaped sail. Each village had its counterpart trading village in the Gulf region and the annual voyage consisted of sailing to this village, trading clay pots and other goods for the sago which grows prolifically along the Gulf then, when the wind direction changed with the season, sailing back. Although the Hiri has ended long ago it still gives its name to an annual festival in Port Moresby. Canoe races around the harbour are one of the highlights of the activities.

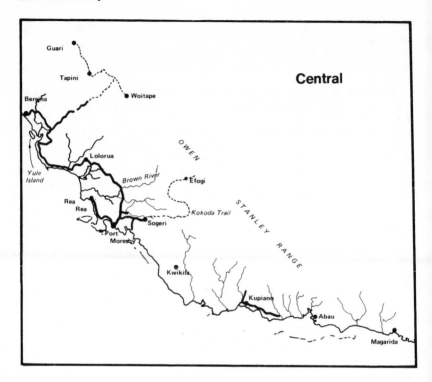

PORT MORESBY

Port Moresby was the capital of first British New Guinea and then, after the handover to Australia, of Papua. Between the wars PNG consisted of two parts — Papua with Port Moresby as its capital and Australian New Guinea with the capital at Rabaul in New Britain. Since WW II the country has been governed as one entity with Port Moresby as its capital. Since Independence in 1975 its role in PNG has taken on even greater importance.

Many people find "Moresby", as it is known locally, a rather dismal place. It's dry, hot and dusty for much of the year and that's only the start of its problems. Expatriate residents, who almost without exception have cars, may not find it annoying, but to visitors one of Moresby's biggest drawbacks is its amazing sprawl. It is not so much a city as a collection of widely separated suburbs. Worse, Moresby suffers from the "big city" syndrome — it's the place in PNG that people go to in search of fame and fortune. Naturally most fail to find either and many people end up living in squalid squatter settlements. They contribute to Moresby's high crime rate, particularly house-breaking which leads to fanatical security precautions by the expatriate population.

The gloom is not all-pervading. There are many interesting things to see and do around the city and there is no better place in PNG to indicate how important contacts can be. "Knowing" somebody can be enormously helpful in PNG so if you do know somebody, look them up! If you don't know anybody then try to find somebody to know — give the Port Moresby bushwalkers a ring for example (tel: 25 6666). They walk somewhere most Sundays and not only will you see something you'll also meet some nice people. But if all else fails and you still dislike Moresby then remember that very important traveller's rule of thumb — never judge a country by its capital city.

Orientation

Getting your bearings in Moresby is no easy task as it's not so much a city as a string of widely scattered suburbs with no discernible centre. It takes a while for the new arrival to work out where things are. Transport is a virtual necessity since the town sprawls so much. The Moresby region is built over and around a series of hills, so getting from A to B, a short distance in a straight line, may involve lengthy detours around the intervening terrain.

The town centre, if Moresby can claim such a feature, is on a spit of land which ends in Paga Hill — good views from the summit lookout. The centre has the majority of Moresby's older buildings, the shipping docks and wharves and most of the major office buildings. If you follow the coast round to the north you'll come to the cultural centre, Konedobu — a hostel and office centre, and Hanuabada — the stilt village where you are recommended not to be at night.

West from the town centre you follow popular Ela Beach until you reach the suburb of Koki — shops, the Salvation Army and the colourful Koki Market. From Koki the road climbs steeply up Three Mile Hill to Boroko the secondary centre with many of Moresby's shops and more offices. Boroko is also known as Four Mile and if you continued out in that direction you'd eventually get to Seven Mile which is another name for Jackson — the Port Moresby airport.

If you'd turned off north-west from Boroko on Waigani Drive you'd pass through Hohola and Gordon, residential areas, then Waigani — the new, and very spread out, government centre. A little beyond Waigani you reach the university campus, the road then bends back towards the coast and eventually runs back into Moresby through Hanuabada.

Port Moresby City

The "old town" is probably the most colourful part of Port Moresby and the part with the most "colonial-Pacific" feel to it. The Australian New Guinea House office block dominates the town, along with the recently completed Travelodge right across the road from it. Fine views from the

Travelodge. At the other end of Douglas St is the new PNG Banking Corporation building, a fine modern building with some interesting traditional decoration on the front.

The National Parliament and the National Museum used to share a building just behind ANG House but the museum moved out to Waigani in 1977 and the parliament will soon follow it. Paga Point, where the old town is situated, ends in a high hill — it's worth getting up to the top for the fine views over the town and surrounding area.

Cultural Centre
North of the town centre, beyond the yacht club and near Konedobu, is the Cultural Centre, an open area with a number of examples of traditional houses and boat building. Here you can clamber around a sea going canoe, crawl into a Haus Tambaran or inspect a yam house.

Hanuabada
A little beyond the Cultural Centre is the stilt village of Hanuabada, which means "big village" in the local dialect. It was the major village along the coast when Captain Moresby sailed by in 1873. Although it is still built out over the sea on stilts, just like it was over a hundred years ago, the addition of large amounts of that all-Australian building material, corrugated iron, has fairly drastically altered the way it looks. Hanuabada is not a good place to be at night, but it's quite OK to wander around and have a look during the day.

Ela Beach
Heading the other way from the old town centre you soon come down to the long sandy stretch of Ela Beach. It's a popular spot for lazing on the beach and has some old, but not particularly interesting buildings. Ela Beach is not much good for swimming because the water is very shallow and weedy.

Koki
Ela Beach ends in the headland at Koki, here there are a cluster of shops, the Salvation Army hostel and a couple of interesting things to see. One is the Koki Market, it may be a long way from being the best market in the country, but it is quite possibly the best know. Saturday is the big market day although there will be some activity here virtually every day. Quite close to the market is the Girl Guides' Handicraft Shop with a good collection of artifacts from all around the country including some which you just don't seem to see anywhere else.

Waigani
It's been dubbed "Canberra in the Tropics" and there's more than a little truth in that description. A handful of flashy modern buildings with a lot of

empty space between them. Totally de-humanising in my opinion, since the only way you can get there or get around them is by car. The parliament building is worth visiting (here or still in the town centre if it has not yet moved) to watch the proceedings which are simultaneously translated into English, Pidgin and Motu — the three main languages of PNG.

National Museum & Art Gallery
The museum moved from its cramped city location into its spacious and dramatic new location in mid '77. Unfortunately the displays don't yet match up to the building — I was more impressed with the old museum than the new one, of course that could soon change as more items are put on display. At first many fine pieces from the old museum were simply put in storage as the budget was too small to show them all. Still it's a very fine building and has a central walk-through aviary. The museum is open 9 am to 3 pm on weekdays, closed Saturdays and open from 1 to 5 pm on Sundays; admission is free. It is difficult to get out to the museum in its remote Waigani location.

University of Papua New Guinea
The very modern university has an attractive and spacious campus just a little beyond Waigani. It's easier to visit than the Government Centre, if you're transportless, since it is closer to the main road and plenty of PMVs run by it. Close to the university is the Botanical Gardens, with a very fine orchid collection. Orchid cultivation is a big deal in Port Moresby and Papua New Guinea as a whole. I managed to get myself invited to an orchid-fanciers' barbecue in Moresby where, despite not knowing an orchid from a sunflower (well almost), I did not feel alone! A little beyond the university is the National Arts School where much interesting work is being done; PNG is a naturally artistically inclined country.

Village Arts
Less than a km past the Six Mile turnoff on Rigo Road is Village Arts, the biggest artifacts dealer in PNG. Government financed, it claims to have over 20,000 items on display and also has a small outlet at the airport. It's certainly a pretty impressive collection, if you can't find what you want just ask and chances are they'll have it hidden away somewhere. Unfortunately very little of it is labelled or grouped so you have to know a little about the various styles to pick things out. Village Arts is open 8 am to 5 pm on weekdays, 9 am to 4 pm on weekends. The 'phone number is 25 4934.

Other
Near the Badihagwa High School, just beyond Hanuabada, is the old Moresby town cemetery where Sir Hubert Murray is buried and the unfort-

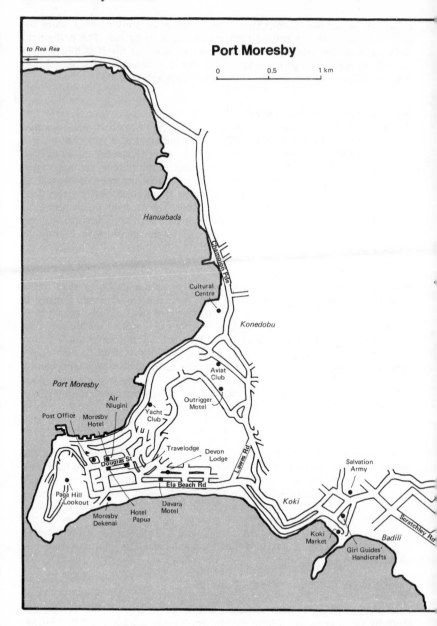

Port Moresby

0   0.5   1 km

to Rea Rea

Hanuabada

Champion Pde

Cultural Centre

Konedobu

Port Moresby

Aviat Club

Outrigger Motel

Air Niugini

Post Office

Moresby Hotel

Yacht Club

Lawes Rd

Travelodge

Devon Lodge

Douglas St

Salvation Army

Ela Beach Rd

Paga Hill Lookout

Koki

Moresby Dekenai

Hotel Papua

Davara Motel

Scratchley Rd

Badili

Koki Market

Girl Guides' Handicrafts

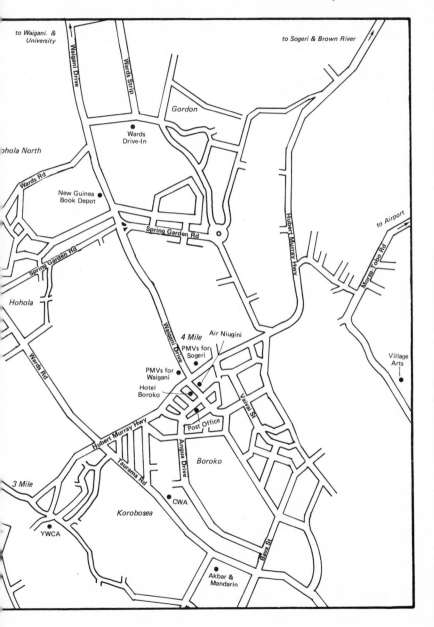

unate Justice Robinson who shot himself in front of Government House after his expedition against the Goaribari — see "Gulf & Western Provinces". If you take the Taurama Road out of Boroko you'll come to the army barracks, which you can drive through to get to Taurama Beach. Pleasant, but like Ela it is very shallow and weedy at low tide. Another popular beach is the small cove of Idler's Bay on the Napa Napa peninsula just north of Moresby. It's a pleasant drive out beyond here to Lea Lea, a large coastal village which you get to by crossing the creek on a dugout canoe "ferry" service.

Biggest of the nearby islands is Manubada — "big bird". Tuaguba Hill is another popular lookout spot, but Burns Peak is the best known in Moresby. In Moresby Harbour, off Hanuabada, the wreck of the Burns Philp cargo ship *MacDhui* can be seen just breaking the surface. It was sunk by Japanese aircraft in the early days of WW II. Other popular Moresby attractions include bushwalking (contact Moresby Bushwalkers — tel: 25 6666 ext 350) and diving (beautiful reefs).

Accommodation in Port Moresby

Places to stay around Moresby are scattered, generally pretty expensive and often hard to get into. It is very wise to book ahead when coming to Port Moresby. This particularly applies to the top end of the market where the squeeze is tightest. The opening of the new Travelodge in late '78 temporarily takes the strain off the room demand but it's likely to be only a short respite.

There is no central accommodation area in Moresby — you'll find places to stay at the airport, Boroko, Waigani, Koki, Ela Beach and in the town centre. A brief survey:

The Top End

The Port Moresby *Travelodge* is the top-rated place to stay in Moresby. It's actually located the old town centre at the corner of Douglas, May and Hunter Sts — right across from Australia New Guinea House; with ANG House it dominates the town. The rooms offer some appropriately stunning views over Moresby and the prices are similarly right at the top of the Moresby scale. Naturally the Travelodge offers all the features you'd expect — air-conditioning throughout, restaurant, bars, souvenir shop, conference facilities, swimming pool, entertainment nightly and even an associated scuba diving instructor. Rooms cost K32 single, K38 double.

Port Moresby Travelodge
Bookings: PO Box 3661,
    Port Moresby
Tel: 21 2266
Cables: Travelodge, Port
    Moresby
Telex: Travlex NE 22248
Rooms: 178
Tariff: K32 sgl, K38 dbl

Davara
Bookings: PO Box 799, Port
    Moresby
Tel: 21 2100
Cables: Davara Moresby
Rooms: 79
Tariff: K24-30 sgls, K32-38
    dbls

Until the Travelodge came into operation a number of places vied for Moresby's "nambawan" position. The *Davara* looks out over Ela Beach from Ela Beach Rd — it's only a short stroll from the town centre. Built in the late '60s it's modern, well equipped, has a swimming pool and a popular bar and restaurant. Rooms cost from K22 to K28 single, K30 to K36 twin — there's an older and a newer wing.

The *Islander* is in Hohola near the Waigani government complex but otherwise it's rather far from anywhere — although that does bring a little quietness and peace with it. Built in the mid '70s it falls in price somewhere between the Davara and the Travelodge. The restaurant serves Melanesian and western food and rooms cost from K29 single, K38 double or twin. The final top drawer hotel is the *Gateway Motel* right beside the airport — convenient if your stay in Moresby is short and you want to be handy for your flight out, but otherwise a rather dull establishment. It's similarly priced to the Davara and has a bar/restaurant with very reasonably priced grills at lunchtimes. In the evenings there is often entertainment — one of the best places for jazz in Moresby.

In the Middle
Moresby's medium price range includes a number of guest houses, serviced apartments, hotels where the emphasis is more on beer than beds and a lower priced motel. If your stay is going to be longer some of these places can offer weekly rates which are much more competitive than their daily prices.

The *Devon Lodge Apartments* are one of the best bargains in this group. They're on Kermadec St, Ela Beach — almost directly behind the Davara Hotel. All the units are fully serviced and fully self-contained so you can fix your own food. Koki Market is just down the road and the Moresby centre isn't too far away — save a few kina that way. It's most economical for couples (even slightly bigger groups if you can squeeze them into the rooms!). Singles

Islander Hotel
Bookings: PO Box 1981, Boroko
Tel: 25 5955
Cables: Islander
Telex: Davara NE 22288
Rooms: 96
Tariff: K40 sgl, K40 dbl

Gateway Hotel
Bookings: PO Box 1215, Boroko
Tel: 25 3855
Cables: Gateway
Rooms: 35
Tariff: K26 sgl, K33 dbl

Devon Lodge Apartments
Bookings: PO Box 105, Port Moresby
Tel: 25 8417
Rooms: 24 doubles
Tariff: sgls K10 per day, K56 per week; dbls K12 & K60

Outrigger Motel
Bookings: PO Box 437, Port Moresby
Tel: 21 2088
Rooms: 21
Tariff: K22 sgl, K29 twin

cost K10 a day, doubles K12, or by the week singles/doubles cost K56/K60.

The *Outrigger Motel*, Vananama Crescent near the city centre, is a smaller motel with a pleasant swimming pool. Room only rates are a notch below the "top end" places — singles at K22, doubles K29. The *Civic Guest House*, Mairi Place, Boroko, offers home style accommodation with all meals included in the tariff — K21 for a single or K19 per person in the twins or family rooms.

Then there are the hotels. The *Boroko* has one big thing going for it — in many ways Boroko is the most convenient place to be, in the centre of everything. Drawbacks are that the nearby public bar can be a bit of a blood bath on Friday and Saturday nights when you venture out only with caution. The fact that the front door of the hotel is locked in the evening is fair warning. Rooms are air-conditioned and reasonably equipped and there's a choice of rooms with or without private facilities — K14 to K18 single, K21 to K23 for doubles.

In Port Moresby there are two hotels — the "top pub" and the "bottom pub". Both of them are more drinking places than staying places although equally they have their own little place in Moresby's history. Both are on Musgrave St, only about a hundred metres apart; as the names suggest the *Papua* at the "top" end of the street and the *Moresby* down at the "bottom" nearer the waterfront.

The *Papua* has 46 assorted rooms — some single, some double, some air-con, some fan. Singles start from around K17, doubles from K23; all charges are room only. The Papua is particularly noted for its good food and is a popular lunchtime meeting place for Moresby businessmen. Down at the *Moresby* there are just 13 rooms, all fan cooled, and nightly cost is K14.50 per person, bed and breakfast.

Finally, round at Konedobu which was a government office centre before Waigani sprung up, there is the *Konedobu Hotel* which costs

Civic Guest House
Bookings: PO Box 1139, Boroko
Tel: 25 5091
Rooms: 16
Tariff: sgl K21, dbl K19 each — incl all meals

Boroko Hotel
Bookings: PO Box 1033, Boroko
Tel: 25 6677
Cables: Borokotel
Rooms: 38
Tariff: sgl K14-18, twins K21-23 incl breakfast

Papua Hotel
Bookings: PO Box 122, Port Moresby
Tel: 21 2622
Cables: Paptel
Rooms: 46
Tariff: K17-21 sgl, K23-28 twin

Hotel Moresby
Bookings: PO Box 122, Port Moresby
Tel: 21 4068
Cables: Mortel
Rooms: 13
Tariff: K15 per person B&B

Konedobu Hotel
Bookings: PO Box 407, Port Moresby
Tel: 21 2211
Rooms: 12
Tariff: K18 inc all meals

K18 per person, per day including all meals. There are just 12 rooms here, all fan cooled. If you're planning a longer stay enquire about their more competitive weekly rates.

The Bottom End

There is a limited choice of cheaper places in Moresby but you should first compare prices with places in the "middle" group like *Devon Lodge*. The *Salvation Army Hostel* is in Koki, near the market and on the main PMV route from Moresby to Boroko. There are six rooms here, actually there are many more than that but most are for long term residents. Nightly cost is K5 per person, room only. There may, or may not, be a dormitory here — the Salvation Army Hostel once had some sort of youth hostel affiliation and the dormitory was still operating in '77 at between K2 and K3 a day (depending on the mood of the moment), but may be out of operation now. Sometimes it is difficult to get a straight answer in PNG — closed can equally mean "full", "temporarily out of operation" or even "dunno".

The *Country Women's Association* (Jessie Wyatt House) is on Taurama Rd right across from the hospital and next door to the Red Cross. The address is Boroko but it is a little way from the Boroko shopping centre. Easiest way to get there is to get a PMV or bus running between Moresby/Koki and Boroko via Badili and Korobosea. That will drop you off right outside, most PMVs go via the shorter Three Mile Hill route. Accommodation here costs K9 per person per night, room only. There are only four rooms and there are cooking facilities so you can save a little on meal costs.

Finally there is the *YWCA Hostel*, also in Boroko but at the top end of Three Mile Hill. There are only four single rooms, otherwise it is all permanent residents. Bed and breakfast costs K7 a night, lunch costs just 50t, dinner K1.50. Ladies only.

Salvation Army Hostel
Bookings: PO Box 4070, Badili
Tel: 25 3744
Rooms: 6
Tariff: K5 per person, K6.50 incl breakfast.

CWA — Jessie Wyatt House
Bookings: PO Box 1222, Boroko
Tel: 25 3646
Rooms: 4
Tariff: K9 per person

YWCA Hostel
Bookings: PO Box 1883
Tel: 25 6604
Rooms: 4
Tariff: K7 B&B

Places to Eat in Moresby

There are probably more places to eat and types of food available in Moresby than anywhere else in the country. Starting at the top of the pile, there is the *Moresby Dekenai*, undoubtedly the classiest restaurant in Papua New Guinea. Situated at the town end of Ela Beach Road, the Dekenai is built into the cliff face and looks out over the beach and harbour. It makes the best possible use of this stunning site — built on two levels, there's a bar and lounge area downstairs and the restaurant above, all fronted by large windows so you can really appreciate the views. The Dekenai is open daily except Sunday, from 6 pm until midnight, or 1 am on Fridays and Saturdays. There is a fixed price of K14 per person for a four course meal plus coffee — drinks are extra. If you want to sample the Dekenai's magnificent location and fine food at more moderate cost, try the Friday lunchtime session when it is open from noon to 2 pm and the set price is K6.50. There is also a lower priced á la carte menu available from 6 to 8 pm nightly, on the condition that you have eaten and left by 8.

A little cheaper but still very pleasant is the *Galley II* at the Aviat Club on Aviat St, Konedobu. You don't have to be a member to use the restaurant. The emphasis here is on seafood, main dishes cost from K6 or so. Telephone for reservations. Other upper range restaurants include the *Mandarin*, pricier Chinese, at Gavamani Mall, Korobosea. A meal will cost K6 to K10, dishes are K4 or K5 each. Telephone: 25 3634.

Moving down a price notch there are quite a few places to try. Very good Chinese food at around K3 to K4 a dish, in somewhat plainer (more Chinese?) surroundings can be found at the *Green Jade Restaurant*, Reke St in Boroko (tel: 25 4013). Yet another Chinese restaurant, the *Rex*, was just around the corner on Okari St — but it had burnt down in mid '78 and I don't know if it has reopened. Places burn down in PNG with stunning regularity.

Indonesian style food can be found in the *Akbar* (don't ask me why the name is Indian) also at Gavamani Mall, Korobosea — close to the Mandarin. 'Phone number here is 25 2347; quite cheap at K4 or even less per person. Back in Boroko there is the *Hun*, Chinese and PNG dishes, meals from K2.50, disco on Thursday, Friday and Saturday nights and licensed till 2 am. It's at Lakatoi Arcade in Boroko. Still in Boroko the *Little White Bull* is a steak and seafood place; count on K4 to K7 per person. It's on Boio St, 'phone 25 5854, and has a band on Friday and Saturday nights. The yacht club has a reasonably priced menu and is open lunchtimes. One problem with restaurants in general in Port Moresby is that it is very difficult to get anything to eat on Sunday nights — if you want to eat out then you may have to fall back on the hotels.

At the bottom end of the market there are a few places definitely worth a look in. The *Oyster Bar* is in the Hugo Building (first floor) almost next to the post office in Boroko. It's a high class fish & chips, hamburger place; take-away or eat there (they have tables and chairs). You can get a snack for around 60t or a complete meal for around K2. Open over lunchtime and then from 4 to 9 pm in the evenings. Almost next door, on the first floor in the next building, is *Pinocchio's Coffee Shop* which is open till midnight on weekdays, but only to 4 pm on Saturday, and not at all on Sunday. Excellent hamburgers, milk shakes and other snacks. Both these places get my recommendation as good, reasonably priced places to eat in Moresby.

Also in Boroko, down by the police station, is *Selamat Makan* which serves vaguely Indonesian style food. Not as tasty as the two above but still reasonable value for money. Another place to try for reasonably priced food is the Ward's Drive-In Cinema out at Gordon. If you're out at the National Museum at Waigani when hunger time rolls around, there's a restaurant in the basement of the New Supreme Court building where you can get a good meal for under a kina. Quick snacks — sandwiches, meat pies, soft drinks and so on — can be had (standing up) in the Burns Philp or Steamship places in Port Moresby or Boroko. There are a number of Haus Kai style places, the majority of which are uniformly dreadful — Australian style greasy takeaways at Australia-minus quality and Australia-plus prices. One or two in Port Moresby city are a little better so the shoestringers amongst us shouldn't give them completely away.

And of course there are the hotels. Most of them serve pretty much exactly what you'd expect for hotels. The *Gateway Restaurant* out near the airport is fairly reasonably priced and at lunchtime its counter style food is excellent value. At the Islander the *Hebou Gabuna* is the pricey place, (K8 to K12 a meal), there's s big smorgasbord lunch (K5 flat charge) on Fridays. The *Boroko* and the *Papua* are both popular at lunchtime, the Papua on Fridays particularly. Good sandwiches upstairs in the Papuan. The *Davara* has good (if expensive) bar snacks and the pricier *Tapa Restaurant*. The *Travelodge* too has dining and snack bar facilities.

Getting to the Airport

Until recently this could be a somewhat difficult problem. Port Moresby's taxis are not noted for their enterprising spirit and finding a taxi to get out to the airport could be a risky operation — particularly if you had an early morning flight. Even getting one from the airport could be a matter of luck, but recently the taxis seem to have deigned to drop by there a little more frequently.

More important, there is now a regular mini-bus service between the main hotels and the airport for (more or less) every flight. It costs K1 to K2 depending which hotel you go from. It is wise to ask at the desk to ensure the bus does come by though, particularly for an early flight. 'Phone 25 7044 or 25 6604 after hours. Unfortunately if you're not staying at a hotel or you're off the main routes you can still have trouble getting there on the bus.

Backpackers can forget the bus and simply take the regular PMV or public bus service which will get you there from anywhere in Port Moresby for just 18t. Look for a sign saying "Jackson" or "Seven Mile". They stop just beside the Gateway Motel at the airport — if you're arriving just walk out of the terminal and across behind the control tower to the open space, it's less than a hundred metres. Of course there won't be many PMVs around for the very early flights — Maureen and I hitched a ride to the airport in a police car once when nothing else seemed to be moving.

Getting around Port Moresby
Moresby has an amazingly frequent bus/PMV service — it's hard to tell one from the other and they all charge the same standard 18t for any trip in town. Buses (pay as you enter) have the destinations on a board on the front, and non-stop radio programmes blasting out music weekdays, hellfire and brimstone preaching on Sundays. On PMVs (pay as you leave) just ask the destination before hopping on, yell "stop" or thump the driver's window when you want to get off. There may be a ferry service across the harbour from Port Moresby to Napa Napa.

Tours
'Phone Trans Niugini Tours on 21 1749 or contact your hotel about tours in Port Moresby. Half day tours cost K8.80 and visit the main city sights and the Moitaka Crocodile Farm. They depart between 8.15 and 8.45 in the morning. The full day tours cost K16 and go out to Bomana War Cemetary and on to Varirata National Park, to Ower's Corner at the start of the Kokoda Trail and to Sogeri.

OUT OF MORESBY
A number of roads lead out of Moresby and there are quite a few places you can head to, either on day trips, weekenders or even longer.

Moitaka Crocodile Farm
A few km out of Moresby on the Sogeri Road, behind Jackson Airport, is the Moitaka Crocodile Farm. Unless you make prior arrangements, it's only open to the public on Friday afternoons between 2 and 4 pm. This is also feeding time — crocodiles are hearty eaters, but infrequent ones. In between those big feeds they lie there waiting for the next meal. There are a whole series of enclosures from those for small ones crowded in on top of one another, to a large, empty looking pond that houses the biggest, ugliest, meanest looking pukpuk you ever saw. The big crocs have neat little flags tacked on their backs with numbers on — you feel like the keepers should yell "come in number 5, your kaikai is ready". The farm also has an enclosure of deer and some native animals and birds, including a Raggiana Bird of Paradise which is a quite amazing show-off. He must wait all week for Friday afternoons when he can put on a non-stop performance — hopping around, displaying his wings and feathers, calling out, whispering hello, presenting his stomach to be scratched and generally acting the clown.

Brown River
About 50 km out of Moresby on the Hiritano Highway towards Yule Island and Bereina, Brown River is a popular picnic spot which also has good

swimming. You're already starting to escape from the dry climate of Moresby by the time you get this far out. En route you'll pass through teak plantations which will eventually become a major industry in this area.

Bomana War Cemetery
Not far beyond the crocodile farm is the large and carefully tended war cemetery where 4000 Australian and New Guinea soldiers who died during WW II are buried. American troops killed in New Guinea were generally shipped back to the US for burial.

Sogeri Road & Rouana Falls
The trip out to the Sogeri Plateau is one of the most popular weekend jaunts for Moresbyites. It's only 46 km all the way to Sogeri, but there is quite enough to see and do to make it a full day trip. You can get out there by PMVs which run regularly from Boroko, near the junction with Waigani Road.

The road runs out of town by the airport, crocodile farm and Bomana Cemetery then follows the Laloki River gorge, at first fairly level then climbing steeply and winding. Although the road is unsurfaced for the last stretch, it is a good quality road. On the way you pass the *Bluff Inn*, a pleasant riverside beer garden and a small animal reserve with a crocodile to look at — it's dubbed a "ples bilong pukpuk". Then you pass the turnoff to Varirata National Park and the *Hotel Rouna*, another good place for a cold beer and it has a popular weekend smorgasbord.

A little beyond the hotel is the lookout point for the spectacular Rouna Falls — before the hydro-electric power plants were installed it was even more impressive. You can have a look at the hydro-power plants and just before reaching Sogeri you pass the Kokoda Trail junction.

Sogeri has other attractions than its cool, 600 metres altitude climate. It also has a good market on weekends with a good selection of fresh vegetables. It is possible to arrange visits to the rubber plantations around Sogeri. The road continues beyond Sogeri, via the Crystal Rapids which is a popular swimming spot, to Musgrave River and Sirinumu Dam. Musgrave River's quite a long way out but it's a delightful spot.

Varirata National Park
The turnoff to the park, the first in PNG, is right after the Number 2 Hydro Station. There are a variety of interesting and clearly marked walking trails in the park and some excellent lookouts back to Port Moresby and the coast. In the park you can inspect a traditional tree house, like the local inhabitants once lived in.

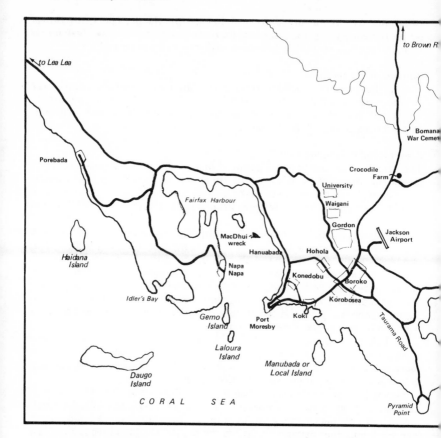

Hombrum's Bluff

A little way down the Kokoda Trail road a smaller road branches off back towards Moresby, paralleling the Sogeri Road but high above it on the top of the Laloki River canyon wall. It leads to Hombrum's Lookout which was used as a retreat for important military brass during the war. Excellent views back towards Moresby.

To the Kokoda Trail

Just before Sogeri the road to the trail branches off from the Sogeri Road. There's a memorial stone at this junction. The road twists and turns and is rather bumpy although quite OK for conventional vehicles (so long as it isn't raining). At McDonald's Corner there is a strange metal sculpture of a soldier, at one time the road ended and the trail commenced here but the

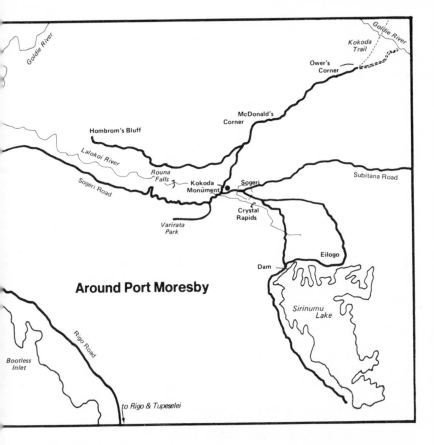

Around Port Moresby

actual trail now starts further on at Ower's Corner where a sign announces the trail. The road actually continues right on down to the Goldie River from Ower's Corner but you would be unwise to try it without 4-WD. I foolishly did and nearly ended up stuck there in my rent-a-car — it would have been very embarassing. This last bit of road was built just a few years ago as a military exercise but it had no real purpose and has not been well maintained after its initial construction.

From Ower's Corner the trail is easily picked up and heads straight down towards the Goldie River. You can easily stroll down to the river if you just want an easy taste of what it is like. On the other side of the river the endless "golden staircase" crawls up to Imita Ridge, the turning point for the Japanese in their attempted assault on Moresby. See the Kokoda Trail section for a full report on walking the trail.

Accommodation out of Moresby

There are a few places to stay outside of Moresby, but really too far out to commute into the city. Nice if you want to escape the big city though.

The *Rouna Hotel* is about a km from the Rouna Falls on the Sogeri Road, about 34 km from Moresby. It's more a drinking pub and place for a weekend meal than a place to stay but it does have six rooms which cost K10 single, K20 double for bed and breakfast, K16 for a single including all meals.

Also on the Sogeri Road is the *Kokoda Trail Motel*, about 40 km out from Moresby. Accommodation consists of 26 units, daily cost is K10 per person, bed and breakfast. There is a restaurant and a pleasant swimming pool — the climate is much cooler than in Moresby due to the altitude. A speciality in the restaurant is crocodile steaks — really!

Much closer to the Kokoda Trail is the *Red Shield Holiday House* which is on the Kokoda Trail road, a good distance from the Sogeri road junction and not too far from the start of the actual walking trail. Accommodation consists of just one cottage that can sleep five people. Nightly cost is K3 per person, worth considering if you want to do a day walk on the trail.

Beyond Sogeri at the Sirinumu Dam there's a campsite run by the Seventh Day Adventists with some accommodation and cooking facilities. It's sometimes possible to use it on weekends. It is also possible to camp in the Varirata National Park — the cheapest accommodation in Moresby.

Rouna Hotel
Bookings: PO Box 67, Port Moresby
Tel: 28 1146
Rooms: 6
Tariff: K10 per person B&B
K16 incl all meals

Kokoda Trail Motel
Bookings: PO Box 5014, Boroko
Tel: 28 2256
Rooms: 26 units
Tariff: K10 per person B&B

Red Shield Holiday House
Bookings: PO Box 1323, Boroko
Tel: 25 5507
Rooms: 1 cottage
Tariff: K3 per person

THE KOKODA TRAIL

Mention walking tracks in PNG and the famed Kokoda Trail is the one most likely to spring to mind. It's a little unfair since the track is far from the most interesting walk in PNG but its historical connections are the big attraction. The trail had an earlier history when it was used by miners struggling north to the Yodda Kokoda goldfields of the 1890s.

Following Pearl Harbour in December '41, the Japanese rapidly advanced across the Pacific, captured New Britain and the north coast of New Guinea.

Then their advance on Port Moresby and Australia was dramatically halted by the naval battle of the Coral Sea. The Japanese decided to take Port Moresby by a totally unexpected "back door" assault. They would land on the north coast near Popondetta, travel south to Kokoda and then march up and over the central range to Sogeri from where the road runs to Port Moresby.

They made one serious miscalculation — the Kokoda Trail was no rough track requiring hard work to upgrade it for vehicles. It was a switchback footpath, endlessly climbing up and then plunging down, infested by leeches and hopelessly muddy during the wet season.

Nevertheless the Japanese landed on 21 July '42 and by 16 September had stormed down the trail to within spitting distance of Port Moresby. On that day their headlong advance was halted — for a whole series of reasons. As they advanced down the trail the Australian opposition had become fiercer and fiercer and a last ditch resistance was planned for Imita Ridge, where the Japanese finally halted. The supply lines had become hopelessly stretched — it was impossible to bring supplies in by air, the intention of making the trail suitable for vehicles was clearly not feasible, and a man could barely carry down the trail sufficient food to get him there and back, let alone supplies for the front line soldiers. Plus at the same time the Japanese were being stretched to their limits at Guadalcanal in the Solomons.

So they withdrew, with Port Moresby virtually in sight. Until the end of January '43, the campaign to dislodge them from Buna on the north coast was one of the bitterest and bloodiest of the Pacific War. If the two sides didn't kill each other then disease or lack of food did. Never again did the Allied forces meet the Japanese head-on during WW II. The policy for the rest of the war was to advance towards Tokyo, bypassing the intervening Japanese strongholds. Thus Rabaul in New Britain was left alone and isolated while the front moved towards Japan.

Today the Kokoda Trail is easily the most popular walking track in PNG for visitors. Somebody is probably making the 90 km trek almost every day of the week and at least once a year the Port Moresby Bush Walkers or some similar club will be organising a mass walk along the trail. The straight line distance from Owers Corner to Kokoda is about 60 km but for the walker it is a bit over 90 km — which gives no impression at all of the actual difficulty. The Kokoda Trail is a continual series of ups and downs, generally steep, exhausting ups and muddy, slippery downs. Over the whole trail you gain and lose 6000 metres, nearly 20,000 feet of altitude.

Of course you should not consider walking the trail during the wet season when the normally muddy trail will be dangerously slippery and many rivers will be high and hazardous to cross. The Civil Defence office in Port Moresby puts out an information sheet on the trail which you can obtain by writing to:

National Emergency Service
PO Box 391, Port Moresby
(tel 25 2999)

You should also inform the Civil Defence office that you intend to walk the trail and notify the authorities at the other end of the trail that you have arrived safely.

You will require normal bush-walking or trekking gear to make the walk, including wet weather gear since even in the dry season it is quite likely to rain. At the high altitude parts of the trail it can get quite chilly at night so come prepared. You'll also need a sleeping bag although there are rest houses, where you can spend the night, in most villages. Bring enough food for the walk, villagers will generally sell some fruit to passing walkers.

Average walking time along the trail is 40 to 48 hours — five or six, eight hour days — although the record across the trail is about 35 hours. If you're not in a hurry you can do it in an easier seven to nine days, there are plenty of villages to stop at. Looking for war mementos is a popular activity on the trail, it's easy to find live ammunition and rusty army helmets — Japanese and Australian.

Distances along the trail from Ower's Corner are Imita Gap 7 km, Ioribaiwa (an old village site) 12 km, Ofi Creek 16 km, Naoro Village 27 km, Menari Village 36 km, Efogi Village 46 km, Kagi 51 km, Kokoda Gap 62 km, Eora Creek 71 km, Alola Village 75 km and finally the Kokoda War Memorial at 94 km. Highest point along the trail is Mt Bellamy at 2300 metres, between Kagi and Kokoda Gap. From Mt Bellamy the trail descends impossibly steeply to Templeton's crossing.

If you want a little taste of the trail without walking the whole distance, you can walk down to Goldie River from Ower's Corner in just an hour or

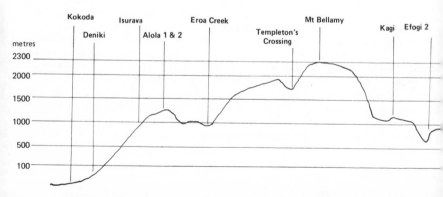

so. And struggle up the "Golden Staircase" to Imita Ridge on the other side if you have the energy. Between Naoro and Efogi the trail is a little easier and there are airstrips at both villages — you could fly in, walk, fly out if you wished. The trail is generally reasonably clear and a guide is not necessary although, back in 1968, a Canadian woman did lose her way on the trail and died of exposure.

LOLOATA ISLAND
Only 22 km out from Moresby, Loloata Island in Bootless Bay is another popular weekend escape for Moresby-ites. Lazing on the beach or skin diving is the order of the day here. To get there you drive out on the Rigo road to the Tahira Boating Centre on Bootless Bay, from there it costs K4 round trip out to the island by launch.

Accommodation on Loloata Island
The *Loloata Island Resort* has nine twin rooms which cost K23 per person including all meals.

Loloata Island Resort
Bookings: PO Box 3260, Moresby
Tel: 25 7914
Rooms: 9 twins
Tariff: K23 including all meals

YULE ISLAND
The missionaries who arrived at Yule Island in 1885 were some of the first European visitors to the Papuan coast of New Guinea. Later it became a government headquarters, from where government and mission workers penetrated into the central mountains in some of the earliest exploration on the island. Today the government centre is on the mainland at Bereina but there is still a large Catholic mission on Yule Island.

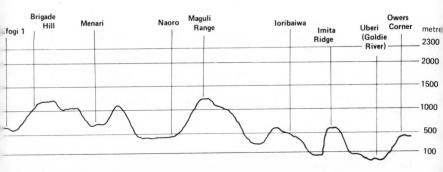

One of the early mission workers buried on Yule Island was a Frenchman named Bourgade who was one of his country's top WW I air aces. You can see his grave in the cemetery. Yule Island is a popular place to get away from Moresby to and there is a small guest house. Bring your appetite as Yule is famous for its tasty prawns which are available in large quantities!

The coast west of Port Moresby, which is connected by road all the way to Bereina, is the home of the Mekeo people who are noted for their colourful dancing costumes and face painting. On ceremonial occasions the men paint their faces in strikingly coloured geometrically patterned designs.

Accommodation on Yule Island

The *Rabao Mareana Hotel* has room for 10 people, tariff is K15 a day per person including all meals. Room only cost is K7.50 per day per person. You must book in advance through Coral Sea Travel Service in Port Moresby (tel 21 4474 or 21 4768). They will also arrange transport to the island from Delena on the mainland. The mission has accommodation available for friends only.

Rabao Mareana Hotel
Bookings: c/o Post Office, Kairuku
Tel: Outstations 109
Rooms: 5
Tariff: per person - K7.50 rm only, K15 all meals

Getting to Yule Island

You can drive out to Delena in a bit under three hours along the Hiritano Highway. It costs K5, for a boat that will carry up to four people, to ferry across to the island. Alternatively you can fly there with Douglas Airways for K23.80 each way. Kairuku is the main village on Yule. You can also fly to Bereina for K26.20.

TAPINI-WOITAPE

If you want to get a look at the high country behind the coastal strip, experience one of the most heart-in-mouth airstrips in PNG, or try a lesser known but extremely interesting walk then Tapini is a good place to go. Tapini is a pretty little station at a bit under 1000 metres. The airstrip is amazing, carved into a hill side it runs steeply uphill ending in a sheer face so you can only come in one way. When you leave, downhill, the strip drops off sheer at the end. You've got a choice of flying or falling. There are many interesting walks around Tapini, the three days it takes to walk to Woitape is an interesting trip and you can fly out back to Moresby. Moresby-Tapini costs K26, Moresby-Woitape K25. There is also a rough road from Tapini to Guari where the once-fearsome Kunimaipa people live. Woitape is particularly noted for its many orchids.

Accommodation in Tapini

There is a small hotel at Tapini, just three minutes walk from the airstrip. There are seven

Tapini Hotel
Bookings: PO Box 19, Tapini

rooms and nightly cost per person is K23, including all meals. The food here has a good reputation.

Tel: Tapini 29
Rooms: 7
Tariff: per person K22.50 including all meals

Accommodation in Woitape
Woitape also has a small guest house — the *Oro Guest House* — where there are six double rooms and daily cost is K20 per person including all meals.

Ororo Guest House
Bookings: c/o Post Office, Woitape
Rooms: 6 doubles
Tariff: per person K20 including all meals

AMAZON BAY
Magarida, at the eastern end of the Central Province, is situated on Amazon Bay. It's a delightful stretch of scenic, palm shaded coastline.

GETTING AROUND
Port Moresby is the centre for much travel in PNG. If you want to fly to the Trobriands, the Gulf, Daru or Tufi in the Northern District then Port Moresby will generally have to be your starting point. There is also a variety of flights to places around Central Province and regular PMVs on the roads out of Moresby. It is very easy to get to Sogeri by PMV.

Lae & Morobe

Area: 33,152 square km
Population: 290,000

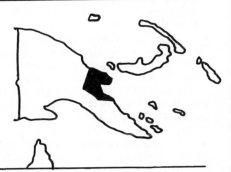

The province of Morobe curves around Huon Gulf with the provincial headquarters, Lae, as its focal point. Morobe is notable for having the best road connections in the country. From Lae you can drive west to the Highlands, north-west to Madang, or south to Wau and Bulolo. The latter two towns were the sites for New Guinea's '20s goldrush.

HISTORY
The first contact with Europeans came right at the beginning of the German

New Guinea Kompagnie's unsuccessful attempt at colonising the mainland. In 1885 they established their first settlement at Finschhafen and soon started to disintegrate from the effects of malaria, boredom, alcohol and various other tropical ills; curses that were to follow them all along the northern coast and which they only finally escaped by transferring to the island of New Britain. The Lutheran Mission followed soon after the company arrived at Finschhafen, but managed to hang on after it departed. It is still a major Lutheran base.

After the Australian takeover, Morobe was a fairly quiet place, no one cared to disturb the ferocious Kukukuku warriors, until the discovery of gold. The legendary prospector "Sharkeye" Park is credited with being one of the first to find gold close to Wau in 1921. By the mid-'20s the gold hunters were flooding in, arriving at the port of Salamua and struggling for eight days up the incredibly steep and slippery track to Wau, a mere 50 km away. As if the conditions of the track, the wet and often cold climate and tropical diseases were not enough obstacle, the miners soon had hostile tribes to contend with. Frequent reprisal raids by angry miners hardly helped matters.

In 1926 a richer field was discovered at Edie Creek, high in the hills above Wau. Although miners made quick fortunes here and at the earlier Koranga Creek Strike, it soon became evident to some of the more far-sighted prospectors that to really squeeze the most out of these gold-rich streams would require large investments and heavy equipment. The rough trail from the port of Salamua up to the sites of Wau. Bulolo and Edie Creek was totally unsuitable for transporting heavy equipment. Even today road building in Papua New Guinea is no easy task and the New Guinea Gold Company took the brave step of flying in the equipment. An airstrip was prepared in Lae and, using three-engined Junker J-31 transport aircraft, a shuttle service was started up and continued for several years. At the peak of the operations more airfreight was lifted in Papua New Guinea than in any other country in the world — in fact more than the rest of the world's airfreight put together!

The goldfields continued to be productive right up until the war, but after the war the recovery rate started to drop, gold was pegged at an artificially low price for many years (US$35 an ounce compared to its current level of over US$200) and the costs of production increased. One by one the eight huge dredges were closed down, the last one in 1965. Although many people still work the fields today, it is mainly a local cottage industry and the old gold companies have diversified into timber and other businesses.

Lae, or Lehe as it was originally spelt, was a tiny mission station before the goldrush. It soon became a thriving little community clustered around its central airstrip in true New Guinea fashion. In 1937 the volcanic eruptions at Rabaul prompted a decision to move the capital of New Guinea to Lae, but WW II intervened before the transfer was really underway. Lae, Salamua and Rabaul soon became the major Japanese bases in New Guinea, but in early '43 the Japanese, reeling from their defeats at Milne Bay and along the Kokoda Trail, their naval power devastated by the Battle of the Coral Sea, decided to make one more attempt to take Port Moresby. This time they attacked through Wau, marching up over the mountains from Salamua in late January 1943. The Australian troops in Wau were quickly reinforced by air from Port Moresby and the Japanese advance was repelled.

A grim campaign now commenced to clear the Japanese from Morobe. It took six months to struggle through the mud and jungle to Salamua and, in September, Australian and American assaults commenced on that tiny port and on Lae. Australian troops landed on beaches 25 km east of Lae on 4 September and the next day a huge allied armada parachuted onto Nadzab airstrip, up the Markham Valley from Lae. Soon transport aircraft were flying vast numbers of men and huge amounts of materials in for the advance on Lae. Salamua had been captured on 11 September and with Lae now surrounded it was easily taken on 16 September. Many Japanese escaped into the mountain wilderness of the Huon Peninsula and started on the gigantic retreat that was to eventually end at Wewak.

Lae, Wau, Bulolo and Salamua were all destroyed during the fighting and Salamua was never rebuilt. Today it is just a tiny, and very pretty, village. Although gold was now giving out and Papua New Guinea was to become one colony, not two, governed from Port Moresby, Lae soon had a new reason for existence. The road between Wau, Bulolo and Lae had been built during the war and soon a road was being carved up the Markham Valley from Lae into the Highlands. The Highlands, terra incognito before the war, were one of the major development areas of the country after the war and soon there were important coffee and tea industries whose production was trucked down the Highlands Highway and shipped out from Lae. Lae became the major port and industrial centre in PNG and is still the only port with extensive road links into the interior.

GEOGRAPHY
Morobe is an arc of land bisected by the Huon Gulf; it's the hump in the New Guinea "dragon's" back. There are two rugged mountain ranges in the province. The Saruwageda Mountains form the spine of the Huon Peninsula — one of the most tangled and impenetrable rain forests in PNG blankets the lower slopes of these high mountains. They march right down to the sea and pop up again further out as the backbone of equally mountainous New Britain.

The mountains in the south-west are equally inhospitable. Here they are part of the central spine of the whole New Guinea island and they rise higher and higher towards the centre. Between the two ranges there is the wide, flat, fertile Markham Valley, which has become a major cattle-grazing area. Morobe also includes a number of volcanic islands between the Huon Peninsula and New Britain.

PEOPLE

Curiously, there were many parts of Morobe which were virtually uninhabited when Europeans first arrived. These included the fertile Wau and Bulolo Valleys. The Leiwomba people were long established in the Lae area and up in the central mountains were a tribe who became the most notorious in Papua New Guinea. The Kukukuku (it's pronounced "cooker-cooker") were tiny people (often less than 5 foot, 150 cm, high) but what they lacked in stature they certainly made up in temper. They lived a nomadic existence interspersed with violent raids on more peaceful villages at lower levels — or upon each other. Despite the bitter climate in their high mountainous homeland, they wore only a tiny grass skirt, like a Scotman's sporran, and cloaks made of beaten bark, which were known as "mals".

J K McCarthy, who between the wars made some of the first contacts with these people, describes them vividly in his book *Patrol Into Yesterday*. His contact even extended to an arrow in the stomach at one point; they are excellent bowmen who make up for their imperfect aim with incredible machine gun like delivery. McCarthy also recounts their first sight of an aircraft: men took turns at crawling underneath it to inspect its genitals — unsure if the giant bird was male or female. One of the more curious habits of these utterly fearless warriors was to simply faint at the sight of something very strange or unusual — like a white man. McCarthy tells of the reaction when he arrived, the first white man, in a Kukukuku village — people fainted all around him.

LAE

The old Lae sat on the flat land to the west of the airstrip, but today that is mainly factories and warehouses. The modern town is built up the rise to the east. It's a green, attractive place which fits easily into its tropical setting. Lae has a reputation as a garden city and there's no place better to appreciate that than in the Botanic Gardens:

Botanical Gardens

Lae has the best botanical gardens in Papua New Guinea — huge trees are virtually smothered in vines and creepers, brightly coloured birds call out raucously and electric green lizards scuttle through the undergrowth. The garden also boasts an exotic orchid collection which is open 10 to 12, or 2 to 4 on the weekends. Within the garden boundaries is the Lae War Cemetery with the graves of thousands of Allied soldiers who died in the fierce fighting with the Japanese during the last war.

Other

Lae has two markets — the local one on the west side of the airstrip is quite interesting. It has food and a few local curios. The Butibum market is a smaller, village market — out of town on the Butibum road. If you want to try bushwalking around Lae, ring the Lae Bushwalkers' Club at the Unitech (42 4999, ext 123). The hill in the centre of town — Luman Hill, or more correctly Lo'Wamung (First Hill) — was used by the Germans and the Japanese as a lookout point. The Germans named it Burgberg, or "Fortress Hill", while the Japanese riddled it with tunnels and caves. It was from Lae airport that Amelia Earhart took off — and disappeared over the Pacific.

Wagan
Eight km from town, across the Butibum River, Wagan is a small village near Malahang Beach which the Japanese used as a landing point. You must ask the villagers for permission to visit the black sand beach where the remains of the landing barge *Myoko Maru* is sinking into the sand. On the way to Wagan you pass by the Lutheran Mission station, Ampo, whose church was used as a field hospital during the war and is one of the few buildings in the Lae area to survive the conflict.

Accommodation in Lae — the Top End
The *Melanesian Hotel* vies with the Huon Gulf for the position of Lae's premier hotel. Situated only a minute's walk from the town centre, the Melanesian has everything you'd expect, including a choice of bars and restaurants and a pleasant swimming pool. Singles cost from K24, doubles from K35 — room only.

Melanesian Hotel
Bookings: PO Box 756, Lae
Tel: 42 3744
Cables: Melanesian
Rooms: 67
Tariff: K24 sgl, K35 dbl

The *Huon Gulf Motel* is on Markham Rd, right by the old airstrip. It's somewhat smaller than the Melanesian, but very similarly priced — K25 for a single, K32 for a double. Like the Melanesian, all rooms are self-contained and air-conditioned and there's a swimming pool.

Huon Gulf Motel
Bookings: PO Box 612, Lae
Tel: 42 4844
Rooms: 30
Tariff: K25 sgl, K32 dbl

Finally there's the *Lae Lodge* on 4th St, not a great distance from the centre. It consists of 12 separate houses, each with three single and two double rooms — singles cost K17.50, doubles K25, room only. The rooms felt a trifle familiar here because they're just like the rooms in my favourite ultra-cheap hotel in Singapore. The only major difference being that my Singapore favourite is about K3 a night for a double! The rooms are not self-contained — you have to wander down the corridor to the shower and toilet. There's a major renovation programme in hand on the Lodge, and in any case part of its attraction is the pool, tennis courts, club atmosphere, grass and video TV.

Lae Lodge
Bookings: PO Box 475, Lae
Tel: 42 2454
Rooms: 60
Tariff: K17,50 sgl, K25 dbl

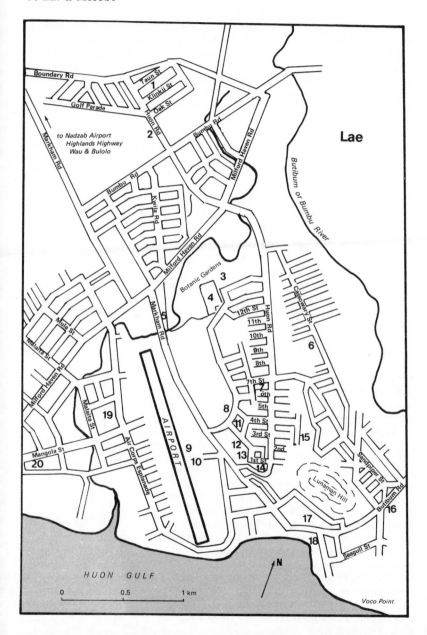

Lae

Boundary Rd
Taun St
Klinkii St
Golf Parade
Oak St
Huon Rd
Bumbu Rd
Milford Haven Rd
to Nadzab Airport
Highlands Highway
Wau & Bulolo
Markham Rd
Bumbu Rd
Kwila Rd
Milford Haven Rd
Botanic Gardens
Cassowary St
Buribum or Bumbu River
Mula St
Malaita St
Milford Haven Rd
Markham Rd
12th St
11th
10th
9th
8th
Huon Rd
7th St
6th
5th
4th St
3rd St
2nd
Mangola St
Malaita St
Air Corps Esplanade
AIRPORT
1st St
Sandpiper St
Buribum Rd
Lunaman Hill
Seagull St
HUON GULF
N
Voco Point
0   0.5   1 km

LAE

1	Klinkii Lodge	12	Terrace Coffee Lounge
2	Salvation Army Hostel	13	Melanesian Hotel
3	Orchid House	14	Lae Club
4	War Cemetery	15	Lae Lodge
5	Huon Gulf Motel	16	Taiping Cafe
6	Buablung Haus	17	Hotel Cecil
7	Corals Restaurant	18	Lutheran Shipping &
8	Post Office		Coastal Shipping
9	Lae Airport	19	Market
10	Air Niugini Office	20	Red Rose Restaurant
11	Islands Carving &		
	Morobe Bakery		

Accommodation in Lae — the Bottom End

Lae has one of the closest things you'll find to bargain accommodation in Papua New Guinea. It's called *Buablung Haus* and is located on Cassowary St, not too far from the town centre. It's a hostel style place with comfortable double rooms at K4 a bed. Apart from the reasonable prices, it's also an excellent place to meet people — travellers or locals. The restaurant is pleasantly cheap too, main courses in the evening will probably be around K1 to K1.50, soup about 25t. On weekends, only lunch is available.

The *Salvation Army Hostel* is on Huon Rd one km or so from the centre. Singles here cost K7 a night, doubles K12 and there are weekly rates, but the supply of rooms is rather limited. The rooms have cooking facilities so you can save money by fixing your own food. Close by, on Klinkii Rd which runs off Huon Rd on the other side, is *Klinkii Lodge* where singles cost K12, doubles K20 for bed & breakfat. The rooms are spartan but quite adequate. Meals are available, in your room, costing K2.50 for lunch, K4 for dinner.

A recent addition to the cheap end of the Lae accommodation scene is the *Lae School of*

Buablung Haus
Bookings: PO Box 1055, Lae
Tel: 42 4412
Rooms: 10
Tariff: K4 per person

Salvation Army Motel
Bookings: PO Box 259, Lae
Tel: 42 2487
Rooms: 5
Tariff: K7 sgl, K12 dbl,
cheaper by the week

Klinkii Lodge
Bookings: PO Box 192, Lae
Tel: 42 1281
Rooms: 20 twin
Tariff: K12 sgl, K20 twin,
incl breakfast

Lae School of Catering
Bookings: PO Box 305, Lae
Tel: 42 2734
Rooms: 4 twin
Tariff: K10 per person incl
breakfast

Catering which has just four rooms available at K10 per person bed & breakfast; other meals are also available. It's at the Lae Technical College.

The *Hotel Cecil* is a long standing name in Lae, the first hotel in town stood on the same site and the Cecil was built in 1932 by the same legendary owner of the first establishment. It even features in a James Michener story from *Return to Paradise*, but today it has seen rather better days. Close to the waterfront, it costs K11.50 single, K19 double including breakfast.

Hotel Cecil
Bookings: PO Box 12, Lae
Tel: 42 3674
Rooms: 30
Tariff: K11.50 sgl, K19 dbl,
  incl breakfast

Eating in Lae

If you're not eating at your hotel, Lae still has quite a range of places to console the inner person. For a snack or light lunch there are a variety of local places. The *Lae Milk Bar* on 4th St is pleasant, you may even be lucky enough to grab one of their two stools and be able to sit down and eat your 20t meat pie in air-conditioned comfort! The *Morobe Bakery* on 2nd St is a little flashier — good sandwiches (and meat pies of course) — but it's take-away only. If you want a guaranteed seat then try the *Terrace Coffee Lounge* also on 2nd St. For a real cooler try the genuine American sno-cones (crushed ice with flavouring) in the snack bar place on 7th St.

In the "real" restaurant category the emphasis is on Chinese — there are two strictly Chinese places but unfortunately, for the visitor, both are rather inconvenient. You really need wheels to get to them. The *Taiping Cafe* is standard Chinese cafe style — it's on Butibum Rd near the junction with Sandpiper Rd; quite a distance on beyond the Hotel Cecil. The *Red Rose Restaurant* is equally inconveniently situated on Mangola Rd out beyond the market on the other side of the airport. Both are really for residents with transport.

Much more central is the excellent, if unimaginatively named, *The Restaurant* which adjoins the Lae Club — just a hundred metres from the Melanesian Hotel on 1st St. It's got the longest menu in town — Chinese and European dishes. The Chinese ones are mainly around the K3 mark, the European ones a little more expensive. My beef curry (not really Chinese) was excellent and the service blindingly fast. You can also skip across into the Lae Club (where you should officially be signed in by a member) for a pre-dinner drink. They also have counter style food here — steak & salad for K2 is a typical example.

Finally there's *Corals* on 4th St next door to the *Wok Take-Aways* — its main fault is it's so anonymous you could walk by it ten times without ever knowing it was there. Once you've entered that faceless door, you'll find it's pleasantly cool and relaxed with a typical Australian/European menu — T-bone steak, wienerschnitzel and the like in the K3.50 to K5 range. Desserts are mainly around K1.50.

So far as hotel eating goes, the cafeteria in *Buablung Haus* is undoubtedly the bargain of the bunch — nothing to write home about of course, but shoestring travellers will find it pleasantly cheap and solid food. The *Klinkii Lodge* and the *Lae Lodge* both do fixed price dinners. I found the Klinkii dinner rather unappetising (breakfast was fine though) at K4 and didn't try the *Lae Lodge*'s (at K6) — I think you'd do better at the Lae Club. The *Huon Gulf* and the *Melanesian* both have licensed restaurants but local opinion is that the food doesn't match the prices.

Getting around Lae

PMVs around Lae cost 20t. Taxis are pretty cheap — 40t flagfall and then you seem to be able to get most places around town for a kina or so. Lae's airport used to be incredibly convenient, right in the centre of town, but now Air Nuigini's flights land out at the larger Nadzab field about 40 km out on the Highland Highway. A bus service operates for each flight and costs K2 for the nearly one hour trip. It will drop off/pick up at most hotels. Talair and other third level carriers still fly to the city airport. If you're feeling energetic you can walk across the road from the terminal, through the little park space and up the hill you'll find yourself in the city centre in about two minutes.

WAU & BULOLO

Wau and Bulolo were the sites for New Guinea's goldrush of the '20s and '30s. Although the gold was petering out by the start of WW II and the mines never got back into full swing after the war, the construction of a road down to Lae on the coast during the war has permitted timber and agricultural industries to develop. They're interesting places to visit both for that taste of gold-days history and for the fresh mountain air. Wau's about 150 km from Lae by road.

Wau Ecology Institute

A privately funded research institution, the Wau Ecology Institute is both a good place to stay and rather interesting in itself. It was originally founded by the Bishop Museum in Hawaii which remains one of the principal benefactors. Research projects include investigations of seed dispersal patterns by birds and ways of regenerating soil exhausted by too frequent burning off and cropping — this form of "shifting" agriculture is still prevalent in Papua New Guinea. The Institute has a small museum and a zoo with tree kangaroos, cassowaries, a crocodile and a hornbill amongst other animals. Down below the zoo in a path of rain forest is a display tree used by birds of paradise — if you're lucky! There are many interesting walks in the area on local footpaths or through the neighbouring coffee plantations. It takes several hours' walk, up and over the hills north of Wau, to the Edie Creek area.

Gold Days

Gold is still found by the New Guinea Gold Company near Wau, but the quantities today are much smaller than in the rush days of the '30s. There are many native New Guineans working smaller finds — you'll see some of their workings along the road between Bulolo and Wau. European residents of Wau are also inclined to have an occasional fossick. A couple of the old pre-war dredges, weighing 2500 tons, all of which was flown in by the old Junker tri-motors from Lae, can be seen near Bulolo. Between Bulolo and Wau the road winds through the deep Wau Gorge, crossing first Edie Creek and then Kotunga Creek — the two creeks which formed the basis of the gold rush activities. Edie Creek is about 20 km from Wau by a winding, rather heart-in-the-mouth road. Mt Kaindi, towering behind Edie Creek, has a small lodge on the top — enquire at the WEI about using it.

Other

The old WW II Bulldog track intended to link Wau with the south coast runs on from Edie Creek. The track never actually got to the coast — from Bulldog you had to travel by river. Since the war, the track has seriously deteriorated and been cut by landslides and slips in many places. Even walking the track is a long hard slog today and by vehicle, even a motorcycle, it would be impossible.

Bushwalkers sometimes follow the old gold miners' route between Wau and Salamua, the path is also rather overgrown and it takes about three days.

Closer to Wau there's said to be a surprisingly intact B-17 bomber a couple of hours' walk to the south-east. It was shot down by Zeroes during the war. An upside down DC-3 with a jeep still inside it is also said to be in the area. Wau airstrip has nothing to remind you of its former level of activity — it's the steepest airstrip in Papua New Guinea, falling 91 metres in its 1000 metre length. Very definitely one way only! If you fly between Wau and Lae with the charter carriers you've got a fair chance of making some additional stops. Aseki is a tiny airstrip approached through spectacular limestone outcrops. On one you can see a cleft in the side of the rock where villagers leave the smoked bodies of their dead. A road from Wau is slowly creeping closer to Aseki through some extremely rough country. further on, is in the heart of the old Kukukuku country.

Accommodation in Wau & Bulolo

Two places in Wau, one in Bulolo. Fairly central in Wau, the *Wau Hotel* is an old pre-war building with old fashioned (no private facilities) rooms. There's a restaurant where lunch and dinner are available. Singles cost from K14.50, doubles from K24 including breakfast.

In many ways the *Wau Ecology Institute*

Wau Hotel
Bookings: PO Box 41, Wau
Tel: 44 6233
Rooms: 11
Tariff: K14.50 sgl, K24 dbl
  incl breakfast

(WEI) is a nicer place to stay — it's also a lot cheaper. The institute is a couple of km out of Wau on a hillside overlooking the town. So get a ride up there or ask your PMV to take you to the "ecology" — or you'll have a hard walk if your bag is heavy. The institute carries on a variety of research projects and has accommodation for visiting researchers and casual visitors. There are five houses which cost K5.50 per person, they all have cooking facilities. One of the houses will sleep up to nine people. There's also a 10 room hostel, each room will sleep three — cost is K5 per person. The hostel is an excellent place for meeting people and meals are available — K1.50 for breakfast, K2.50 for lunch, K3 for dinner; solid, straightforward sort of food. It's one of the most pleasant places to stay in the country for the budget minded traveller.

Wau Ecology Institute
Bookings: PO Box 77, Wau
Tel: 44 6207/41
Rooms: 18
Tariff: K5 per person, K12 incl all meals

In Bulolo the *Pine Lodge Hotel* is the best equipped of these high country places. Singles cost K17.50, twins K20, family room K30 — all including breakfast. Whenever you're staying in Wau or Bulolo, it's worth remembering that you're a lot higher than on the coast — it can get chilly at night so come prepared.

Pine Lodge Hotel
PO Box 26, Bulolo
Tel: 44 5220
Cables: Pinelodge
Rooms: 12
Tariff: K17.50 sgl, K26 twin incl breakfast

Getting to Wau & Bulolo

Drive or fly. Talair operates an aircraft Lae-Bulolo-Wau-Port Moresby every morning and back every afternoon. Lae-Wau costs K19 and Port Moresby-Wau costs K48. Charter flights are also often operated — per person costs could be slightly cheaper. Just enquire around the various operators who might fly there.

The road to Wau splits off the Highland Highway only a few km out of Lae. It crosses the wide Markham River on a single lane Bailey Bridge then twists, turns and winds up into the hills. Mumeng, around the mid point, is the only town of any size it passes through. It's easy to find a PMV out of Lae — just wait by the roadside, go to the market or wait at one of the main junctions in town. Lots of PMVs shuttling back and forth. Most are open trucks, just a few minibuses, so you'll most likely get very dusty and dirty. The trip takes four or five hours, sometimes even longer, and costs K3 for Lae-Wau.

Back in the gold mining days, miners used to walk up from Salamua — a hard, dangerous slog taking eight days. Keen bushwalkers can still follow that historic old trail and are now highly unlikely to get an arrow between the shoulder blades for their troubles. During WW II a rough track was cut through from Wau to Bulldog in Papua. It was only kept up by constant repair work and is now badly overgrown, often broken and totally impossible for vehicles. But good walkers, preferably with a guide, can walk to Bulldog in about three days from where you may be able to get a boat downriver to the south coast.

EAST OF LAE
The Labu Lakes, right across the Markham River from Lae, were used to hide ships during the war. The maze of waterways and swamps are full of crocodiles. Further along the coast is pretty Busama Village, then Salamua — the picturesque peninsula has little to indicate its role in the gold rush days, when it was the largest town on the north New Guinea coast, or the part it played in WW II. It's only about half an hour from Lae to Salamua by speedboat.

TO THE HIGHLANDS
See the Highlands section for details on the Highlands Highway and the trip up from Lae.

HUON PENINSULA
Lae is situated on the Huon Gulf and the Huon Peninsula bulges out to the north-east. In a few years' time there may be a road running around the gulf from Lae to Finschhafen and Sialum. There is already a track negotiable by 4-WD vehicles between Finschhafen and Sialum or you can fly or ship to these places. They're popular sun, sea and sand escapes from Lae — which is not too well endowed with good swimming facilities.

Finschhafen
The town of Finschhafen was the German New Guinea Kompagnie's first unsuccessful attempt at colonising New Guinea. Between 1885, when they arrived there, and 1892, when they shifted west to Stephansort, the Germans had a miserable time and died like flies from malaria and assorted tropical ills. They did scarcely better at Stephansort and soon shifted to Madang and then to Rabaul, where they finally found peace from the mosquitoes.

The modern town of Finschhafen is not on the original site as it was shifted after WW II. Little remains of the original town apart from an early mission building. Towards the end of WW II the town was used as a staging post for American troops and vast numbers of GIs passed through. The war's abrupt end left millions of dollars worth of equipment here which the US forces disposed of by digging a huge hole into which hundreds of aircraft were bulldozed. Off the coast there are also a number of sunken ships and downed aircraft, many of which have not yet been touched by divers.

The beautiful Tami Islands, offshore from Finschhafen, are another of those idyllic tropical islands places, but can be a little expensive to get out to — even though the islands are only 12 km from the coast. Tami Islanders are renowned for their beautifully carved wooden bowls. There are other islands off the coast, particularly the Siassi Group between the mainland and New Britain. Umboi Island is the largest island. They are all in the volcanic belt which extends through New Britain and down to the north coast of New Guinea.

Accommodation in Finschhafen

Dregerhafen Lodge, five km from Finschhafen, was built and is run by Dregerhafen Provincial High School. It consists of three chalets, each with room for four people. There are communal cooking facilities — no food is provided so bring it from Lae. Cost is K5 per person and you can book through Dregerhafen High School, Box 126, Finschhafen, Morobe Province.

Dregerhafen Lodge
Bookings: PO Box 126, Finschhafen
Tel: 44 7050
Rooms: 3 chalets each for 4 people
Tariff: per person K5 bed only

Accommodation in Sialum

Further round the coast from Finschhafen, Sialum has the pleasant *Paradise Springs Holiday Inn* run by a District Officer who married a local girl and set up a delightful "get-away-from-it-all" resort. Situated right on the beach, it has a half dozen individual units and a pleasant swimming pool. Very much a lay-around-and-watch-the-grass-grow place, it's renowned for its excellent food, all of which is locally grown, including strawberries! Cost is K25 per person, per day, including all meals; bar prices are a little steep. To get there take a 25 minute Talair flight, costing K20 each way, then a 45 minute drive — you'll be met from the resort. There is a K80 weekend deal — two days plus the flight there and back. Bookings can be made through Talair, or by writing to PO Box 34, Lae.

Finschhafen Community Hostel
Bookings: PO Box 196, Finschhafen
Tel: 44 7046
Rooms: 4 dormitories
Tariff: per person - K1.50

Paradise Springs Holiday Inn
Bookings: Sialum via Lae
Tel: 019 and ask for Paradise Springs
Rooms: 7 units
Tariff: K25 per person all inclusive

Getting There

The weekly Luthern Shipping Service boat will drop you off in Finschhafen for about K10 — the service takes about eight hours. Or you can fly there in 20 minutes with Talair for K21. During the war, the road used to extend all the way from Lae to Finschhafen.

GETTING THERE

Flights from Port Moresby climb up and over the central mountain range, at 5000 metres in an F27 you're still not too high off the ground, and in the old days you flew through, rather than over, the mountains. These days you whistle across in an Air Nuigini F-28 in 45 minutes; cost is K39 and there are at least two flights every day of the week. Lae is also connected daily to Goroka (K25), Rabaul (K59) and Madang (K28). There are less frequent connections to other parts of the country.

Shipping

Lae is the centre for the only regular passenger shipping services from the main island of PNG. The choice is rather limited, although there are other less certain ships coming through. Madang or Rabaul are the regular choices; you'll find both companies at Voco Point, across the road from the Hotel Cecil.

The Lutheran Shipping Service operates a number of boats, but only the MV *Totol* takes passengers. It operates a weekly service Lae-Finschhafen-Wasu-Yara-Biliau-Madang. The total run takes two or three days and cost K18.

Coastal Shipping Services are also at Voco Point; find them in the Namasu Wharf. Every Friday they have a ship departing on the 38 hour run to Rabaul. On the way back, the ship stops at Kimbe and Kilanga. Costs are from K25 deck, K36 cabin.

Both companies enforce maximum number of passenger regulations (unlike shipping services in Indonesia) and they may also refuse to take passengers if they have a potentially dangerous cargo on board — such as compressed gas bottles. There may also be a Popondetta-Lae shipping service.

The Highlands

Area: 65,248 square km
Population: 1,135,000

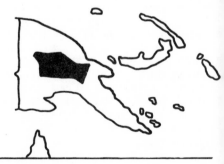

It is rather surprising that the great Highlands area, the most densely populated and agriculturally productive region of Papua New Guinea, should be the last to be discovered. It was not until the 1930s that the first contact was made with the Highlands tribes. Prior to that time it was thought that the mountains rose up from the north coast into a rugged tangle of virtually unpopulated central peaks which eventually sloped down to the south coast. It was definitely a shock when the long series of Highland valleys, stretching right up across the border, were discovered. The Highlands were barely touched when WW II intervened, so it was not until the '50s that they were really opened up. For the visitor it is the Highland people who are the great interest in this region — with their colourful customs and dramatic "sing-sings".

HISTORY
The first contact with the Highlands came as a result of the gold rush; if there was so much gold in the Wau-Bulolo area in Morobe there must be more elsewhere was the thought and in 1930 Mick Leahy and Mick Dwyer set off south to explore the headwaters of the Ramu River. To their amazement the river they followed south, expecting it to bend north-west to join the Ramu, continued south all the way to the Papuan coast where they discovered it was the Purari. This major river had been thought to rise in that inhospitable central range; in fact it started close to the northern coast and ran through densely populated valleys all the way through the central mountains to the south coast.

In 1933 Mick Leahy returned with his brother Danny to further investigate the Highlands and this time stumbled upon the huge, fertile and heavily populated Wahgi Valley. With government officials they then made an aerial reconnaissance of the Wahgi and walked in with a large patrol party. An airstrip was built at Mt Hagen but the hoped for gold was never discovered in any great quantity.

In true tradition where a government expedition and the miners had been the missionaries soon followed. Missions were established near present day Mt Hagen and in the Chimbu Valley near present day Kundiawa. Equally predictably, two missionaries managed to get themselves killed and the government moved in. A patrol post was set up at Kundiawa and the whole Highlands area was made "Restricted Territory" where Europeans were not allowed in without good reason. WW II intervened before too much more development could take place so it was the 1950s before the European presence was really felt. The construction of the Highlands Highway had a major impact on the area, as did the introduction of cash crops, particularly coffee.

The fertility of the Highlands and the consequent dense population has caused more than a few problems for the country. Today the population pressures have pushed many Highlanders out to other parts of the country in the search for work. Ritual warfare was a way of life in the Highlands and "payback" feuds to settle injuries done (or even supposed to have been done) are another facet of Highlands life that the government has to spend much time combating.

THE COUNTRY & THE PEOPLE
The Highlands are a whole series of valleys and intervening mountains. For

administrative purposes it is divided up into five provinces — Eastern Highlands (around Goroka), Chimbu or Simbu (around Kundiawa), Western Highlands (around Mt Hagen), Enga (around Wabag) and Southern Highlands (around Mendi).

The Eastern Highlands

The Eastern Highlands is probably the best known to Europeans and has longest been in contact with the west. The people here have largely abandoned their traditional dress although you'll still see the odd person from the hills down in Goroka market. The villages are recognisable for their neat clusters of low walled round huts. The Eastern Highlands are a less cohesive group than other parts of the Highlands.

Chimbu

Travelling west from Goroka the mountains become much more rugged and the valleys smaller and less accessible. This is the region where some of the highest mountains in PNG stand, including Mt Wilhelm, at 4800 metres the highest of them all. Despite this rugged terrain, the Chimbu Province is the most heavily populated region in PNG and the Chimbu people are the single largest language group. They have turned their steep country into a constant patchwork of gardens which spread up the side of every available hill. The Chimbus have a reputation for being avid capitalists who keep a good eye on their coffee profits and also for being great believers in the payback raid. Minor warfare can still be a way of life in the Chimbu region where aggrieved parties are all too ready to claim an eye-for-an-eye.

The Wahgi Valley & Mt Hagen

Continuing west from the Chimbu Province you descend into the large Wahgi Valley. The people of the valley are proud and handsome and often still dress in their traditional ways. For the men, who are generally bearded, that means a wide belt of beaten bark from which hangs a drape of woven string in the front, while behind hangs a bunch of tanket leaves, descriptively known as "arse-grass". The name has nothing to do with the fact that it covers their arses — it comes from the pidgin word "arse" for "behind of", or "already happened"!

The women can be just as decoratively dressed as the men with string skirts and fur from the cus-cus hanging between their breasts. Today that attire is usually reserved for sing-sings and bright lengths of printed cloth are more likely to be the everyday wear. For men the traditional dress is still the everyday attire. At sing-sings both sexes will have beautiful headdresses with bird of paradise plumes and other feathers.

The Wahgi people are also notable for their carefully tended vegetable gardens, their neat villages where the paths are often bordered by decoratively planted flowers, and the ceremonial parks with lawns and groves of trees. Sing-sings are an everyday occurence in the Wahgi area and you should make every effort to see one.

The Wigmen

Beyond the Wahgi/Hagen area, both south to Mendi and west to Wabag, is the area of the wigmen. The men of all the tribes in this region are notable for their huge wigs of human hair — wives and children, who are consequently short-haired, have to donate their hair for the elaborate wigs the men wear. The whole ensemble is held together by string woven as in a bilum (string bag). It is possible to tell which tribe a man is from by the way he wears his hair or decorates it. This most remote and least touched region of the Highlands is still relatively primitive and little developed. There was no permanent government station here until 1951 and in 1954 the discovery of the beautiful Lavani Valley in the Southern Highlands set newspapers off with high flown stories of the discovery of some lost Shangri-La.

THE HIGHLANDS HIGHWAY

The only extensive road network in Papua New Guinea starts in Lae and runs up into the central Highlands. The highway finally terminates in Mendi, on the Papuan side of the border, although rougher roads continue on a little further. The Highlands Highway is not sealed except in odd sections; at times it can be rather rough and easily effected by the weather. Roadslips or patches which become very boggy after rain are not uncommon. The first part of the highway out of Lae to Nadzab airport is paved. Beyond that it is generally sealed only where the road is especially steep or slippery when wet.

From Lae the road runs out through the coastal "jungle" then emerges into the wide, flat Markham Valley. Pause at the interesting pottery village of Zunim, about 130 km from Lae and 15 km past Kaiapit. It continues on this rather dull stretch to the Kassam Pass where it starts to twist, turn and climb. At the top of the pass there are some good lookout points across the Markham Valley to the Saruwaged Mountains. It continues up and down through Kainantu, the only reasonable size town before the road drops down to Goroka.

From Goroka the road continues through the valley to Asaro, then climbs steeply to the 2450 metre high Daulo Pass, about 25 km from Goroka. It continues twisting, turning and generally descending all the way to the Chimbu district and Kundiawa, about the mid-point between Goroka and Mt Hagen. This section of the road is probably the most interesting but also the roughest and toughest of the whole highway. During 1978 some of the worst sections were upgraded but until it is sealed this will continue to be a reasonably hard drive.

From Kundiawa the road descends to the Wahgi Valley and it's a fast run by Minj and Banz to Mt Hagen. At one time that was the end of the highway, but it now continues a further 137 km to Mendi in the Southern Highlands. Again it's a spectacular and interesting run and the general road condition is probably the best of the whole highway.

This central spine isn't all there is to drive on in the Highlands of central

New Guinea. Shortly after leaving Lae a road branches off to the left, crosses the wide Markham River on a Bailey bridge and then twists up to Bulolo and Wau. A rougher track continues to Edie Creek and once-upon-a-time the old Bulldog Track started there and crossed over to Bulldog in Papua.

On the main spine at Watarais, before Kainantu, a road branches off south-west and runs along the Ramu Valley to Madang. This is still a very rough track with frequent creek crossings and it can be 4-WD only if conditions are bad.

Between Goroka and Mt Hagen there's also the "old" Highlands Highway that parallels the new road for part of the distance. An "old" road also runs to Mendi from Mt Hagen, on the other side of Mt Giluwe to the "new" Men-

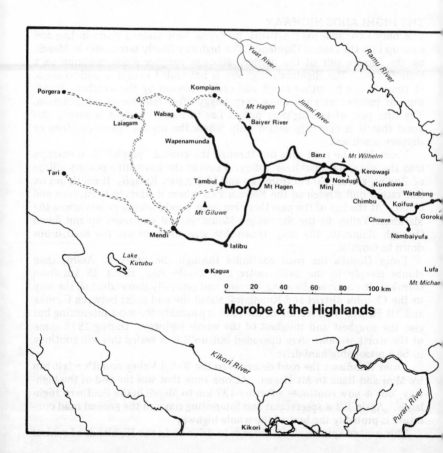

Morobe & the Highlands

di road. The new road runs through Ialibu while the old road, which at 109 km is about 28 km shorter, goes through Tambul. About 10 km out of Mt Hagen, at the junction of the old and new roads, a sign still resolutely points to Mendi on the old road, which was superseded in the early '70s. A German couple I met in PNG rented a car in Mt Hagen and having been carefully instructed as to where they were not allowed to drive it, blithely bounced off to Mendi on the old road — which in places is rough going even for a Land-Rover.

A reasonable road runs north from Mt Hagen through the spectacular Baiyer Gorge to Baiyer River and another road branches off the Mendi road and continues on to Wabag. The adventurous with a sturdy 4-WD vehicle could keep right on beyond Wabag and eventually loop back to Hagen

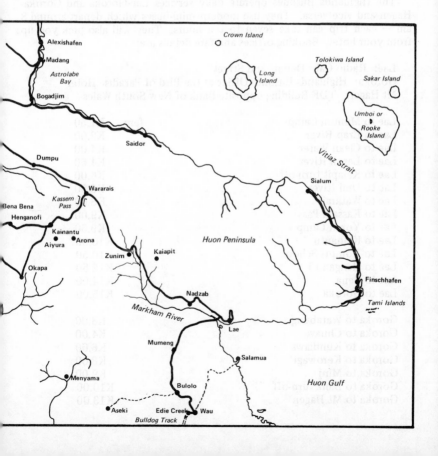

through Kandep and Mendi. There's a breathtakingly precarious road north from Kundiawa to Kegusugl if you're intending to climb Mt Wilhelm.

Transport on the highway? Well you can drive yourself at a suitably high price — see the notes on car hire about restrictions on "out-of-town use" which particularly apply in the Highlands. Only a couple of years ago it was quite easy to arrange to deliver cars or trucks from Lae to the Highlands. A quick scout around the Lae car dealers would often find a vehicle to be driven up. Unfortunately many cars are now delivered by truck so there is less opportunity for this convenient "free" trip. You might still be lucky.

Although an early start and late finish, plus non-stop driving, could get you from Lae to Mt Hagen in a day, it's really two day's drive. You don't average high speeds on these roads, especially if you're held up by vehicle breakdowns or road repairs. Anyway, what's the hurry?

The Highlands Buslines operate daily services Lae-Goroka and Goroka-Hagen and vice versa. They use modern mini-buses which depart around 8 am — each trip can take seven to ten hours. They will also pick you up from your hotel. Booking offices and fare details are:

Lae: Radio Cabs Depot, 2nd Street
Goroka: Highlands Buslines Office at the Bird of Paradise Hotel
Mt Hagen: TDE Building opposite Bank of New South Wales

Lae to Munum Camp	fare	K1.50
Lae to Erap River		K3.00
Lae to Clean Water		K4.00
Lae to Leron River		K4.50
Lae to Kaiapit turn-off		K6.00
Lae to Umi River		K6.50
Lae to Watarais		K8.00
Lae to Kassam Pass		K9.00
Lae to Yonki Camp		K9.50
Lae to Kainantu		K10.00
Lae to Kompri School		K10.50
Lae to Henganofi		K12.50
Lae to Bena		K14.00
Lae to Goroka		K15.00
Goroka to Watabung		K3.00
Goroka to Chuave		K4.00
Goroka to Kundiawa		K6.00
Goroka to Kerowagi		K8.00
Goroka to Minj		K9.00
Goroka to Banz turn-off		K10.00
Goroka to Mt Hagen		K13.00

Finally there are the PMVs, lots of them with all the usual plus and minus points. I don't actually think that they're any more or less safe then anything else in PNG. If you do fall off the road you've just got a long way to fall! Fares are K6 for each sector, Lae-Goroka or Goroka-Mt Hagen. I did Hagen-Goroka by PMV once in an incredibly speedy five hours — yet the driver was extremely safe and steady, my adrenalin flow never increased once for the whole journey.

Pigs, Bride Prices and Mogas

If you need convincing that the concepts of materialism, possessions and capitalism are not purely a modern invention a visit to the New Guinea Highlands should soon do the job. Wealth here is enormously important and the men of consequence in a village are invariably also the men of affluence. In the Highlands just being wealthy is not enough, you have to show it and much of the ceremonial life of the Highlands is centred around displays of wealth. Ostentatious displays.

The old shell money has been seriously devalued since European contact, both by shell money becoming more readily available and by the advent of modern currency. Pigs, however, still retain their value, for a pig is not just food — it's the most visible and important measure of a man's solvency. Cassowaries are also extremely important in the Highlands and they're even less edible!

The most vivid wealth displays are the "mogas" — in Enga Province the "tee" ceremonies are very similar. There is no better way of showing just how rich you are than giving it way and a moga is the approved way of doing it. Mogas follow a pattern, every few years the time rolls round and the ceremonial exchanges begin — for wealth is never really given away, whatever you give results in an obligation to give back and eventually you expect to have those pigs and kina shells returned. The moga ceremonies flow from village to village with one group displaying their wealth and handing it on to the next. Even your enemies get a look in, they have to be impressed by how much you are able to give away to your friends. During these festivals vast numbers of village pigs will be slaughtered and cooked and all present indulge in an orgy of eating. Attempts to convince the Highlanders, many of whom live on the borderline of protein deficiency, that pigs could be used more sensibly, rather than in this feast or famine manner, have been mainly unsuccessful.

Bride price is another occassion for proving just how much you can afford to pay. The bride's clan has to be paid by her new husband and although local councils have tried to put top limits on how much can be handed over, the average price is around 20 pigs and K400 or more in cash. An interesting earlier description of the tense negotiations of fixing a bride price, and the prestige that goes with it, can be found in Kenneth Read's book *The High Valley*.

Another example of this cash society concept comes up in the payback feuds. An eye for an eye is not just a basic concept — it is virtually a greater sin to fail to "payback" than to have committed the initial wrong. Again it is not specifically aimed at the wrongdoer, his whole clan is responsible for his actions. Under this concept if a man murders somebody then it is the responsibility of the murdered person's clan to kill someone in the murderer's clan. Preferably the murderer himself, but if not any man, woman or even child will do. Naturally this sort of thing has been very firmly clamped down on by the government but even today substantial financial compensation will be required from the villan's clan — whether western style justice has also been done or not. Car accidents are a rich source of payback feuds.

THE HIGHLAND SHOWS

During the 1950s, as the Highlands first came into serious contact with Europeans, the Highland Shows were instituted as a way of gathering the Highland tribes and clans together and showing them that those people from across the hill really weren't so bad after all. They soon became an amazing success and grew from the original concept of a local get-together into a major tourist attraction. As many as 40,000 warriors would gather together in the show arena in a stomping, chanting, dance that literally shook the earth. The drums beat, the feathers swayed, their bodies glistened with tree oils or pig grease, it was extremely colourful.

Unfortunately, over the last few years the shows have suffered a serious decline. The days of the warring between the clans, on a serious level at least, are now far behind. With improved transport and better roads it is no longer an effort to get from place to place; something you save up for an annual gathering. Plus, the soaring price of coffee has made a lot of Highlanders comparatively wealthy, with a consequent loss of interest in picking up a little money from the show. Still, the shows go on and could well have a revival. They take place in even numbered years in Goroka (in 1978 it took place in September) and in odd years in Mt Hagen.

KAINANTU

The major town on the Highlands Highway from Lae up to Goroka, Kainantu is an important cattle and coffee production region. At one time there was also some gold found in this area and very minor production still continues. Nearby is the Summer Institute of Linguistics headquarters where the Bible is being translated into local languages.

Accommodation in Kainantu

The *Kainantu Lodge-Motel* has seven rooms in the cheaper lodge part and 10 in the motel. Singles/doubles cost K15/K24 in the lodge, K19/K30 in the motel — both including breakfast. There are a variety of charges for larger groups.

Kainantu Lodge/Motel
Bookings: PO Box 28, Kainantu
Cables: Lodge
Tel: 77 1021
Rooms: 17 twin & fmly
Tariff: sgl K15-19, dbl K24-30, & so on incl breakfast

OTHER PLACES IN THE EASTERN HIGHLANDS

Okapa is south of Kainantu. It's notable for the disease known as Kuru which appears to be totally unique to this area. Kuru has been dubbed the laughing disease since it attacks the central nervous system and the victims die with a peculiar "smile". Tribes in this area have been decimated by Kuru which appears to attack women, with invariably fatal results, far more often than men. It is thought the disease developed from ritual cannibalism of tribal dead.

Lufa is south of Goroka and a good base for climbing Mt Michael, named after those two original Highland "Michaels" — Mick Dwyer and Mick Leahy. Near Lufa there is a cave with some interesting pre-historic cave paintings.

GOROKA

The town of Goroka has grown from a small outpost in the mid '50s to its current position as the commercial centre of the entire Highlands. It's still a typical PNG town — clustered around the airstrip. At an altitude of 1600 metres the climate is perpetual spring — never too hot, never too cold. The town centre itself is small enough to walk around, although you'll need transport to get to the further out attractions.

Lookout

Wisdom St, beside the post office, leads to a track that climbs to an excellent lookout over Goroka. It's a long, steep walk if you've not got wheels, but the reward is an excellent view over the valley.

J K McCarthy Museum

McCarthy was one of Papua New Guinea's legendary patrol officers and wrote one of the classic books on New Guinea patrolling — *Patrol into Yesterday*. The museum that bears his name is off to the side of the airstrip, in a corner of the showgrounds. To my mind it's the best museum in Papua New Guinea but that is partly because the new National Museum in Port Moresby is not fully developed. Among the exhibits here in Goroka are a variety of pottery styles, weapons, clothing and musical instruments, even some grisly jewellery including a necklace of human fingers! Admission is free and there is a shop with a good selection of artifacts and handicrafts, including paintings by PNG's best know modern artist, Jakupa — at K300 a time. Behind the museum there's a P-39 Aircobra left behind by the USAF after the war. One catch about the museum — it's a lengthy walk from the town centre and it's only open from 9 to 11 in the morning and 1 to 3 in the afternoon.

Bena Bena

About 10 km out of Goroka on the old road to Kainantu (it must have been a hard trip) is the village of Bena Bena with the biggest of the Highlands weaving set-ups. Curiously the hand looms are all operated by men, quite the opposite of most Asian countries where weaving is a woman's skill. A couple of women do weave shoulder bags in an adjoining hut. The men weave pleasantly coarse rugs, bedspreads and place mats. They're not

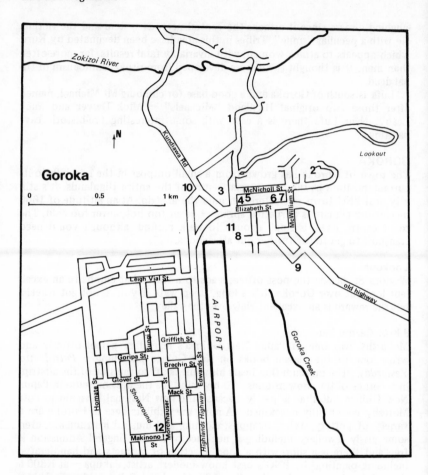

GOROKA

1 Salvation Army Flats
2 Minogere Hostel
3 Club
4 Post Office
5 Lutheran Guest House
6 Trans-Niugini Office
7 Bird of Paradise Hotel
8 Air Terminal & Air Niugini
9 Lantern Lodge
10 Market
11 Talair Office
12 J K McCarthy Museum

cheap — rugs start from K20 and go up to K66. There are other weaving centres around the valley and a shop in town, but the prices are fairly standardised.

Kotuni
A relatively new Highlands enterprise and one with great potential, is the trout farm at Kotuni — about 15 km out of town off the Hagen road. Here they hatch out trout eggs which are flown up from Australia and breed them up for consumption or to be released as fingerlings into the many excellent (but little fished) Highland streams. Apart from putting trout on the local menus, the trout farm is a popular weekend spot as it's very beautiful — a rocky little river, bouncing through the jungle close to the fish tanks.

Asaro Mud Men
Many years ago, so the story goes, the village of Asaro came off second best in a tribal squabble. The warriors of Asaro coated themselves with grey mud and made huge masks of mud then went off on the inevitable payback raid. Seeing these ghostly apparitions emerging from the trees, their unfortunate opponents thought the dead had risen and scattered. The mud men recreate this little caper for tourists but unfortunately it has become rather commercialised and dull. The number of mud men appears to be in direct proportion to the number of kina paying tourists. I think it would be much better if the mud men were to perform, say, once a month and really make a show of it rather than the current half-hearted, "if there's a tourist bus coming", affair. Mud men "tours" cost K17 each for two people, K14 for four, K12 for six. Asaro is about 20 km from Goroka on the Hagen road.

Daulo Pass
The road out to Hagen runs fairly flat through Asaro then hairpins its way up to the 2450 metre high Daulo Pass. It's cold and damp up there but the views are spectacular, particularly if you're heading down from the pass towards Goroka.

Other
You can easily arrange visits to coffee plantations or coffee processing plants around Goroka. Tea is also an important Highlands crop. The Goroka market is particularly busy on Saturdays although, like other PNG markets, it also operates on other days of the week.

Accommodation in Goroka — the Top End
The *Bird of Paradise Motel* on Elizabeth St in the centre of town is the top hotel in Goroka. It's recently been bought out by the same enterprising couple who run the Lantern Lodge.

The "Bird" has 62 rooms and a licensed restaurant. It's only a few minutes walk from the airport — which may be just as well since Goroka only has one taxi! Rooms cost from K20 single, K32 double or twin — room only. If it has a drawback it is probably its central position; people in the lower level front rooms may find the street noise annoying. At lunchtime the rooftop *Flight Deck* has hamburgers and salad for K2, other dishes for K3.

The *Lantern Lodge* is equally close to the airport — it is smaller and a little cheaper. Just nine rooms with prices from K18 single, K26 double, K28 twin. Pleasantly warm atmosphere here in the evening plus an excellent restaurant, which is said to have some of the best Chinese food in PNG (I'm inclined to agree!); most dishes K3.50 to K4.

Goroka's third hotel, which bridges the gap to the low price end of the market, is the *Minogere Lodge*. It is run by the local town council, has 64 rooms and costs K12 single or K9 per person in a double, K10 in a twin. Breakfast is included in the tariff, the rooms are fairly spartan, without private facilities or even a washbasin in the room. The Minogere has a pleasant outside patio area where a good barbecue lunch with smorgasbord salad is available — cheap too, from only K2. Right below the patio area is the council swimming pool, 30t admission and very convenient. The Minogere also has a licensed restaurant (dinner is a fixed price, K5, which is quite good value) and its only drawback is that it's on a steep hillside overlooking the town — a tough walk carrying bags if you don't find that elusive taxi. 'Phone and ask to be picked up.

Accommodation in Goroka — the Cheap End

Just a couple of places to try — there used to be a third (the CWA Hostel) but that has closed. The *Lutheran Guest House* is right in the centre of town, behind the post office. Cost is K5.50 per person, bed and breakfast. Although there is a kitchen you can only use it for making tea or coffee. Sandwiches are available in the even-

Bird of Paradise Hotel
Bookings: PO Box 12,
    Goroka
Tel: 72 1144
Cables: Birdpara
Rooms: 52
Tariff: K20 slg, K32 dbl

Lantern Lodge
Bookings: PO Box 58,
    Goroka
Tel: 72 1776
Rooms: 9
Tariff: K18 sgl, K26 dbl

Minogere Lodge
Bookings: PO Box 450,
    Goroka
Tel: 72 1009
Cables: Gorokaunsil
Rooms: 64
Tariff: K12 sgl, K18 dbl, incl
    breakfast

ing, but other than that you may have to eat out — at least that was the situation while I was in Goroka. It may be different when the regular manageress is back.

The *Salvation Army Flats* are a km or so out of town — a ten minute walk from the post office. They're self contained with their own well-equipped kitchens. They're also often full, so it's wise to book ahead if possible. Cost is K8 per night for one person, K13 for two.

CHIMBU (SIMBU) PROVINCE

Squeezed between the Eastern Highlands (Goroka) and the Western Highlands (Mt Hagen), Chimbu is the smallest of the mainland provinces and the most densely populated. The name is said to come from the first patrol handing out steel axes and knives to which the recipients replied that they were "simbu" — "very pleased". The area was accordingly named Simbu which became Chimbu. The name has officially reverted to Simbu.

The Chimbu area is the centre of the Highlands "payback" concept and was also notable for the battle of the sexes often becoming outright war. The old customs are breaking down, but at one time all the men in a village would live in a large men's house while their wives lived in individual round-houses — with the pigs.

Chuave and Kundiawa are the main towns along the Highlands Highway, surrounded by some of the most mountainous country in the Highlands. There are a number of interesting caves including some near Kundiawa which are used as burial places. There are other large caves, suitable for caving enthusiasts, only a few km from Kundiawa or the Keu Caves which are very close to the main road near Chuave. The Nambaiyufa Amphitheatre is also near Chuave and noted for its rock paintings.

Accommodation in Kundiawa

There are two places to stay in Kundiawa and neither is cheap. The pleasant *Chimbu Lodge* is the quality establishment — room only rates start at K14 for a single, K22 for a double. It has a pleasant licensed restaurant and is close to the town and the airstrip. The *Kundiawa Hotel* is even more central but it is only marginally cheaper (K10.50 single, K18.50 double) and is a bit of a hellhouse on drinking nights.

Chimbu Lodge
Bookings: PO Box 191, Kundiawa
Tel: 75 1144
Rooms: 20 family
Tariff: K14 sgl, K22 dbl

Kundiawa Hotel
Bookings: PO Box 12, Kundiawa
Tel: 75 1033
Rooms: 10 twin
Tariff: K10.50 sgl, K18.50 twin

MT WILHELM

Climbing to the 4509 metre summit of Mt Wilhelm is a popular activity. You start out from Kegusugl about 43 km from Kundiawa, you can get there by PMV (K4 or K5) up a road that has to be seen to be believed. Or you can fly in to the airstrip at 2469 metres — the highest strip in Papua

New Guinea and higher than the top of Mt Kosciusko, the highest mountain in Australia. The local council have a rest house close to the the airstrip and can recommend guides, although the path is clearly marked and a guide is not really necessary. It may also be possible to stay, reluctantly, in the Catholic Mission.

The first stage of the climb entails walking up to Pindaunde Lakes at about 3500 metres, there are a couple of rest houses here — it costs slightly more (K2 against K1) to use the University of Papua New Guinea one but it is much warmer at night and well worth the extra expense. You book the rest houses before you commence your climb. The next morning you make the three or four-hour climb to the top. At times the peak is snow covered and on a clear day you can see both coasts.

It's a long, fairly hard walk and some walkers reckon it is better to spend a day acclimatising at the lake rest houses. It can also become very cold, often windy and foggy at the top. The clouds roll in around 9 am so it is wise to start up from the rest house as early as possible — certainly before 5 am. While in the Mt Wilhelm area a visit to the little village of Gembogl is also interesting — a very pretty little place with people in native undress and an old swing bridge.

Exactly How High?

My $64,000 question could be "How high is Mt Wilhelm?" According to a map from the National Mapping Office it is 4509 metres (14,795 feet), the *Papua New Guinea Handbook* says 4697 metres (15,412 feet) as does a tourist brochure I picked up, while an Air Niugini brochure goes all the way to 4800 metres (15,750 feet). The Office of Information simply says "nearly 4500 metres". Will the real Mt Wilhelm please stand up?

BANZ & MINJ

These two towns are mid-way between Kundiawa and Mt Hagen, Banz on the Highway, Minj a few km south of the road. There are a number of pleasant drives around this area. Nondugl, back towards Kundiawa, has a small Bird of Paradise Sanctuary — the remnants of the Sir Edward Hallstrom collection that formed the basis for the Baiyer River sanctuary.

Accommodation in Minj

The *Ramada Inn* in Minj has 12 twin rooms and costs K34 a night including all meals. It's a flashy establishment used mainly by tour parties who make it their Highlands' base. Cultural performances in the evenings are part of the package.

Ramada Lodge
Bookings: PO Box 20, Banz
Tel: 56 2348
Telex: NE 52012
Rooms: 12
Tariff: K34 per person with
    all meals, K56 incl tours

Accommodation in Banz

The *Banz Hotel* has rooms at K10.50 a single, K18 a double.

Banz Hotel
Bookings: PO Box 16, Banz
Tel: 56 2245
Rooms: 12
Tariff: K10.50 sgl, K18 twin

MT HAGEN

The major town in the Western Highlands, Mt Hagen was just a patrol station before WW II and only in the past ten years has it really expanded to its present size. The airstrip was moved from its middle-of-town position to a new location a few km east of town in the late '60s.

The town acquired its name by a rather round about route. It is named after nearby Mt Hagen which in turn was named after the German administrator, Kurt von Hagen. In 1895 two Germans started off on a badly planned and ill-fated attempt to cross the island from north to south. They were murdered by two of their carriers, although one wonders if they would have survived the trip in any case. The carriers later escaped from custody and in the subsequent hunt for them von Hagen was shot and killed near Madang in 1897; he was buried at Bogadjim.

The Market

Mt Hagen market on a Saturday is one of the most interesting in PNG because the people here are still very much seen in traditional costume — unlike in more "modern" Goroka. It's a bright, colourful affair with many men wearing bark belts, "arse grass" and plumed headdresses. Women may be a little less traditionally dressed, but they make up for that with the sheer brightness of their lap-laps or dresses. But don't just look at the people, there are plenty of interesting goods on sale including, of course, those very valuable pigs and, when I was there, a cassowary tightly trussed up in lengths of bamboo. There is a small artifacts shop in the market.

Sing-Sings

Not an everyday occurrence but one you should definitely try to see while in Hagen is a sing-sing. Actually there quite probably are sing-sings on almost every day of the week, but finding where they are and getting to them can be a problem. Many places around Hagen are still inaccessible except on foot. A sing-sing can be for any of a number of reasons — it might be associated with paying off a bride price, a moga gift-exchange ceremony or even some more mundane activity like raising money for a local school. Whatever the reason, the result will be much the same — a lot of people, brilliantly costumed, singing and dancing around. Bring lots of film if you're keen on photography — the people love being filmed. A good place to find out about sing-sings, if you're not on an organised tour that is, is the market or the post office. Just ask if anybody knows of a sing-sing coming up.

Other Highlands activities which, while you may not get to see them "for real", are often staged for tourists, are the courting rituals known as "Karim Leg" (Carry Leg) or "Turnim Head". Ceremonially dressed young couples meet in the long houses for courting sessions where they sit side by side and cross legs (Carry Leg) or rub their faces together (Turn Head).

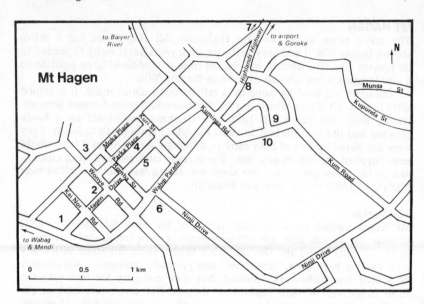

Mt Hagen

to Baiyer River

to airport & Goroka

Highlands Highway

N

Munga St

Kupunda St

Kupunda St

Moka Place

Kum St

Parka Place

Kuminga Rd

Wabag Parade

Bonny Drive

Hagen Rd

Womye St

Kei Nor Rd

Kum Road

Ninji Drive

Ninji Drive

to Wabag & Mendi

0   0.5   1 km

MT HAGEN	
1 Highlander Hotel	6 Botanic Gardens
2 Hagen Eagle	7 Kimininga Hostel
3 Hagen Park Motel	8 Market
4 Post Office	9 Mapang Hostel
5 Air Niugini	10 Hospital

Other

In the car park circle in front of the Country Club (next to the Highlander Hotel) is the Hagen Eagle — symbol of the family of von Hagen, it was moved here from his memorial near Madang. Not many people in Hagen seem to know about it. The "Sunken Gardens" are nearby. Hagen is an important centre for tea and coffee cultivation. It's also a good base for trips further afield to the Baiyer River, Nebliyer and Wabag Valleys.

Accommodation in Mt Hagen — the Top End

Top of the top end is the *Highlander Hotel*, just a hundred metres or so from the town centre. It's got two wings and rooms in either wing have private facilities and tea/coffee making

Highlander Hotel
Bookings: PO Box 34, Mt
   Hagen
Tel: 52 1355

equipment. The new wing rooms also have a radio, telephone and newer furnishings. Cost, including breakfast, is K19.50/K29.50 singles/ doubles in the old wing, or K26/K38 in the new. There are also some family rooms. The licensed restaurant provides you with a substantial breakfast. The K3.50 lunch and K6 dinner are equally generous — bring your appetites. The Highlander is situated in pleasant gardens and is quiet and peaceful, if a little colourless.

In contrast, the *Hagen Park Hotel* is rather more noisy and active. Bed and breakfast here costs K21 single, K33 double or twin. The restaurant is not as good as the Highlander's and it's more expensive — main dishes for dinner start from K5. The third "better" place is the *Airport Hotel* which, as the name suggests, is out at the airport — inconveniently far from the town, but very handy for when you fly out! Rooms here cost K20 single, K32 double or twin — again including breakfast. The restaurant is similarly priced to the Hagen Park. The Highlander is the best of the three hotels for eating in.

Apart from the hotels, the only other place in Hagen to eat is *Val's Place* near the Talair and Air Niugini offices — or the take-aways, of course.

Accommodation in Mt Hagen — the Bottom End

The *Kimininga Hostel* on the Goroka side of town about ten minutes walk from the centre is the best known cheaper place. If you're coming up from Goroka by road, get off before you get into town. It's good value for PNG — K5.50 for a bed, breakfast K1.50, dinner K3, and the food is really quite good. The rooms are comfortable and clean and some of them are very modern — they don't have private facilities of course. There's a lounge with coffee, free, on tap in the evenings. A nice little touch is the xylophone player who tinkles around to announce it's mealtime. Packed lunches are available if you're off for the day — just K1, a

Cables: Hotel
Rooms: 38
Tariff: K19.50-K26 sgl,
K29.50-K38 dbl, incl
breakfast

Hagen Park Motel
Bookings: PO Box 81, Mt
Hagen
Tel: 52 1388
Cables: Harpark
Rooms: 32
Tariff: K20.50 sgl, K33 dbl,
incl breakfast

Airport Hotel
Bookings: PO Box 86, Mt
Hagen
Tel: 55 1326
Rooms: 16
Tariff: K20 sgl, K32 dbl, incl
breakfast

Kimininga Hostel
Bookings: PO Box 408
Tel: 52 1865
Cables: Kimininga Hostel
Rooms: 21 twin
Tariff: K5.50 per person,
K7 incl breakfast

very pleasant contrast to the Highlander's over-priced K4 effort.

Otherwise try the *Mapang Hostel* beside the hospital — it's a mission place, but will take travellers if there's room available — cost is K12 a head. Finally the *Red Cross* may have a couple of rooms in their cottage which is just across the road from Mapang — check in the hospital, but keep your fingers crossed.

BAIYER RIVER

The 120 hectare Baiyer River wildlife sanctuary is 55 km north of Mt Hagen. There are tours operated to the sanctuary or the do-it-yourselfers can get there by PMV for K2. On the way you pass through the spectacular Baiyer River Gorge.

Admission to the sanctuary is K1 and there are many animal and bird enclosures dotted around the rainforest — and some good picnic spots. A large hornbill watches you eat from his perch in the trees around the picnic area. It's an excellent place to view many of PNG's spectacular birds of paradise and noisy parrots. They also have a large collection of PNG's possums and tree kangaroos. Like many other zoos and wildlife sanctuaries, I would like it better if there were fewer animals and in larger enclosures. But even when cages get you down you can still get those magic moments — when a bird of paradise swoops through the trees high above you.

Accommodation at Baiyer River

There is a reasonably priced lodge at the sanctuary, the *Baiyer River Bird Sanctuary Lodge*. Costs are K5 per person in the 10 twin rooms — students and children are free. You can also camp here for K1 per night. There is no food available at Baiyer River, although the lodge has cooking facilities. You must bring your own food from Mt Hagen.

Baiyer River Lodge
Bookings: PO Box 490, Mt Hagen
Rooms: 10 twin
Tariff: K5 per person, students free, camping K1

A Two men clowning around at a sing-sing
B A chilly warrior in Mt Hagen market
C The Highlands Highway between Goroka and Mt Hagen

THE SOUTHERN HIGHLANDS & MENDI

This was one of the last parts of PNG to be opened up for before the war it came under the Papuan jurisdiction whereas physically it is very much part of the Highlands area, which is more accessible from the northern, New Guinea, coast. The Mendi Valley is the best known part of the Southern Highlands but even this part was first explored only in 1936 and mapped in 1938. It was 1950 when the first airstrip was constructed and 1952 when that sure sign of the arrival of civilisation, the prohibition of tribal warfare, took place. Not unnaturally the Mendi tribesmen turned their energies to attacking government patrols who were still fighting them off in 1954.

This is the area of the Wigmen with their fantastically decorated wigs of human hair. Widows in the Southern Highlands coat themselves with grey mud and drape themselves with immense strings of the grey kunai grass seeds known as Job's tears. Supposedly they cannot wash the mud off until all the seed necklaces have been removed at the rate of one string per day. The Mendi Valley is on the trade route from the Gulf of Papua into the Highlands along which salt, kina shells and the body oil tapped from trees was distributed.

Mt Giluwe, 4362 metres high, is the second highest mountain in PNG and the highest on the Papuan side of the border. It stands between Mt Hagen and Mendi, the old and new roads pass either side of it. The Southern Highlands is also starting to attract caving expeditions as the limestone nature of the hills here is ideal for the formation of extremely deep caves. Some caves of enormous depth have already been explored and it is a distinct possibility that some of the deepest caves in the world await discovery in this region.

The drive from Mt Hagen to Mendi is an interesting one, passing several spectacular waterfalls along the way. Saturday is, naturally, the best day to visit Mendi when tribespeople crowd into town from the surrounding country. Mendi is a centre for handloom weaving and has an interesting small museum on a hillside just beyond the town.

Check with Mongol Business Inc (Private Mail Bag, Mendi — tel: 59 1193) about tours further out from Mendi. Also about their twice weekly mini-bus service between Mendi and Mt Hagen.

Accommodation in Mendi

The *Mendi Hotel* is the main hotel in this "end of the road" town. It's comfortable and has a licensed restaurant, but is decidedly on the expensive side. Singles at K23, doubles at K31,

Mendi Hotel
Bookings: PO Box 108,
Mendi
Tel: 59 1188/9

A The old cemetery in Madang
B Haus Tambaran in Palembai village on the Sepik
C Malanggan carvings in New Ireland

both room only. Alternatively try the *Mendi United Church of Christ* which may, or may not, offer accommodation at K10 full board.

Rooms: 22
Tariff: K23 sgl, K31 dbl

ENGA PROVINCE

Beyond Mt Hagen the roads deteriorate and the country becomes more primitive. Even in the '60s much of this region was still "uncontrolled". Control may have arrived but tribal warfare is still common enough up here to be known as "Highlands Football". From Mt Hagen the Wabag road starts out in the same direction as the Mendi road, then branches off north-west. It's a rougher road than the Mendi one, particularly over the nearly 3000 metre high Kaugel Pass before Wapenamunda. Wabag has a cultural centre and museum and a stunningly frightening airstrip. If you've got a sturdy 4-WD vehicle and the ability to go with it you can loop back from Wabag through Kompiam to Baiyer River and down to Mt Hagen; or continue on beyond Wabag to Laiagam or down to Mendi. Hard going.

Accommodation in Wabag

The *Wabag Lodge* has 14 rooms and costs K19 single, K30 double or twin, for bed and breakfast. Tours out from Wabag can be arranged from the Lodge.

Wabag Lodge
Bookings: PO Box 2, Wabag
Tel: 57 1069
Rooms: 14
Tariff: K19 sgl, K30 dbl,
incl breakfast

ARTIFACTS

The Highlanders do not carve bowls, masks or other similar items, their artistic abilities are shown almost entirely in personal attire or in weapons. Best known would probably be the fine ceremonial axes from Mt Hagen. The slate blades come from the Jimi River area north of Hagen on the Sepik-Wahgi divide. They are bound to the shaft with decorative cane strips and were never intended for use either as weapons or tools, their use is purely ceremonial.

"Killing Sticks" from Lake Kopiagu had a much more obvious use, the

ceremonial axe

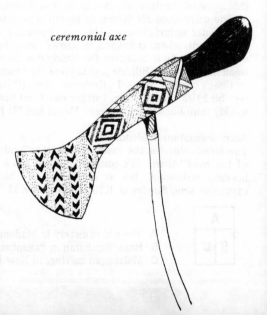

pointed fighting stick is tipped with a sharpened cassowary bone to make a lethal weapon in close fighting. Other traditional items you may see are the fine kina shells made from the gold lip pearl shell or the aumak necklaces of bamboo rods. In the Highlands, kina shells are often mounted on a board of red coloured resin. At traditional wealth displays, such as the moga ceremonies, long lines of these mounted shells will be formed on the ground.

Far from traditional, but extremely attractive, are the Highlands weaving articles found mainly around Goroka. Blankets, rugs, bedspreads, bags and other items are all available in pleasantly coarsely woven wool.

GETTING THERE & AROUND

Air Niugini have regular connections to and from Goroka and Mt Hagen and Wewak, Madang, Lae and Port Moresby. In addition there is a comprehensive third level network around the Highland centres. The chart below details some of the connections and fares:

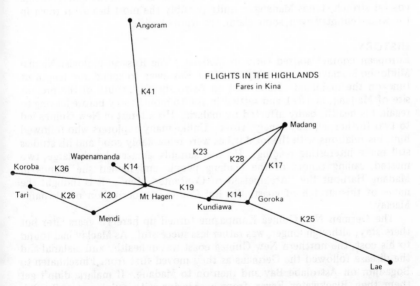

The major third level carrier, Talair, has its headquarters in Goroka. There are also convenient flights to the Sepik River or south to the Gulf and Western Provinces. If you are going to Bensbach Lodge in Western Province you'll find it as easy to get there from the Highlands as from Port Moresby.

For details on road travel in the Highlands, see the section on the Highlands Highway.

Madang

Area: 27,970 square km
Population: 192,000

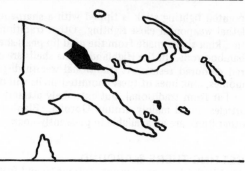

Madang province consists of a fertile coastal strip backed by some of the most rugged mountains in New Guinea — the Adelbert and Schrader Ranges to the north, the Finisterre Range to the south. Offshore are a string of interesting, and still active, volcanic islands. More or less in the middle of the coastal stretch stands Madang — quite possibly the most beautiful town in the whole country even, some claim, the whole Pacific.

HISTORY
European contact started early in Madang. The Russian biologist Nicolai Miklouho-Maclay was probably the first European to spend any length of time on the mainland. He arrived on Astrolabe Bay, south of the present site of Madang, in 1871 and settled in for 15 months stay before leaving to regain his health, badly affected by malaria. His interest in New Guinea led to two further, equally lonely, visits. Unlike many explorers who followed him, his relations with the local tribes were remarkably good and his studies still make interesting reading. He was suitably amazed by the large, two masted, sailing canoes of the Madang people and named the islands in Madang Harbour the "Archipelago of Contented Men". It is thought the name of this stretch of coast, the Rai Coast, is a derivation of his name Maclay.

The German Neu Guinea Kompagnie turned up here 13 years later but there stay, although longer, was rather less successful. As Maclay had found to his cost, the northern New Guinea coast was unhealthy and malarial and the disease followed the Germans as they moved first from Finschhafen to Bogadjim on Astrolabe Bay and then on to Madang. If malaria didn't get them then Blackwater Fever, from overdosing with quinine, usually did. From 1884 to 1899 a total of 224 officials worked for the company, of whom 54 died and 133 either resigned or were dismissed. Gavin Souter's book *The Last Unknown* depressingly describes the sheer misery of working for "the bloody bone" as the company became known. On the point of failure, the German government took over and swiftly moved to the healthier climate of Kokopo near Rabaul on New Britain, but the coast still has

116

many German names and large mission stations although gravestones are almost the only reminders of the old company.

In WW II the Japanese soon took Madang but after the recapture of Lae, Australian troops slowly and painfully pushed the Japanese along the coast to their final defeat at Wewak. The bitter fighting for control of "Shaggy Ridge" and the route over the Finisterre Range to Madang, started in late '43 and took a full month to finally push the Japanese down to the coast and on towards Wewak.

As with other towns, Madang was virtually demolished during the war and had to be totally rebuilt. Even the old German cemetery bears scars from the vicious fighting. Madang's importance as a major north coast port, from where freight was flown up to the Highlands, was drastically changed when the opening of the Highlands Highway shifted the business to Lae. Timber cutting development has since rejuvenated the town which is also an important ship building and repair centre. Madang is now linked to the Highlands by road but it is a lengthy and roundabout route. The long projected, but still far distant, direct road to Kundiawa in the Chimbu district will have to be built before Madang is conveniently "on-line" to the Highlands.

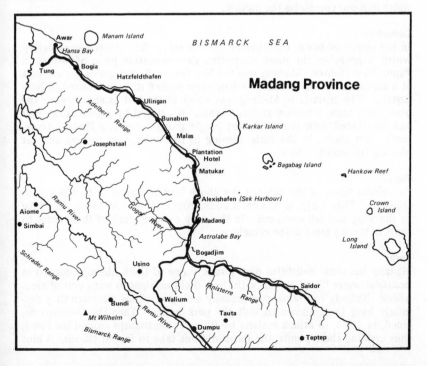

GEOGRAPHY

The Madang area is composed of strips of lowland and mountain. Along the fertile coast coconuts and cocoa have been growing since the German days. Inland, mountain ranges rise, parallel to the coast then slope down to the Ramu River Valley which also parallels the coast. This is some of the most productive cattle country in PNG and only a low divide separates the Upper Ramu from the Markham Valley, in which the Highland Highway runs to Lae. Inland from the Ramu, the Bismarck and Schrader Ranges rise to the highest peaks in the country, including Mt Wilhelm which stands on the border to the Chimbu Province. The volcanic islands off the Madang coast are still periodically active.

MADANG

The title of "prettiest town in the Pacific" may not be an official one but it could well be correct. The town is perched on a peninsula, jutting out into the sea and liberally sprinkled with parks, ponds and waterways. The warm, wet climate and fertile soil leads to luxuriant growth and many of the huge shade trees, planted by the Germans, survived the war and still tower over Madang's gently curving roads. A scatter of islands around the town's deep-water harbour completes the picture.

Cemetery

In the centre of town, right behind the market, is the old German cemetery which is probably the most interesting European-style piece of history in Papua New Guinea. Madang was the Neu Guinea Kompagnie's last attempt at a foothold on the mainland before they packed it in and moved to New Britain. The malaria in Madang was every bit as bad as elsewhere — the overgrown little cemetery attests to that. It's ringed by a solid stone wall and smothered with that luxuriant jungle growth that is a Madang trademark. Up above, in the early evening in particular, you can see another Madang trademark — bats.

Bats

At certain times of the day the sky above Madang seems to be black with fruitbats. They hang, as is a bat's wont, from trees all over town, then take to the wing and sail overhead. In the early evening many of them come to roost in the tall trees in the cemetery.

Parks

Madang has some delightful park ponds — one of them liberally decked in beautiful water lilies. But all with those ominous signs to warn you of crocodiles. Nobody can remember actually seeing a pukpuk although they definitely have been known to visit the park ponds. When the Germans decided, in 1904, to attack malaria by filling in the swamps around the town, thus creating these ponds, the locals did not take to forced labour. A plot

against the Germans was stifled by the drastic action of rounding up the ringleaders and shooting them. They were buried on Siar Island in the harbour.

Harbour Cruise

Madang has possibly the nicest harbour in Papua New Guinea so it's worth getting out on it. There's a harbour cruise every morning operated by Melanesian Tours — departs at 9 am and costs K8. You get picked up from your hotel and the boat takes you out to an island where you'll see the rusting wreckage of Japanese landing craft. Then it's across to Kranket Island where you can view the fish and coral formations through glass bottomed viewing boxes. You then cross the harbour again to Siar Island where you stop for an hour, wander around (it's a small, very green island), or you can snorkel with the masks and equipment they provide if you wish. The day I was there the water was far too murky to see, although it had been very clear at Kranket.

Siar Island is a popular spot for picnics and barbecues and on the beach you can see some large chunks of aircraft wreckage. With a fellow amateur aircraft expert we decided it was American, WW II of course, twin engined, possibly a B-25 or a P-38. Any answers? Somewhere on the island are the graves of those unfortunate victims of the anti-swamp-filling conspiracy.

Do-it-yourself Harbour Cruises

If you want to organise your own voyage around the harbour you can do it easily and cheaply. If you wander down to the Lutheran Shipping wharf you'll find a small ferry service that shuttles across to Kranket Island for

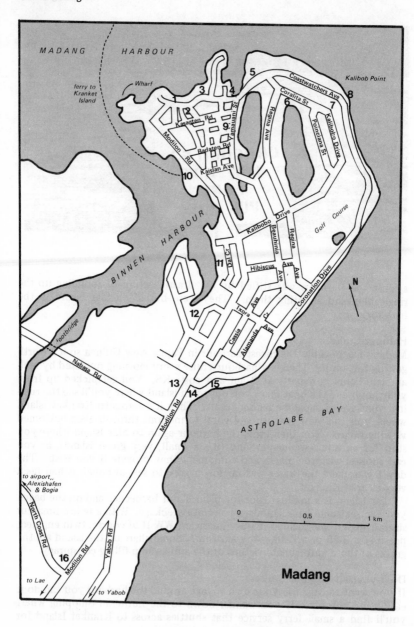

MADANG   HARBOUR

ferry to
Kranket
Island

Wharf

BINNEN   HARBOUR

Coastwatchers Ave

Kalibob Point

Coralita St

Regina Ave

Kasagten Rd

Tamauani St

Modilon Rd

Badaten Rd

Kaislan Ave

Poinciana St

Kalibobo Drive

Golf Course

Kalibobo Drive

Beauhinia

Regina

Dal Cr

Hibiscus

Ave

Ave

Coronation Drive

Ixora Ave

Cr

Cassia

Alamanda Ave

footbridge

Nabasa Rd

Modilon Rd

ASTROLABE   BAY

N

to airport,,
Alexishafen
& Bogia

North Coast Rd

Modilon Rd

Yabob Rd

to Lae

to Yabob

0   0.5   1 km

Madang

```
MADANG

 1  Air Niugini                   9  Market & Old Cemetery
 2  Post Office                  10  Lutheran Wharf
 3  Madang Club                  11  Bicycle Hire
 4  CWA Cottage                  12  Lutheran Hostel
 5  Hotel Madang                 13  Tusbab High School
 6  Lutheran Guest House         14  Smugglers' Motel
 7  Coastwatcher's Motel         15  Lions Reserve Beach
 8  Coastwatcher's Memorial      16  Government Centre
```

just 10t. It's irregular but frequent and you could hardly have a cheaper harbour tour than that. Once on Kranket you could wander around, swim, or find somebody to take you further on an outrigger canoe.

Another method is to take a PMV round to Siar village, just 30t, and negotiate a ride across to the island. It's only a short distance and shouldn't cost more than a kina at the outside. It's easy to find canoes here for longer "cruises". Two names to ask for are Paul Muz in Siar village or Saimon Tewa on Siar Island. The Madang Hotel has outboard motor boats for hire, with skipper, for K30 a day.

Coastwatcher's Memorial
The 30 metre high beacon is visible 25 km out to sea, a lasting reminder of those men who stayed behind the lines during the last war to report on Japanese troop and ship movements. The coast road from the memorial is one of the most pleasant in Madang, fringed by palm trees and poincianas and backed by the golf course with fine views across Astrolabe Bay towards the Rai Coast.

Around Town
Tusbab High School, on Modilon Road almost directly opposite the Smuggler's Motel, has a small museum and an interesting little zoo with a crocodile pond and a couple of very talkative cockatoos. Down beside the Madang Club you can still see the old German steps.

Yabob Village
If you take Modilon Road out of town, shortly before the right turn to the airport and north coast road, a road branches off left to Yabob village. You pass a lookout point and a Japanese war memorial on the way to this pretty little village with its offshore island which you can easily arrange to visit by canoe. Long before Europeans arrived in the area, Yabob was well known for its fine clay pots which were traded far up and down the coast. You can still buy them today as it's a continuing craft. Further down the coast is Bilbil which also makes pots, similar to the Aibom pots from the Sepik area.

Accommodation in Madang — the Top End

The *Smugglers Inn* has long had a reputation as one of the top hotels in Papua New Guinea — certainly you could hardly beat its delightful setting. Built right on the waterfront, the open air restaurant actually juts out into the water. There's a swimming pool and the Lion's Reserve Beach is only 50 or so metres away — excellent coral and tropical fish for the snorkel enthusiasts just a few strokes from the shore. The Smugglers' also boasts a Haus Wind, open air room by the swimming pool, for private functions. There are three wings — the difference being in standards of fittings and room size. Singles from K14.50 to K22, doubles K22 to K27. Meals in the restaurant are a la carte — at lunchtime main dishes are in the K3.50 to K4.50 range, at dinner they start from about K4.50. You're summoned to meals by the thump of a garamut drum.

All Madang's other hotels are along the same straight line — about 200 metres takes them all in and they're all within reasonable walking distance of town; in contrast to the Smugglers' which is rather far out from the centre. The *Hotel Madang* has a setting almost as good as the Smugglers' but until recently insufficient advantage was taken of this. A major renovation programme in 1978 upgraded all the rooms and facilities. It has a swimming pool, outdoor waterfront-restaurant, and a pleasant open dining room/bar area by the pool and harbour. The new prices for the upgraded rooms are in the K15 to 18 bracket for singles, K25 to 30 for doubles.

The *Coastwatcher's Motel* is on Coastwatcher's Avenue near the Coastwatcher's Memorial. It's a smaller motel with just 14 family sized rooms. The tariff here includes breakfast and runs from K15 for a single, K24 a double, K33 for a family. There's a licensed restaurant where the fixed price dinner costs K6.

Accommodation in Madang — the Bottom End

The *CWA Cottage* is very close to the Madang

Smugglers' Inn Hotel
Bookings: PO Box 303
  Madang
Tel: 82 2744
Cables: Smugglers
Telex: NE 82722
Rooms: 50
Tariff: K14.50-K22 sgl; K22-27 twin

Hotel Madang
Bookings: PO Box 111,
  Madang
Tel: 82 2655
Cables: Tourist
Telex: NE 82707
Rooms: 42
Tariff: K15-18 sgls; K25-30 dbls

Coastwatcher's Motel
Bookings: PO Box 324,
  Madang
Tel: 82 2684
Cables: Cowamo
Rooms: 14 family
Tariff: K15 sgl, K24 dbl incl breakfast

Hotel, just a little bit closer to the town. It only has four twin rooms and costs K8 per person room only or K40 per week. CWA members of three months standing enjoy a reduced tariff of K5/K25 for the day/week. The cottage has fully equipped kitchens so you can prepare your own meals.

The *Lutheran Guest House* is on Coralita St, about midway between the Hotel Madang and the Coastwatcher's Motel. It moved from its old harbour side location in late '77. The new building is considerably more modern than the old, each of the rooms has its own bathroom. Price per person for bed and breakfast is K7. The interesting (if a little gruff at times!) Dutch lady who runs the place, operates with military precision. Breakfast is punctually at 7 am and, if available, lunch arrives at 12 noon, dinner at 7 pm.

There is also a Lutheran Hostel in Madang — variously reported as being for locals only or open to anyone. Shoestringers may care to investigate, it's on Dal Crescent.

CWA Cottage
Bookings: PO Box 154,
    Madang
Tel: 82 2216
Rooms: 4 twin
Tariff: K8 per person

Lutheran Guest House
Bookings: PO Box 211,
    Madang
Rooms: 4
Tariff: K7 per person, B&B

Eating in Madang

Steamships has the usual lunchtime sandwiches and milkshakes but the *Coral Seas Snack Bar* next to the cinema is also open in the evenings — until the interval of the movie. Round beyond the market place there's a *Haus Kai* where the food looks a little more edible than in most of them.

For a good, down to earth meal at a reasonably low price the best place in town is the *Madang Club*. See the "what to see" section for its tenuous historical connection. It's officially members-and-their-guests only but if you hammer loudly on the door someone will come and sign you in. They need the business! You can get snacks, omelettes, hamburgers, sandwiches and there will be a few nightly specials — pork chops, salad and french fries for K1.80 is a typical example.

Getting around Madang

There are frequent PMVs around Madang with a standard 20t fare in town. There are also plenty going further out at pleasantly low fares. One thing you can do in Madang, which (if you're reasonably fit) you may wish was possible in many other PNG towns, is hire a bicycle. Supa-Valu bicycle hire is in the Business Development Centre on the harbour side of Modilon Rd near the Kalibobo Rd intersection. The bikes are not in the greatest shape but quite adequate for a jaunt out to Yabob village, or even further if you felt like it. Cost is 50t per hour, K4 per day.

OUT OF MADANG
Roads run out of Madang in both directions — south-east towards Lae and north-west towards Wewak.

The Lae Road
Until a few years ago the road to Lae used to run to the Gogol River, a comparatively short distance south of Madang, where it crossed on a bridge and then abruptly stopped. Now it continues, or at least tries to as bad weather can make it impassable, all the way to the Highlands Highway in the Markham Valley. Further south from the Gogol River it branches along the coast to Saidor and south-west to the Ramu Valley. Dumpu, in the Ramu Valley, was the base from which the attack on Shaggy Ridge was commenced during WW II. At the old German station of Bogadjim nothing remains apart from the cemetery. Balek Wildlife Sanctuary, with walks, caves and good views, is also off the Lae road.

Nobanob & Nagada
A little beyond the Siar village turn-off on the north coast road, there are turnoffs to the left and right. The right hand turn leads to the Lutheran Mission on Nagada Harbour. The left hand turn leads up to Nobanob lookout which also has a Lutheran Mission out-station and was used as a Japanese lookout during the war. There is a fine view here over the north coast, Madang and the harbour.

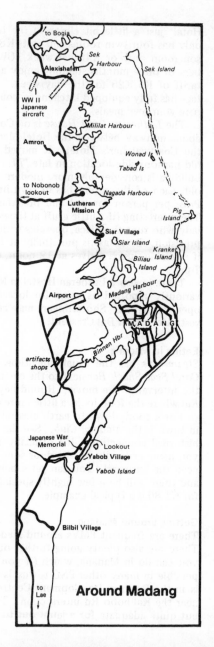

Around Madang

Up the Coast
The road runs a long way north of Madang and will eventually reach all the way to Wewak — it already runs to the Ramu River although the last stretch is not too good. It's expected to meet the Sepik somewhere downstream from Angoram where vehicles will cross the river by ferry. A road already runs from Angoram into Wewak — that final short section from the Ramu to the Sepik is still some distance in the future.

Heading north from Madang you pass the turnoff to Siar village, 10 km out. At about 14 km there are turnoffs to Nagada and the Nabanob lookout while at 16 km the Japanese WW II HQ at Amron is off to the left of the road.

Alexishafen Catholic Mission is off the road to the right, 21 km north of Madang. Like so much else of the area it was badly damaged during the war, although the old graveyard still stands as a firm reminder of the number of early missionaries who died for their cause. There is a fine old teak forest along the north coast road — totally unusable since the trees are riddled with shrapnel from the fierce fighting during the war.

A little beyond the mission you can see the site of the old mission airstrip, now virtually overgrown. The WW II Japanese airstrip is a little off the road to the left, between the mission airstrip and Alexishafen. You can easily recruit a couple of kids from the villages to guide you to some of the Japanese aircraft still standing close to the strip. The rotting wreckage of one Japanese twin engined bomber is only a wingspan away from the bomb crater which immobilised it. Closer to the north coast road is the fuselage of an early Junkers mission aircraft.

The road continues north to the Plantation Hotel, 43 km up the coast, and Bogia, jumping off point for Manam Island. The road peters out soon after Bogia, only a short distance before the mighty Ramu River.

Accommodation — North Coast
The *Plantation Hotel* is 43 km north of Madang across from Karkar Island. It has seven units, a licensed restaurant specialising in fresh, locally caught fish and a swimming pool. Diving equipment can be hired if you want to explore the offshore reefs. Accommodation costs K10 for a single including breakfast, K18 for a double.

There is also a small hotel at Bogia — the *Bogia Hotel* where room only cost is K12.50 per person.

Plantation Hotel
Bookings: PO Box 302, Madang
Tel: VHF 82 0184
Rooms: 7
Tariff: K10 sgl, K18 twin incl breakfast

Bogia Hotel
Bookings: PO Box 3, Bogia
Rooms: 4 twin
Tariff: per person — K12.50 room only, K23 all meals

Inland
Although it is the coast that attracts in the Madang area, there are also some isolated and interesting places inland towards the Highlands, some of them only recently contacted. Simbai and Bundi are the main stations, both very remote. Bundi, is wedged between Mt Wilhelm and Mt Herbert in some of the roughest country in PNG. Some of the people living in these primitive areas are almost small enough to be termed pygmies.

ISLANDS
The volcanic islands off the Madang coast can make interesting visits — they are accessibly by air or sea.

Manam
The island of Manam, or Vulcan, is only 15 km off the coast at Bogia. The island is 83 square km in area and is an almost perfect volcano cone, rising 1829 metres high. The soil is extremely fertile and supports a population of about 4000 but from time to time the entire population has had to be evacuated as the volcano is still rather active. There is a seismological observatory on the side of the cone. Bogia is 193 km from Madang and easily accessible, a boat runs across to the island every day, fare is K1. Hansa Bay, near Bogia, has many wrecked WW II ships.

Karkar
William Dampier made an early landing on the 362 square km island but later Lutheran missionaries had a hard time both from malaria and the local natives. A volcanic eruption finally evicted them but they came back and today Karkar has both Catholic and Lutheran missions as well as some of the most productive copra plantations in the world. The volcanic cone here is just two metres higher than Manam's at 1831 metres; it's a full day's walk up to the crater and back. The volcano erupted violently in 1974, leaving a cinder cone in the centre of the huge, original crater. A road encircles the island and it takes about four hours to drive right round. You can fly to Karkar from Madang with Talair for K19.

Bagabag
Situated close to Karkar, Bagabag is a sunken crater 36 square km in area. It too is inhabited.

Long Island
The largest of the volcanic islands, Long Island is 414 square km in area and 48 km off the coast. It has two active craters, one of which contains a lake surrounded by crater walls up to 250 metres high. The human population of remote Long Island is only about 600 but it is renowned for its prolific bird life and the many fish which swarm around its surrounding reefs. Turtles come ashore here to lay their eggs at certain times of year.

ARTIFACTS & CULTURE

The clay pots from Yabob and Bilbil villages are the most interesting locally made items. If you buy them make sure they are very carefully packed as, like other PNG pottery, they are extremely fragile. In the evenings there's a thriving little artifacts marketplace at the Smugglers Motel — carvings are often done by Sepik people who have moved down to Madang.

Tusbab High School has a cultural group which often performs sing-sings at Smugglers. Bamboo bands or other performances also occur at the Madang Hotel. Around June to August of each year the Maborasa festival takes place in Madang with sing-sings and groups of bands from Madang and villages up and down the coast.

GETTING THERE & GETTING AROUND

Flights into Madang are operated from Lae, Goroka and Wewak — all direct by Air Niugini. The flight from Goroka is very brief and quite interesting as you climb up and over the southern fringe of the Highlands then over the Ramu Valley and drop down to the coast. It looks like an interesting and manageable walk — from above. You can also get to Madang by road from the Highlands or Lae, PMV fare from the turnoff at Watarais is about K4 to 5 but beware, traffic can be very light and you can easily get stranded. It costs K5 up the coast from Madang to Bogia by PMV.

Shipping

Check with Lutheran Shipping (tel 82 2577) about the *Totol*, their weekly K18 service to Lae, and about other shipping possibilities. They also operate a monthly service to Rabaul. It is fairly easy to find ships along the coast to Wewak — simply ask around the dock area.

The Sepik

Area: 74,915 square km
Population: 339,000

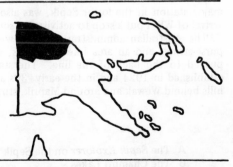

The Sepik region is quite possibly the most interesting area of Papua New Guinea for the visitor. Although there is a long streatch of open coastline with a number of fair sized towns and a range of hills rising behind the coast — then sloping down to the Sepik, it is the mighty river which commands interest. The Sepik is one of the largest rivers in the world in terms of annual waterflow and although it is rivalled in size by the Fly River in the south of the country, it is far more significant in terms of local importance, as an avenue of communications and in cultural and artistic substance. It is the Sepik which is the core of Papua New Guinea's thriving artistic skills. It has the same relevance to PNG as the Congo does to Africa, the Amazon to South America. River-boating down the Amazon is said to be a pretty amazing experience but people who have been on both say the Sepik is even better. Go there!

HISTORY

The Sepik's first contact with the outside world was probably with Malay Bird of Paradise hunters for the feathers from those beautiful birds have been popular long before European ladies of society had their fling with them during the last century. First European contact came in 1885 with the arrival of the Germans and their Neu Guinea Kompagnie. Dr Otto Finsch, after whom the German's first station — Finschhafen — was later named, rowed about 50 km upstream from the mouth and named the river the Kaiserin Augusta, after the wife of the German Emperor.

During 1886 and 1887 further expeditions, using a steam boat, travelled 400 km upriver beyond the present site of Ambunti and then, when the river was higher, 600 km inland. These early expeditions were soon followed by more mercenary explorers, traders, labour recruiters and, inevitably, the missionaries — for here was a whole new parcel of headhunters waiting for the word.

The Germans established a station at Aitape on the coast in 1906 and in 1912-13 sent a huge scientific expedition to explore the river and its vast, low-lying basin. They collected insects, studied the tribes and produced maps of such accuracy that they are still used to this day. Angoram, the major station in the lower Sepik, was also established at this time but the arrival of WW I put a stop to activity for some time.

The Australian administration of New Guinea suffered from very tight purse-strings and an area like the Sepik, with little economic appeal, was pushed to the back of the line. The station at Ambunti was, however, established in 1924 and in the early '30s a small flurry of goldrushes in the hills behind Wewak and around Maprik, stirred further interest. Then WW II

A The *Sepik Explorer* on the Sepik
B The Chambri Lakes
C The Sepik finally reaches the sea

arrived and once more development and exploration of the Sepik went into reverse.

The Japanese held the Sepik region for most of the war but the struggle for control was bitter and prolonged. As the Australian forces pushed along the coast from Lae and then Madang, the Japanese steadily withdrew to the west. Then in early '44 the Americans seized Aitape and an Australian division started to move west from there. When a huge American force captured Hollandia (Jayapura in Irian Jaya today) in April '44, the Japanese 8th Army was completely isolated. The enormous number of rivers flowing to the sea, and the extensive coastal swamps, made the fight along the coast a drawn out affair. It was over a year later, in May '45, when Wewak finally fell and the remaining Japanese troops withdrew into the hills behind the coast. Finally, with the war in its last days, General Adachi surrendered near Yangoru. He was so weak he had to be carried on a chair. The formal surrender took place a few days later on 13 September '45 at Wom Point near Wewak.

Since the war government control has been re-established and extended further upriver although the uppermost limits of the Sepik are still amongst the most primitive and isolated parts of the country. It has been a touchy area ever since the Indonesian takeover of West New Guinea, although the border was jointly mapped and marked in 1968. During 1978 the flaring up of the Irian Jaya resistance campaign again made the border region a politically difficult area. There are periodic movements of refugees across the border from Irian Jaya and in '78 this reached a flood at times. In addition the guerrilla forces opposing the Indonesians in Irian Jaya often duck across the border to take refuge in PNG.

GEOGRAPHY

The Sepik River is 1126 km in length and navigable for almost that entire distance. It starts up in the mountains in central New Guinea, close to the Irian Jaya border, and very close to the source of the country's other major river — the southward flowing Fly. At first the Sepik flows almost due north and meanders back and forth across the Irian Jaya border four times. At its final exit it is only 85 metres above sea level and from there it winds gradually down to the sea; a huge, brown, slowly coiling serpent.

The Sepik is not a straightforward river — it turns back on itself and has often changed its course leaving dead-ends, lagoons, ox-bow lakes or

A
B

A Japanese tanks rust on the beach near Namatanai, New Ireland
B The Panguna mining complex in Bougainville

huge swampy expanses which turn into lakes in the dry season or dry up to make grassland when the river is low. It's an indicator of its age and changing course that along much of the river there is no stone or rock whatsoever within about 50 km of its banks. Villages often have "sacred stones" that have been carried in from far away and placed in front of the village spirit house.

At the end of the wet season the sudden drainage of water from adjoining lakes and swamps tears great chunks of mud and vegetation out of the riverbanks and these drift off downstream as "floating islands" — often with small trees and even animals aboard. At times it is almost possible to walk across the river and small channels clog up completely. At the mouth there is no delta and the river stains the sea brown for 50 or more km from the shore. It is said that islanders off the coast can draw fresh water straight from the sea.

For much of the distance from the coast the Sepik is bordered by huge expanses of lowland — either swamp or covered in wild sugarcane known as pitpit. Further inland there are hills and eventually the Sepik climbs into wild mountain country near its source. Between the river and the coast the Prince Alexander Range rises to over 1000 metres then descends to a coastal plain. There are no natural harbours on the whole Sepik region coastline.

WEWAK
Wewak is really just a transit stop — people pause here on their way to the Sepik or out to Irian Jaya. There's no real attraction to the town itself. Wewak does have something pretty rare for Papua New Guinea coastal towns though — good and easily accessible beach. There's a sweep of that romantic golden sand, backed by the proper swaying palm trees, right round from the town headland to Moem Point.

Wewak is built on a high headland poking out from the coast — you can see similar proturbances to the east and west. Cape Wom, to the west, is historically interesting as the place where the Japanese General Adachi surrendered to the Allied forces in WW II. To the east Cape Moem is an army base. In between there's a long shipping wharf jutting out into the sea, Wewak is a poor harbour.

Behind the town the hills climb steeply, you don't have to travel very far back from the coast to enjoy a very good view.

War Mementos
Wewak's most vivid legacy of the bitter fighting in WW II is the enormous number of bomb craters that pockmark the area. Around the Boram airport runway and the now disused Wirui airstrip, there are almost more craters than clear ground. But even well away from the airport you'll see the circular, water-filled reminders of the violence of 30 plus years ago.

Heading out of town on the Dagua road you'll pass a scrapyard on the right, known locally as Roy Worcester's, with a pile of badly damaged bits and pieces of Japanese Zero fighters. At Mission Hill there's a Japanese War Memorial, the remains of the many troops buried here in a mass grave were later exhumed and returned to Japan. Further along is Cape Wom where the Japanese surrender took place. If you travel a couple of km out of town on the Maprik road, a right turn will take you to the Japanese lookout point where anti-aircraft guns were mounted — there's a fine view over the airport and coast. The Japanese caves on the top of Wewak Hill have been filled in.

Other
Near the new wharf, the rusting remains of the *MV Busama* are rotting away in the sand. Further down at Kreer, the wooden hulks of two Taiwanese fishing junks are heading the same way. They were seized a few years ago for infringing PNG's coastal fishing limits. Kreer market is one of two big markets in Wewak, the other is at the end of the main street in the centre. Saturday is the big market day, as usual. Michael Somare, a Sepik man from the Murik Lakes, has his house on Wewak Hill; it's pointed out to you but is really just another suburban house. At Brandi High School the students have built a traditional village within the school grounds.

Accommodation in Wewak — the Top End
There are just three hotels in Wewak, none them particularly cheap, and the cheap accommodation story is a complete disaster. Two of the hotels are close together on Hill St, up the hill that tops the end of the promontory. They are convenient for the town centre.

The *Sepik Motel* is the first place up the hill and has 16 family rooms, all air-conditioned and with private facilities. Room rates are K22.50 single, K30 double for room only. The *Wewak Hotel*, right at the top of the hill overlooking the sea, has 16 singles and 17 twins, some air-con, some with fans. Room only prices run from K18 single, K26 twin.

The third place, the *Windjammer Motel*, is a km or two round the bay from town towards the airport. It certainly has the nicest location since it's right on the beach — only a couple of steps into the sea from the rooms at the front. It's also a popular local eating place at lunch time and dinner and a particularly good place for meeting people. Bed and breakfast costs K14 for a single without private facilities, K20 with. Doubles are K20/28 without/with. There are also family rates and rates for larger groups. The rooms are fan cooled.

Sepik Motel
Bookings: PO Box 496, Wewak
Tel: 86 2422
Cables: Sepikmotel
Rooms: 16 family
Tariff: K20 sgl, K26 dbl

Wewak Hotel
Bookings: PO Box 20, Wewak
Tel: 86 2155/2554
Rooms: 33
Tariff: K18 sgl, K26 twin

Windjammer Beach Motel
Bookings: PO Box 152, Wewak
Tel: 86 2548
Rooms: 22
Tariff: K14 to K20 sgl, K20 K28 dbl, incl breakfast

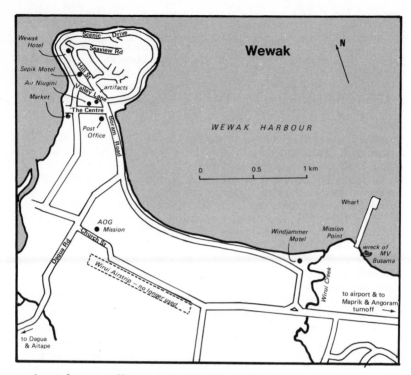

Apart from a coffee shop in one of the trade stores and a Haus Kai at the junction of Dagua Rd and Church St, the only places to eat are the hotels. The Windjammer does good sandwiches or meat pies from the bar and the dinner menu has main dishes at K5.

Accommodation in Wewak — the Bottom End

Very bad, which is a problem for people travelling in from or out to Jayapura in Irian Jaya, who may be forced to spend at least a night in Wewak. Your only hope is the mission rest houses, none of which are too enthusiastic about offering accommodation or, for that matter, have too much available. The *South Seas Evangelical Mission* on Wewak Hill has a three bedroom flat which may, but improbably, be able to offer space at K7 a night, per person, room only.

South Seas Mission
Bookings: PO Box 214, Wewak
Tel: 86 2278
Rooms: 1 flat
Tariff: K7 per person

The Assembly of God mission on Church St, near the Dagua Rd junction, has a guest house with a number of rooms, but in late '77 they stopped offering accommodation to visitors. Very often this sort of policy switches around when somebody else takes over so it may be worth checking just in case. When last available, accommodation costs K5 a night per person. The rooms have (or had) cooking facilities. Otherwise you're on your own.

Artifacts
There are a number of locally run artifact sellers around but the main gathering place is on the beach front of the Windjammer Motel every evening. You'll see quite a selection of items on sale here, most rather touristy but the odd unusual piece. The sellers are patient, they hang on till almost the last guest has departed for bed, and the prices are very reasonable. There's a permanent artifacts display in the shop on Valley Lane, just off Hill St behind the centre.

ANGORAM
Angoram is the oldest Sepik station, established by the Germans before WW I. It's a pleasant, sleepy place with a bit of frontier town atmosphere. If you were just going to "see" the Sepik without actually travelling on it then Angoram would be the best place to do it — much more interesting than Pagwi, the other point on the Sepik accessible by road. It's also possible to hire canoes to make trips from here although it is not as interesting as the middle Sepik area around Pagwi. The road from Wewak to Angoram is good but traffic is light — see "Getting There". Eventually Angoram will also be connected with Madang — slightly downstream from the town a barge will cross the river and a road will be put through to the Ramu River.

Haus Tambaran
Angoram has a large Haus Tambaran which is a mixture of local styles and contains a large and varied display of artifacts. It was originally intended that this be a Sepik cultural centre but although that worthy idea fell through, there is a fairly representative collection of the styles seen all along the Sepik plus items carved by Angoram's resident craftsmen. They're all price labelled — often with 1st and 2nd prices! Don't miss the lounge and dining room of the Anoram Hotel where there are a number of very interesting pieces including some particularly fine Kambot storyboards.

Other
Ominously perched right on the end of the airstrip is a tiny graveyard. Amongst those buried there is the legendary labour recruiter "Shanghai" Brown who, according to his headstone, "died in 1956 of Blackwater". He features briefly in Colin Simpson's book *Plumes and Arrows*. At the wharf

is the "place baim pukpuk skin", where crocodile skins are purchased, treated with salt and despatched to Singapore. As you walk along the river, notice the "Nile cabbage" floating by — it has only appeared on the Sepik in the last few years and plays havoc with outboard motors.

A small memorial on your right marks the spot where the 11 survivors of an Indian army group held prisoner by the Japanese were rescued towards the end of WW II. The local village stretches along the riverbank, you'll see carvers at work on artifacts at a number of the houses. Angoram's old colonial feel will be reinforced by the frequent greetings of "mornin masta."

Accommodation in Angoram

The *Angoram Hotel* is another place that seems to fit the PNG outstation mood — you sort of expect laconic conversations in the bar and after a fashion you'll get them. Including all meals singles are K22, doubles K40 — you can also have room only rates, but the food is good. The manager can organise canoe hire if you want to get out on the river. The Sepik art hanging in the lounge and dining room is particularly fine — worth a look even if you are not staying here.

Angoram Hotel
Bookings: PO Box 35, Angoram
Cables: Arshak
Tel: 52 1589 (x 14)
Rooms: 2 sgl, 11 twin
Tariff: K22 sgl, K40 dbl or twin incl all meals

Getting to Angoram

The road to Angoram is the shorter of the two access routes to the Sepik. It branches off the Maprik road only 19 km out of Wewak. The 113 km road from Wewak to Angoram is generally excellent by PNG standards, but traffic is very light. To avoid getting stranded by the roadside, it's wise to set off very early in the morning or arrange a straight through ride. Wewak-Angoram by PMV costs about K5 and takes two to three hours if you travel through non-stop.

MAPRIK

The Maprik area is noted for its distinctive Haus Tambaran style and for the yam cult of the region. The population around Maprik is quite dense and there are many small villages, each with its distinctive forward-leaning spirit house. The front facade of the towering Haus Tambaran is brightly painted in browns, ochres, whites and blacks. Inside the carved spirit figures are similarly treated. As in the Trobriand Islands at the other end of PNG, yams are a staple food and also have great cultural significance. Their harvesting entails considerable ritual and you may often see festivals or singsings during the May to August harvest time. The woven fibre masks made around Maprik are yam masks. Maprik has a very fine Haus Tambaran which also doubles as an artifacts store and cultural centre. There is also a traditionally decorated, open courthouse.

Pagwi, futher down the road and actually on the Sepik, is important as the most used road access point to the Sepik — it is the only road access to the most interesting and significant middle Sepik area. There is little of interest in Pagwi, despite this vital role. A couple of km before Pagwi the road passes the large government funded crocodile farm and this is the one place in Pagwi which the visitor should not miss.

Accommodation in Maprik

There is one rather dull hotel in Maprik — the *Maprik Waken* — with six twin rooms. Nightly cost per person, room only, is K10.50 for the rooms with private facilities, K8.50 if you're willing to share a bathroom. I have been told that the Catholic Mission at Maprik offers accommodation for K3 per person — they emphatically did not when I was last in Maprik, but in PNG things can change very rapidly.

Maprik Waken Hotel
Bookings: PO Box 104,
    Maprik
Tel: 89 1221
Rooms: 6 twins
Tariff: K8.50 to K10.50 sgl

Getting to Maprik and Pagwi

The road from Wewak runs to Pagwi with a branch off to Maprik which will eventually extend beyond there all the way to Aitape and Ambunti. It already continues for some distance beyond Maprik. If the Frieda River mining project takes off this may speed up the road building. From Wewak the road climbs up and over the Prince Alexander Mountains then continues to Maprik, 132 km from Wewak. Maprik is actually eight km off the Wewak-Pagwi road, the junction is called Hayfields. Wewak-Maprik costs K5, Maprik-Pagwi K2 by PMV, or you can get a straight through PMV at a slight saving. It is 53 km from Maprik to Pagwi and there is quite a lot of traffic on this road.

THE SEPIK

The mighty Sepik (pronounced "sea-pick") reverted to its local name when the Australians took over from the Germans and Kaiserin Augustin had her name deleted from the river. It is said, by some people, to mean "great river", but nobody is certain. Due to its lack of natural resources the Sepik has attracted little development and remains remarkably untouched by western influences.

Seeing the Sepik is one of those PNG activities where you either have to grit your teeth and spend the money or have a lot of time and persuasive ability. There is only road access to the Sepik at two points — Angoram on the lower Sepik and Pagwi on the middle Sepik. The most interesting areas are concentrated on the middle Sepik and if you want to see a reasonable amount of the river at not too considerable cost, Pagwi is the best base to use although it is also possible to get out on the river from Angoram.

Lower Sepik

The lower Sepik starts a little upstream from Angoram and runs down to the coast. The major station is Angoram; about two hours downriver is the Marienberg Mission station which has been operated by the Catholics for many years. Near the mouth of the river are the Murik Lakes, vast semi-flooded swamp lands, narrowly separated from the coast.

Middle Sepik

The middle Sepik region commences up from Angoram and continues to a little beyond Pagwi — only a short distance before Ambunti. This is the "cultural treasure house" of PNG and almost every village has some distinct artistic style. The Haus Tambarans, in which the carved figures are stored, are the one consistent connection. Although the whole middle Sepik region is of great interest the largest concentration of villages is just below Pagwi and it is possible to see many of them in day trips by canoe from Pagwi.

Upper Sepik

Above Ambunti the river becomes increasingly primitive as it climbs up towards the Irian Jaya border. Although there is not the same concentration of artistic skills that you find in the middle Sepik region there is still much to be seen. Getting to the remote upper Sepik regions is much more exped-ition-like than visiting the middle or lower Sepik.

A SEPIK GLOSSARY

A few of the terms and words you're likely to come across while on the Sepik:

Pukpuks Pidgin for crocodile, they still have enormous cultural and economic importance on the river. In their initiation rites, young men are scarred so that it looks like crocodile scales on their arms, legs and trunk. Crocodile heads are still carved on the prows of the handsome Sepik dugout canoes. And, of course, crocodiles are still one of the most important sources of cash for the Sepik villagers.

Sak sak Sago is still a staple food for the Sepik people. Preparation of sago is a long and tiring process and it is neither very appetising or very nutritional — but in a land where it is often too swampy to grow anything else, it is very important. Certainly there is no shortage of it, since sago palms grow prolifically. To prepare a meal of sak sak, first cut down your sago palm, chop off the leaves, break open the trunk and pound the starchy pith into small bits. That's the male work over, now it's the wife's turn. She crushes the pith and kneads it with water to dissolve the starch — an old dugout canoe makes a fine trough to perform this operation in. The fluid is drained off and stored either by keeping it liquid or drying it out like flour. Sak sak is either steamed or fried in little cakes or boiled up like a gluey porridge. Either way it's very starchy but supplemented with bananas, vegetables or fish it will keep you going.

Haus Tambarans Tambarans are spirits so the Haus Tambaran is the house where they live — or at least where the carvings that represent them are kept. You will also hear them referred to as the "spirit houses" or the "men's houses", since only initiated men (and tourists — male or female) are allowed to enter the village Haus Tambarans. Once upon a time a women who ventured inside could expect to meet instant death — times probably have not changed. Every village has to have a spirit house and although they may have lost some of their cultural importance they are still very much the centre of local life. Haus Tambaran styles vary, the high, forward leaning style of the Maprik region is probably best known. During the early days of contact with the west, some missionaries allowed their Christian zeal to get the better of them and burnt down Haus Tambarans and destroyed the village "idols". One brave district officer actually took the commendable action of charging a missionary with arson and these days a more enlightened attitude is usual.

Head Hunting Not any more — but at one time no man could take his place in the tribe until he had killed — whom he killed was irrelevant, an old woman or a small child was just as good as a rival warrior. The skulls were brought back and hung in the Haus Tambaran and the men could now wear the skin of a flying fox as an apron — a symbol that he had killed. At one time no Haus Tambaran could be erected without first putting a human skull under every post. Some of them had a lot of posts. The arrival of European administration put an end to this endless inter-village raiding.

Barets Man made "short cut" channels across loops in the river or from the river to adjoining lakes.

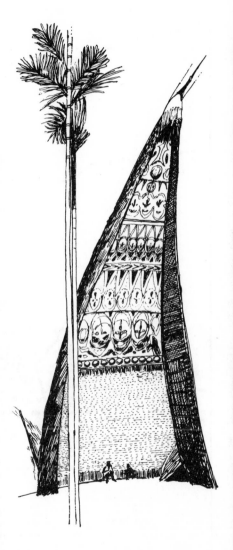

Maprik Haus Tambaran

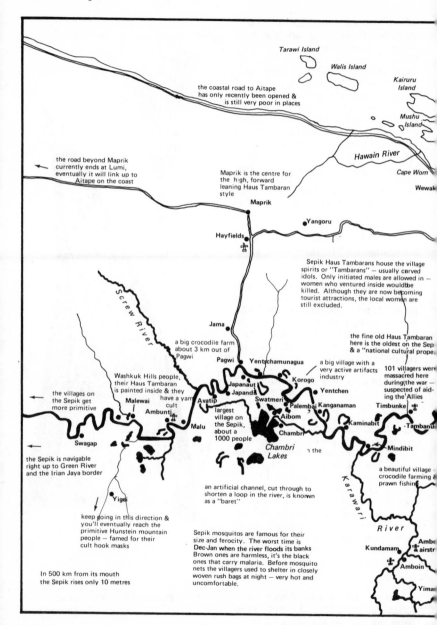

Tarawi Island

Walis Island

Kairuru Island

the coastal road to Aitape has only recently been opened & is still very poor in places

Mushu Island

Hawain River

Cape Wom

the road beyond Maprik currently ends at Lumi, eventually it will link up to Aitape on the coast

Maprik is the centre for the high, forward leaning Haus Tambaran style

Wewak

Maprik

Yangoru

Hayfields

Sepik Haus Tambarans house the village spirits or "Tambarans" — usually carved idols. Only initiated males are allowed in — women who ventured inside would be killed. Although they are now becoming tourist attractions, the local women are still excluded.

Screw River

Jama

the fine old Haus Tambaran here is the oldest on the Sepik & a "national cultural prope..."

a big crocodile farm about 3 km out of Pagwi

Pagwi   Yentschamunagua

a big village with a very active artifacts industry

101 villagers were massacred here during the war — suspected of aiding the Allies

Washkuk Hills people, their Haus Tambaran is painted inside & they have a yam cult

Korogo

Japanaut

Japandi

Yentchen

the villages on the Sepik get more primitive

Malewai

Avatip

Swatmeri

Palembai

Kanganaman

Ambunti

largest village on the Sepik, about a 1000 people

Aibom

Timbunke

Malu

Chambri

Kaminabit

Tambanu

Swagap

Chambri Lakes

Mindibit

the Sepik is navigable right up to Green River and the Irian Jaya border

a beautiful village crocodile farming & prawn fishing

an artificial channel, cut through to shorten a loop in the river, is known as a "baret"

Karawari

Yigei

keep going in this direction & you'll eventually reach the primitive Hunstein mountain people — famed for their cult hook masks

Sepik mosquitos are famous for their size and ferocity. The worst time is Dec-Jan when the river floods its banks. Brown ones are harmless, it's the black ones that carry malaria. Before mosquito nets the villagers used to shelter in closely woven rush bags at night — very hot and uncomfortable.

River

In 500 km from its mouth the Sepik rises only 10 metres

Kundamam

Amboin airstrip

Amboin

Yimas

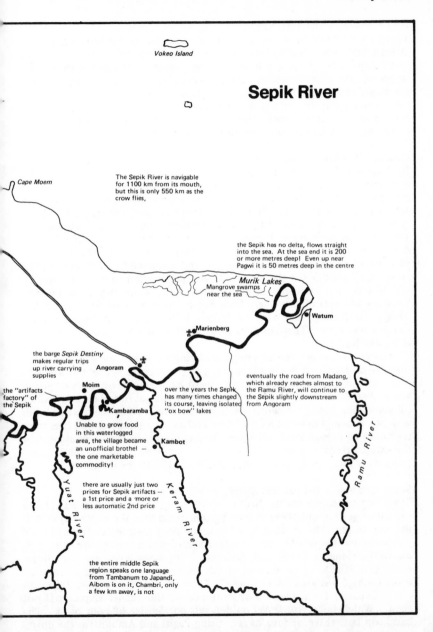

Vokeo Island

Sepik River

Cape Moem

The Sepik River is navigable for 1100 km from its mouth, but this is only 550 km as the crow flies,

the Sepik has no delta, flows straight into the sea. At the sea end it is 200 or more metres deep! Even up near Pagwi it is 50 metres deep in the centre

Murik Lakes
Mangrove swamps near the sea

Watum

Marienberg

the barge *Sepik Destiny* makes regular trips up river carrying supplies

Angoram

Moim

the "artifacts factory" of the Sepik

Kambaramba

Unable to grow food in this waterlogged area, the village became an unofficial brothel — the one marketable commodity!

Kambot

over the years the Sepik has many times changed its course, leaving isolated "ox bow" lakes

eventually the road from Madang, which already reaches almost to the Ramu River, will continue to the Sepik slightly downstream from Angoram

there are usually just two prices for Sepik artifacts — a 1st price and a more or less automatic 2nd price

the entire middle Sepik region speaks one language from Tambanum to Japandi, Aibom is on it, Chambri, only a few km away, is not

Yuat River

Keram River

Ramu River

GETTING OUT ON THE SEPIK

There are basically three ways of getting out onto the big brown river — or at least there may soon be three ways, at the moment there are two and one possibility. The cheapest is to hire a canoe, either by the day or from point to point. The most expensive, but quite possibly the most in-depth (at least for those not planning to spend a long time on the river), is to close your eyes, grit your teeth and pay out the money to travel on the *Sepik Explorer* houseboat. The third alternative, the "maybe" one, is the projected Sepik ferry service which may be in operation in early '79.

Canoes — the Shoestring Sepik

In Angoram, Pagwi or Ambunti it is relatively simple to hire a canoe plus outboard motor (and a river-savvy pilot) by the day. So long as you have a reasonable number of people, up to six in a large canoe, this can be a very economical way of seeing the river. In Pagwi ask for local trader Ken Dowry who even offers some fairly standard-priced Sepik tours. An interesting and fairly comprehensive three day tour could be made; out to Chambri and down the river as far as Kaminabit then back up to Pagwi. There is reasonably priced accommodation at Chambri and Kaminabit. Daily cost will be about K25 per day for the canoe. If you just wanted to go downriver to, say, Korogo and back that would be about K11. A day trip to the most interesting and accessible villages from Pagwi could be done for around K25 to 30. To Chambri and back would cost K25 to K40 depending on which channel was open. The trip right down river to Angoram would cost something like K125.

You're not going to be superbly comfortable (did you expect to be?) but the biggest drawback is uncertainty — you could arrive at the river and find there are no canoes available and have to hang around for days or give it away. People do tour the Sepik by simply arriving at one place and waiting till something goes by heading for the next. You'd really see the Sepik this way but it would demand a lot of time and an easy going nature. Plus some resistance to mosquitoes! Of course having your own canoe would also be the way to really explore the river — find a canoe with suitable pilot, negotiate a daily rate, stock up with supplies, head off into the unknown.

Sepik Explorer — the top-end Sepik

Travelling by canoe has its "will it, won't it" problems, if you want to be certain of getting out there and seeing something then the *Sepik Explorer* is the way to go. The Madang based tour company Melanesian Tours operate flat-bottomed houseboat style "mother ships" which run regular trips starting or finishing at Pagwi and Ambunti. The houseboats are your home while you shuttle up or downriver but excursions out to the villages are made on high powered "river trucks". There are actually two *Sepik Explorers* — Explorer I can take 20 or more people, the smaller Explorer II just eight. Which boat you travel on depends on the size of your party. The basic trip lasts three or four days — using Pagwi and Ambunti as the downriver and upriver points, although you will travel both further down and up the river. Connections from Wewak are made by air to Ambunti, by road to Pagwi. No two trips are exactly alike — conditions on the river change and your itinerary has to be altered to suit. Plus, of course, every trip varies with the interests of the people aboard. If they're elderly art enthusiasts then the emphasis is going to be more on art and less on chasing crocodiles!

The houseboats are quite comfortable — you have bunk beds in the rooms, bathrooms with purified drinking water and filtered river water (solar heated no less) for the showers. There are three solid meals a day, a bar (with beer at a kina a can) and a fairly mosquito proof lounge area (nothing on the Sepik can be totally mosquito proof). Your captain, Jeff Liversidge, is a knowledgeable river-veteran and you can be fairly well guaranteed an exhausting three or four days on the river! If you can afford the price, K70 per day per person including meals, you will probably decide you've got your money's worth. On top of the daily charge you'll have another K45 to front up for your transfers to and from the river — minibus to Pagwi, Douglas Airways' Islander to Ambunti. Of course most Sepik Explorer adventurers will book themselves aboard as part of a larger tour of the country but if you want more details write to Melanesian Tourist Services, PO Box 707, Madang.

Ferry — the "maybe" Sepik

A Wewak based group has firm plans to buy a Japanese inter-island ferry (will there be a glut of these when the inter-island tunnel opens in Japan?) to operate a regular service on the river. The intention is that this boat should do a regular three day trip up river from Angoram with overnight stops at Timbunke and Ambunti then turning round at Iniok on the Frieda River and repeating the three day trip back down. There would be accommodation for 52 passengers in air-conditioned cabins at a projected fare of around K50 for the three day trip. In addition there would be room for deck passengers — no fares decided yet but if there were, say, six stages in a day's trip then each stage might cost about K2.

The big drawback would seem to be that travel on the Sepik isn't a matter of sitting back and watching the riverbanks go by. Visitors to the Sepik want to stop, wander off into the villages and look around. You can't do that with a ferry schedule to keep to. The deck passage idea might have some appeal to the budget traveller, but once you're off the ferry you've got a week's wait for it to come by again. Time will tell.

There is already one regular service up the Sepik — the barge *Sepik Destiny* carries fuel and supplies to the Frieda River copper mining project and will take anything else for anyone else either up or downriver, for a suitable charge.

What to Take

Whether you're going in a canoe or on the Explorer you're well advised to plan what you need to take with you. On a canoe you're going to be very limited for space and on the Explorer you won't want to be hauling bags full of gear around with you — you can't on the light plane flight anyway. This is really no problem since you really don't need too much on the Sepik. For men or women a pair of shorts and a T-shirt will be all you'll need to wear most of the time although women will probably have to wear a skirt or dress into the villages. If you're there at a time of year when the mosquitoes are bad you may want to cover up more skin — long trousers or long sleeve shirts in the evening. A sun hat is probably a necessity, particularly if you travel by canoe, a swimsuit too if you take a Sepik swim. On your feet — tennis shoes are ideal, thongs nearly as good.

Camera and plenty of film are an essential if you're a photographic freak, binoculars too can be very useful. A shoulder bag is good for carrying odds and ends when you're walking to the villages — but you'll probably acquire a bilum while you're on the river anyway. Plastic bags are necessary to keep your camera dry or to protect artifacts you purchase. A rain-cape or umbrella will be welcome if it rains.

Finally, but far from least important, insect repellant will make things more comfortable at any time of year but during the wet it will be vital. People talk about their insect repellants on the Sepik with much the same professional interest that travellers in India bring to bear on their stomach condition. Actually I didn't think the mosquitoes on the Sepik were anywhere near as bad as they were cracked up to be, but then I'm fairly immune for some unknown (but I'm grateful anyway) reason, and it was the dry season. If you're travelling by canoe and staying in villages you'll also need a sleeping bag, some sort of mosquito netting, and food.

Accommodation on the Sepik

Angoram is virtually the only place on the Sepik with a proper, western style hotel, but there are a number of places where you can find a place to stay, particularly in the most interesting middle Sepik area. Of course there are always Haus Kiaps in many villages, so you can be fairly sure of at least finding a roof over your head if, for example, you should be canoeing down river.

At Timbunke contact the Catholic Mission who will probably be able to provide accommodation. Ditto at Chambri Village on the Chambri Lakes, nightly charge here is K3 per person. At Kaminabit there is a lodge which is currently being upgraded — cost seems to be a little variable at the moment (depending on how close it is to completion?).

Accommodation in Amboin

For those with the money, the *Karawari Lodge* at Amboin is another possibility for exploring the Sepik. Amboin is up the Karawari River, well off the main Sepik, and is usually reached by air to Amboin airstrip from where you travel by river to the lodge. Built in the form of a traditional Haus Tambaran (but with all mod-cons!), the lodge has 20 twin rooms which cost K56 per day per person — this includes all meals and tours from the lodge. The lodge river trucks will take you to nearby villages like Maraba, Marvwak and Simbut — where the trad-itional Sepik style tree houses are still used. Sing-sings, mock head-hunting raids and re-en-actments of the Mangamai skin-cutting cere-monies are alll part of the performance at the lodge. Contact Trans-Niugini Tours for more details.

Karawari Lodge
Bookings: via Trans-Niugini Tours
Rooms: 20 twin
Tariff: K56 per person incl meals, tours, transfers

SEPIK DIARY

This is my diary of four, probably fairly typical, days I spent on the Sepik River on the *Sepik Explorer II.*

Day 1

Flew from Madang to Wewak and after a phone around the Wewak hotels found our reluctant mini-bus driver and started off on the long haul to Pagwi. It took nearly five non-stop hours, after Hayfields (the Maprik turn-off) the road is flat but badly corrugated and the shock absorbers on our bus are definitely on their last legs. On the way we pass clearings in the bush with large mesh nets spread across them. Flying foxes (bats) fly into the net, become entangled, and end up in the cooking pot. It's 4 pm by the time we finally arrive at the Sepik so we set off almost immediately. Our boat, the *Sepik Explorer II,* is houseboat style — two double berth and one four berth cabin, so there is capacity for eight passengers. Upstairs there's a lounge (mosquito proof, although this isn't the worst season for them) and a sundeck out back. Jeff Liversidge, the captain, has been on the Sepik for 17 years, 10 of them as a crocodile hunter, and is married to a Sepik girl. There's a crew of three — Wee the engineer, Crosby the cook, and James the young Jack-of-all-trades.

That evening we only travelled downstream for about 35 minutes before mooring at the village of Korogo, one of the villages most "into" art on the whole river. The Haus Tambarans on the river have a totally different style to the forward leaning Maprik ones which are commonly though of as typ-ical of the whole Sepik area. The one here is packed full of saleable art — and the artists to sell it. They say that three out of four men in the village carve — they also carve dug-out canoes of course. One old guy is acknow-

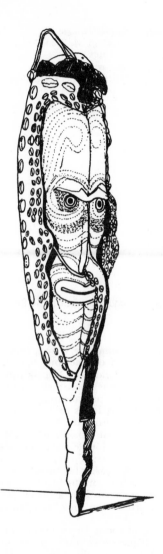

Korogo mask

ledged as the village expert and is often called in to carve the traditional crocodile head canoe prows. It takes a month to axe out a dug-out and they may last three or four years before falling apart. Every village seems to have plenty of cracked discarded canoes lying around. The villagers fish, catch prawns and shell fish from the lakes behind their village — there are many lakes all along the Sepik, a lot of them are the ox-bows left when the river changed its course. Korogo is a very beautiful, green village but as evening draws in there are plenty of mosquitoes — and this is the dry season!

After a substantial dinner Jeff brings two small crocodiles in to show us the difference between a saltwater and a freshwater pukpuk. Both are found all the way up the river, but the salt variety can also venture out to sea. They're more valuable due to their smaller scales and better colouring, they also grow larger but by the end of the trip I still have trouble telling one from the other. Even these small ones are fiesty little buggers and will go for you if given a chance, but held firmly they're surprisingly placid. If held down on their backs they soon go completely limp and would eventually die; flipped over they immediately spring back into action!

Crocodiles are still very important commercially although it is now illegal to take ones over seven foot (two metres) — the illegal size is actually determined by girth, not length. A seven foot crocodile is about 20 inches (50 cm) in girth. The skin from a good condition saltwater crocodile can be worth K6 an inch (in girth), a freshwater only K4. Below 10 inches they're worth much less. Many villages have crocodile farms but they're generally not grown beyond four and a half foot in length (one and a half metres) as they take a long time to grow larger than that. The complete hide must be presented for sale, so you can't cheat on the maximum size limit by cutting the skin down. Crocodiles are edible but only really the tail, the rest is very sinewy. According to the connoisseurs it has a sort of fish/meat taste. Crocodiles won't bite underwater so villagers catch them by feeling in the mud with their feet — I wouldn't want to test that theory! Many are caught in fishing nets.

A young man from the village comes on board to show us his initiation scars. His arms, legs and trunk are patterned with little scars made by cutting with a razor blade then rubbing clay in to simulate crocodile scales. They used to use bamboo knives. Great importance is attached to initiation on the Sepik and ceremonies are conducted just as often now as they ever were — even Prime Minister Somare has been initiated. It takes about an hour, a painful hour, to make the many tiny cuts. During that time the Haus Tambaran is totally shielded off by a high fence and the drums, flutes and bull roarers play continuously.

Day 2

We depart at 7 am and breakfast on the rear sundeck as we head down river, there's positively no chance of starving on this trip — the meals are big. It takes two hours to reach Yentchen where there is a two storey Haus Tambaran — it was built from photographs taken at the turn of the century by German explorers of the Haus Tambaran here at that time. You climb upstairs between the legs of a female figure carved into the end posts — a fairly graphic fertility symbol. Yentchen is noted for its wicker work dance costumes — figures of crocodiles, pigs, cassowaries, two headed men. One of them is shown on the cover of this book. We also see the sacred flutes here — they're always played in male/female pairs, alone they have no great importance.

Downstairs there are two recent initiates waiting for the end of their three week stay in the Haus Tambaran. Their cuts are nearly healed, coated in river clay. As in nearly every Haus Tambaran we visit, there's a large orator's stool there; the Sepik people are noted for their oratorical skills — it's probably no accident that the Prime Minister is a Sepik man. Orators don't sit on the stools, they stand beside them and slap a bunch of leaves on the seat, placing one down each time they make an important point.

We walk through the village, crossing a precarious tree trunk bridge, to see Michael — a large, recently captured and very bad tempered, young cassowary. They don't have the same significance here as in the Highlands, but the villagers think they may transport it there in order to sell it. They say they may get K1000 for it — the small cassowary I saw for sale in Mt Hagen market was K160. Once again this village is very pleasant — clean and green.

We speed further downriver in our river truck — this is the furthest point downriver that the houseboat goes, we travel on from it by the flat bottomed river truck with its 115 HP outboard motor. Palembi village is a couple of km inland from the river, a pleasant walk through the gardens and the village is quite stunningly beautiful. There are two Haus Tambarans with a lush, grass dancing place between them. The ruins of an old Haus Tambaran was said to have been bombed out by the US during the war as Japanese troops were hiding out here.

There is a cluster of "sacred stones" in front of the larger Haus Tambaran. The wide meanderings of the Sepik has totally swept away all stones for a great distance on either side of the river's present course. Yet every village has a number of stones that have been there as long as anyone can remember — they've obviously been carried in. Palembi, like a number of other villages we visit, is built on stilts due to the annual flooding. Although all the flooded vegetation dies, the subsequent regrowth is fantastically fast. The coconut trees have all formed their own little mound to grow from, that little extra clearance from the flood waters.

There are always fires burning in the Haus Tambarans and the clay pottery fireplaces all come from Aibom on the Chambri Lakes. Palembi is a centre for making bilums, the string bags here are finely made and very cheap compared to the coastal town prices. Kids in the village have a wedge tailed kite and an unfortunate blue kingfisher with its wings clipped. Throughout Asia our concept of kindness to animals is totally alien to the children who have no qualms about cruelly mistreating them.

In the afternoon we make a long trip downriver then in to the Chambri Lakes — a vast, flat expanse of shallow water a large part of which periodically dries up. At the finish of the wet season vast amounts of water flood out of the lakes into the Sepik and carry huge pieces of land with them, often in the form of "floating islands". The recent end of the wet this year has blocked most of the channels into the Chambri Lakes so we are forced to take this longer route.

We stop at a fishing village on a hilly island in the centre of the lake then

Aibom pot

double back to Indagu — one of the three villages that make up Chambri. There is a new Haus Tambaran here with a huge collection of carvings — mainly in the polished Chambri style. They sell for only K1 to K3, there are also many ornamental spears. We then head back to Aibom, the pottery village, where a soccer match has the whole village enthralled. The distinctive Aibom pots sell from only a kina or two. All the way along the channel between the Sepik and the lake we continually scare up egrets and other water birds that rise up from the riverbank and wheel away from us.

Back on the main river we carry on to Kaminabit, not an exciting village but it does have a trade store selling cold drinks. Amongst the artifacts for sale were penis gourds — those items of attire for every well dressed stone-age man. It's strictly for the tourists as you have to get way up into the upper Sepik region to find places where they are still worn.

We leave the village and wait for dusk before crocodile hunting on our way back to the *Explorer*. A powerful spotlight, swept along the bank, picks up the red, cat-like eyes of the reptiles. Then you simply swoop in and grab them (if they're small), spear them (if they're large), or leave them strictly alone (if they're very large). Big pukpuks have got that way by being crafty, they submerge before you get to them, but we do grab one small one. At the boat, almost a mother-ship to us now, an Austrian artifact collector has stopped by. He's been on the river for several months collecting from villages way up the Kariwari.

Later in the evening we set off on another croc hunting — or should it be called a wildlife terrorising? — expedition. Anything goes, "if it moves, grab it" seems to be the motto of our crew who see anything feathered, furred or even scaled as a potential addition to the village cooking pot. We caught a small leaf wader, failed to grab a tiny crocodile then got a slightly larger one. We then jammed in a baret and all hands were overboard into the shallow mud to try to push us free. I ended up as gamekeeper — a crocodile in one hand, the leaf wader in the other, no hands left free for the mosquitoes; a handicap which they took immediate advantage of. We grabbed one more small crocodile and then headed back to the *Explorer*, Crosby has a crocodile farm back in his home village.

Day 3

We all rise groggily, after our late night croc hunting, and then travel by river truck to Kanganam village which has the oldest Haus Tambaran on the river. It's a fine, large old building — totally open. The carved columns are particularly well done. The artistic style here seems to specialise in thin, open worked food hooks. There are interesting combinations of women and crocodiles or birds — there are many Sepik legends of women with crocodiles or birds as children. The village spiritual life remains a totally male preserve in which women have no part at all, but they now realise that much of it is a little hokum!

We soon head back to the *Explorer* where I'm relieved to hear that our leaf wader has taken advantage of an open window and disappeared. The boat heads off upriver and we breakfast on the way. Next stop is Swatmeri, a centre for carving orator's stools but overall the crafts here are fairly crude compared to other villages we have visited. From there it is a few hours travel (and lunch) before we stop for the villages of Kandagai and Yentschamunngua. The first village is a longish way up a baret and a tree has fallen across the channel so we are unable to get there. Yentschamunngua is directly across the river, a long walk along a trunk path to the village — it floods easily. Here we are invited inside a big family house — the owner has two wives and plenty picanniny. The food hooks with clusters of bilums hanging down give the place a strange look. It's really just one large room, many Aibom fire pots scattered around.

The Haus Tambaran here burnt down a few years ago, the men are still in temporary accommodation. The artifacts here too are crude, but two men play the garamut drum for us — a fine, stately sound. On the way back to the river a man takes us to see the skin and head of a pukpuk he recently caught, inadvertently, in his fishing net. It's a big one, right on the legal limit, and he's relieved to hear from Jeff that it's OK and he can sell it. Of course he has to get it to Angoram where all the skins are bought, a long trip.

On upriver to Japanat, a small village that specialises in "trinkets" — little black masks or other carvings on shell or seed necklaces. Although every village has its own distinctive style there is also almost always a some strange little item which is completely out of character. Here it's a couple of carvings with an almost Egyptian look to them. In other villages we saw a mask with Maori like swirls on the face, a curious roof top figure of a women with a crocodile arched across her back, or a modernistic, almost Balinese style, fish or frog.

It's almost dusk when we reach Japandi, a brief stop because it is really too dark to see very much. Like Japanaut the artifacts house is hardly a Haus Tambaran, just a shack with a collection of carvings. The speciality of this village is oval "moon faced" masks, some of which are black and highly polished. A little further upriver we tie up by the bank for the night.

carved column in Kanganam Haus Tambaran

After dinner the evening's entertainment is a "jungle walk". Using the croc hunting spotlight, a 12-volt car battery comes along in a trusty bilum, we make off for the jungle, joking about the possibility of coming face to face with a hairy bird-eating spider — or worse. Actually we come face to face with nothing threatening at all — although a few birds definitely feel threatened by us! Along the way we find a brush turkey's mound — a huge hump of dirt and leaves, perhaps two metres high and five across, inside of which the eggs are left to incubate in the heat generated by the rotting vegetation. James digs one egg up — for our breakfast tomorrow Jeff assures us.

Tiny green frogs stare at us from plant stems and butterflies and moths flutter by, or just pose prettily. A beautiful paradise kingfisher sleeps in a branch high above us until he's rudely awakened by a hurled stick. We see luminous mushrooms, a flying fox swoops overhead, two tiny yellow birds perch quietly side by side and a tawny nightjar also gets the rude awakening treatment. Curiously none of the sleeping birds are at all disturbed by the light or the noise of our party. Twice Crosby sees a cuscus but the rest of our party is not fast enough. James gives a totally false, startled yelp at one point which prompts one of our ladies to leap, with amazing agility, on to her husbands back! It takes ten minutes to calm James' hysterical laughter. Back at the boat we're all surprised to find the walk took two hours.

Day 4

After breakfast we rivertruck to Avatip while the mother ship continues upriver. Although it is the largest village on the upper Sepik, it's not greatly interesting. The Germans burnt it down twice and the old carving skills have been totally lost. The man's house is a dull place. Simon, a very English anthropologist, is staying in the village. He has already been here ten months but his initial intention of studying the lending/giving practises and their connection with leadership — as in the Highlands — has been shelved. It doesn't seem to happen here so he has switched to a general social study. The village has three initiations the second of which is involved with the yam cult while the third is only for old men. Debating is of great importance — they try to find the meanings of names, information which the owners of the names are very reluctant to part with. Simon says it's a much more interesting structure than the Highlands.

Malu village, almost at Ambunti, is interesting for its variety of fruit trees and flowers. We're not allowed into the Haus Tambaran here, in other villages we were not allowed in with hats on or, alternatively, with hats off. After a short pause at Ambunti, the big upriver town used by many missions as a base, we head on to Melawei by rivertruck. Here we meet Crosby's amazing old uncle and his two wives — the third one died. They all have bits of string threaded through holes in the tops of their ears. Above the village the Haus Tambaran is decorated inside with panels of brightly painted bark. Some of the village boys give us a virtuoso demonstration of garamut drum playing. Melawei is on a lake which was once a curve of the Sepik.

That was as far as we got upriver but on the way back to Ambunti we detour to Yigei, a very poor and primitive village well off the river. The women here wear grass skirts, the men loin cloths.

After a pleasant final dinner we're off spear fishing. Shine the light till you see a fish in the murky shallows then spear it with a multi-pronged spear. At least that's the way it's supposed to be done. Score — Crosby 3, the rest of us 0.

Day 5
Pack up and leave the boat. Ambunti has an interesting open court house perched on the hill overlooking the airstrip. Then it's back down to the strip, sit under a shady tree until our Douglas Airways Islander comes in. It's an incredibly tatty aircraft and most of the way back to Wewak it's solid cloud below. I'm always happier in light aircraft when I can see the ground but it clears up well before we reach the coast. End of trip.

AITAPE
There is some push in PNG to have the West Sepik HQ transferred from Vanimo, near the politically sensitive Irian Jaya border, to more tranquil Aitape. It's a tiny, picturesque little town with evidence of its long, by PNG standards, history. The Germans established their station here in 1905 and the jail they built in 1906 still stands above the town. It was used by the Japanese during the war.

There are some bits of aircraft wreckage near the wartime Tadji airstrip, it was the first place captured by the Allies in their advance on the Sepik district. A Japanese war memorial is situated between the town and the Santa Anna Mission. The offshore islands, about 15 km from the coast, are interesting — particularly beautiful Ali or Selio, which has an airstrip.

Accommodation in Aitape
There are single and double rooms at the *Tamara Hotel* in Aitape.

Getting to Aitape
The road from Wewak to Aitape has only recently been completed and is still rough going and has little traffic. Douglas Airways will fly you Wewak-Aitape for K31 or on to Vanimo for a further K31.

VANIMO
Only 30 km from the Irian Jaya border, a resident told me you could hear the bombs falling when the Indonesians were having trouble with their guerrilla opponents. Vanimo is situated on the isthmus of a neat little peninsula poking out into the sea. There are fine beaches on both sides of the peninsula. There is a road along the coast from Vanimo right to the Irian Jaya border which is marked by the PNG patrol post of Watung. Here you can see one of the 14 markers which the joint Australian-Indonesian border mapping party erected in 1968. On the way to the border you'll pass some tidy little villages such as Mushu and Yako and excellent white sand beaches.

Accommodation in Vanimo

There is a hotel and a guest house. The *Narimo Hotel* has 14 rooms and costs K17 room single, K25 double for room only. The rooms are air-conditioned and tours to the Irian Jaya border can be arranged or 4-WD vehicles can be hired. The *Vanimo Guest House* has four twin rooms and costs K8 per person including meals.

Narimo Hotel
Bookings: PO Box 49,
Vanimo
Tel: 87 1113
Rooms: 14
Tariff: K17 sgl, K25 dbl

Vanimo Guest House
Bookings: PO Box 82,
Vanimo
Tel: 87 1141/58
Rooms: 4 twin
Tariff: K8 per person all meals

Getting to Vanimo

The coastal road has only reached Aitape so it will be a long while before it extends to Vanimo. There are two flights a week between Wewak and Vanimo with Air Niugini for K34. Douglas Airways have flights to a number of Sepik centres from Vanimo; to Aitape costs K31. If you're flying from Wewak to Jayapura in Irian Jaya you can clearly see Vanimo as you descend into Jayapura. I once met an adventurous young English couple who arrived in PNG from Irian Jaya by the highly unofficial method of getting a local fisherman to drop them off just across the border; from where they got a ride into Vanimo. Probably completely illegal but they got away with it.

THE BORDER

The border between Papua New Guinea and Indonesia (Irian Jaya) has always been a rather curious place. It's a typical example of a colonial border — draw a straight line across a totally unknown area of the world, with scant regard for who might be living near it. Or, as it has turned out, actually on it. There have been a whole series of Dutch-English, Dutch-German, Dutch-Australian and most recently Indonesian-Australian attempts to define exactly where the border is and today it is pretty clear just which unfortunate villages straddle the line.

For many years, villagers near the border, but on the Papua New Guinea side, were much more under Dutch influence than Australian for Hollandia was close while Wewak was a long way away. Many people close to the border still speak Indonesian as (in its virtually identical Malay guise) this was the lingua franca of Dutch rule. Apart from their other insecurities, villagers within 20 miles of the border on the PNG side are not allowed to grow coffee or raise cattle due to fears of disases being spread across the border and eventually reaching the productive PNG coffee and cattle industries. Further south in the Sepik region the high Star Mountains of Irian Jaya continue across the border to form the watersheds for both the Sepik and Fly Rivers.

TELEFOMIN

The remote and tiny station at Telefomin was only opened in 1948 — it's still one of the most isolated and primitive places in the country and, due to its inaccessible location high in the central mountains, likely to remain that way for some time. Oksapmin station, a short flight from Telefomin, was only established in 1961. Up here the penis gourd is still often the only item of male attire.

Western & Gulf

Area: 134,100 square km
Population: 150,000

The two western Papuan provinces are amongst the least developed in the whole country. The coastline is a series of river deltas, huge expanses of swamp run inland before rising to the foothills and then the mountains of the Highlands. In the far west the border with Irian Jaya runs north through the open expanses of seasonally flooded grassland. Two of the greatest rivers in the country, the Fly and the Strickland, run almost their entire length through Western Province.

HISTORY

The coastal people of the provinces have had a long history of contact with European and other outside influences. The annual "hiri", trading voyages along the south coast, were still a regular feature long after the establishment of Port Moresby. Due to its easy access from the sea the coastal villages were also the first hunting grounds for representatives of the London Missionary Society who were in operation here from the early 1880s.

In 1827 Durmont D'Urville had surveyed part of the north-east coast of New Guinea and in 1842 he returned in *HMS Fly* to chart the western side of the Gulf of Papua. He discovered the Fly River and decided a small steam powered boat could travel up this mighty river far into the interior of the country. It was some years before this idea was put into action but when the controversial Italian explorer, Luigi D'Albertis, did make his second, and most successful, trip up the Fly in 1876 lost time was quickly made up. In his tiny steamer, the *Neva*, he travelled over 900 km upriver, far further into the unknown interior of New Guinea than any previous explorer. He returned from this epic voyage with a huge collection of botanical specimens, insects, artifacts, even painted skulls from village spirit houses.

It was his method of appropriating many of his finds and the general level of his relationships with the villagers which coloured opinions about D'Albertis. He was a great believer in the philosophy of "shooting first and asking questions afterwards" and travelled upriver with a huge arsenal of fireworks, rockets, gunpowder and dynamite. At the slightest sign of even the mildest difficulty with river people he was inclined to launch off fusilades of dynamite loaded rockets! It was certainly not sheer chance that led to so many of his artifacts being found in strangely "deserted" villages. When he returned to the Fly in 1877 he found the villagers much readier to attack him than on his previous expedition, nor did he manage to penetrate so far up river and along the way he lost five of his Chinese crew, one of whom it would appear died at his hands.

Much of D'Albertis' "difficulties" with the natives may have been self-inflicted but later missionaries were also to have their problems although the best known case, that of the Rev James Chalmers, was also partially his own fault. Chalmers was one of the earliest missionaries in New Guinea, had been involved in some of the first expeditions into the interior, and was a highly respected man. Yet somehow, after 25 years in the country, an act of sheer stupidity led to his death and at least 50 others. In 1901 Chalmers visited Goaribari Island on the Papuan Gulf and his boat was besieged by hostile tribesmen. He managed to persuade them to leave the boat by promising to come to their village in the morning. Chalmers would surely have known that the people here were practising cannibals and all too ready to execute their captives in the *dobus* or men's house. Any sane man would have departed immediately, yet next morning Chalmers with another missionary, a friendly chief and nine local mission students, went ashore — perhaps looking for some sort of martyrdom. He quickly found it, for all 12 had their skulls crushed with stone war clubs and were soon cooking up nicely in a sago stew.

His boat managed to escape and retribution soon followed from Port Moresby. When the government ship *Merrie England* arrived at Goaribari the bill for that meal was rather more than the villagers might have expected. At least 24 were killed in their first encounter with white justice and 12 *dobus* were burnt down. A year later Chalmers' skull was recovered and all might have been allowed to settle down had not Christopher Robinson arrived in Moresby in 1903 to become temporary administrator. Robinson decided another visit to Goaribari, to recover the skull of Oliver Tomkins, Chalmers' assistant, was in order. As on the first punitive expedition, the visit quickly turned into a massacre and somewhere between eight and 50 villagers were killed. When Robinson returned to Moresby he found Australian public opinion violently against his over-reaction and early one morning, before the official enquiry had commenced, he stood beside the flagpole in the garden of Government House and put a bullet through his head.

Although the Gulf and Western coasts were well charted and the Fly, Strickland and other major rivers were soon comprehensively surveyed, it was not until the late '20s that the mountains north of the coast were explored. In 1927 Charles Karius and Ivan Champion set out to travel up-river from Daru, near the mouth of the Fly, to cross the central mountains and then to go downriver on the Sepik to the north coast. Their first attempt failed when they ran out of supplies while trying to find a way through the jagged limestone mountains which they named the "broken bottle country". A year later they managed to complete their journey, one of the last great exploratory expeditions. It is an indicator of how far the psychology of dealing with primitive, uncontacted tribespeople had improved that, in complete contrast to D'Albertis, they did not fire one shot in anger on the whole trip.

Exploration apart, not much had happened in the region for there proved to be little agricultural potential due to the frequent flooding and little mineral wealth despite a massive expenditure over many years in an unsuccessful search for oil. Today there is a major copper mining project underway at Ok Tedi, high in the central mountains near the border with Irian Jaya, but a very large percentage of the population continues to migrate to other areas, either temporarily or permanently, in the search for work.

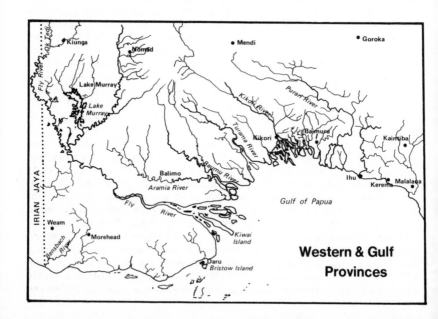

GEOGRAPHY

The border region with Irian Jaya is composed of vast, open, seasonally flooded grasslands to the south, rising up into the mountainous backbone of the country. The Fly River starts from high in this central divide and turns south-east towards the sea where it ends in a huge, island-filled mouth. The Strickland River, nearly equal in size, joins the Fly about 240 km from the coast. Despite its size the Fly does not have the same importance or interest as the Sepik. Because it tends to flood so far over its banks, villages are usually some distance from the river. It is not so usable as a means of travel due to colossal tidal bores that can rush down it at times of full moon.

From the mouth of the Fly on eastwards to the Purari River the Gulf of Papua is a constant succession of river deltas, backed by swamps which run 50 to 60 km inland. East of the Purari the land rises more rapidly from the coast, is less subject to flooding and more heavily populated.

Headhunting

Angry protests were once made to the Dutch colonial officials about "their head hunters" poaching across the border into British New Guinea. The Tugeri people, whose land once spread across both sides of the border, were ferocious headhunters who believed they had to collect a head for every child born. But a head was no good unless it had a "name" to pass on to the child. So their unfortunate victims had first to be persuaded to say something before they were despatched. Presumably even "don't do it" was good enough.

DARU

The HQ town for the Western Province is Daru, a small island off the coast that used to be a pearl and bêche de mer trading port. It is a busy shipping port and an important fishing industry is starting to develop from Daru — that apart there is not much of interest. The unfortunate Rev Chalmers was based in Daru and his "grave" and that of his wife can be seen here and his Tamate Memorial Church; built by the Kiwai Islanders and given his native name. Daru is also the town from which the skins of crocodiles, caught in the Western Province, are exported.

Accommodation in Daru

Daru has a guest house and a hotel which has a bad reputation for value for money even by PNG standards. The *Daru Guest House* has seven twin rooms and costs K18 per person per day including breakfast. The *Daru Hotel* has 14 rooms and costs K30 per person including all meals. Five of the rooms are air-conditioned.

Daru Guest House
Address: Cameron Rd
Bookings: PO Box 51, Daru
Tel: 65 9104
Rooms: 7 twin
Tariff: per person - K18
    bed & breakfast

Daru Hotel
Bookings: PO Box 6, Daru
Tel: 65 9120
Rooms: 14 sgl
Tariff: per person — K30
    all meals

BENSBACH

Only a few km from the Irian Jaya border, Bensbach Wildlife Lodge is the premier tourist attraction in the Western Province — well-off-tourist attraction that is! The mouth of the Bensbach River forms the border between Papua New Guinea and Irian Jaya but the border runs due north while the river bends off north-east into PNG territory. This area is a vast expanse of grassland and swamp, lightly populated due to the effects of heavy head hunting in earlier years.

What it lacks in people it makes up for in wildlife — the area is alive with animals and birds, many of them amazingly fearless since they have had little contact with man. The Dutch introduced Rusa deer into West New Guinea in the 1920s and, untroubled by natural predators, they have spread far into PNG — there are over 20,000 west of the Bensbach in PNG territory. Wallabies, wild pigs and crocodiles are also prolific and the bird life is quite incredible. It's a photographer's paradise. Keen fishers will also enjoy themselves since the Bensbach River is renowned for the size and number of its barramundi which feature frequently on the menu at the lodge.

Accommodation in Bensbach

The *Bensbach Wildlife Lodge* is situated near Weam, 96 km north of the river mouth, on the east bank. The low-lying lodge is built of local materials and has two wings, each with four twin rooms, flanking a central complex of bar, lounge and dining room. The rooms are simple, fan cooled rather than air-conditioned (unnecessary in the generally cool climate), but with a refrigerator in each room. There are shower and toilet facilities for each wing. Cost per person per day is K72 but this includes all meals, tours, boats, fishing equipment and park entrance fees. Bookings are made through Trans-Niugini Tours.

Bensbach Wildlife Lodge
Bookings: Trans-Niugini Tours
Rooms: 8 twin
Tariff: from K50 per person per day

Getting to Bensbach

Air Niugini fly from Port Moresby to Daru three times a week; the one hour and 25 minute flight costs K50, from there it is a further K43 by Talair. It is also possible to charter from Mt Hagen to Bensbach. The lodge is reached from the airstrip by river.

OTHER

Lake Murray, in the centre of the vast Western Province, is the biggest lake in Papua New Guinea but during the wet it can spread to five times its 400 square km dry season area. There is a crocodile research station at the lake. Nomad, to the north, is one of the most remote and inaccessible patrol stations in the country. There is accommodation available at the *Balimo*

Lodge, at Balimo on the Aramai River.

In 800 km to the sea the Fly River falls only 20 metres, it flows (slowly) through 250,000 square km of swamp land where mosquitoes appear to be the only successful inhabitants. It is nowhere near as easy to visit the Fly as it is to get out on the Sepik, and in any case there is not so much to see.

The Kiwai people, who live on the islands in the mouth of the Fly, are noted for their seagoing abilities and their interesting dances. They have close cultural links with the Torres Strait Islanders off Cape York Peninsula in Queensland, Australia.

THE GULF

The Turama, the Kikori, the Purari and the Vailala are just some of the great rivers that flow into the swampy, delta-land of the Papuan Gulf. Nor is the water just at ground level, the dry climate of Port Moresby and the Central Province gets progressively damper as you move west around the Gulf. When you get to Kikori in the centre of the Gulf the annual rainfall is an astounding 600 cm per year, nearly 20 feet of rain! Between May and October, the worst part of the wet season, the airstrip at Kikori was socked in so often that in 1960 the district HQ was moved east to drier Kerema.

The people of the delta-land build their houses on piles high above the muddy riverbanks. As the rivers change their courses they frequently have to move their villages. Each village centred around the men's longhouses, known as a *dobu* or *ravi*, in here weapons, important artifacts, ceremonial objects and the skulls of enemies were stored. Men slept in the longhouse, women in smaller, individual huts outside. Today the longhouses are no longer so culturally important, the Gulf people have been fairly well bombarded with Christianity for nearly a century and been persuaded to give up some of their unsavoury habits — cannibalism in particular.

Cannibalism was partly a cultural activity but probably more important was its value as a source of protein. As on the Sepik the main food is sago, the tasteless, starchy food produced from the pith of the sago palm. There is no shortage of sago, which grows prolifically in the Gulf area, so nobody starves, but as a food source — even supplemented by the fish they catch and the small amount of vegetables their inhospitable land will allow them to grow — a sago diet leads to severe protein deficiencies.

In the hills behind the coastal swampland live the Kamea people, a sparse and scattered population who are the same as the small in stature, but large in temper, Kukukuku tribespeople of the south-eastern part of the Highlands. They raided villages on the south coast just as often and just as violently as on the north. The last major Kukukuku raid took palce at Ipisi near Kerema just before WW II. Today there is a government station at Kaintiba in the heart of their land and all is fairly peaceful.

KEREMA

The tiny government HQ town is situated where it is, mainly because of the more pleasant (ie drier) climate. There is a sketchy road network around Kerema and it is possible to travel by boat up river behind the town.

Accommodation in Kerema
The *Hotel Kerema* has eight twin rooms and costs K25 per person inclusive of all meals.

Hotel Kerema
Bookings: PO Box 25,
 Kerema
Tel: 68 1041
Rooms: 8 twin
Tariff: per person - K25
 all meals

KIKORI & BAIMURU
The two major delta-country towns are situated well back from the coastline. Both have small airstrips and it is possible to get from one to the other by boat, through the maze of waterways. There are some interesting villages along the way. Kikori is one of the oldest stations in Papua.

Accommodation in Kikori
The *Gulf Hotel* has 12 twin rooms and costs K10 per person, room only. Tours in the area can be arranged by the hotel.

Gulf Hotel
Bookings: Post Office,
 Kikori
Rooms: 12 twin
Tariff: per person - K10

ELSEWHERE
Ihu is the main station between the delta-country and Kerema and it will be the centre for the proposed Purari River power project. It has a guest house. Kaintiba, in the foothills behind the coast, is in the Kamea/Kukukuku country, there is only one scheduled flight a week into Kaintiba. Malalua is a starting point for following the old WW II Bulldog track up to Wau.

Accommodation in Ihu
The *Ihu Guest House* has 10 rooms and costs K18 a single with all meals included.

Ihu Guest House
Bookings: c/o Post Office,
 Ihu
Tel: Outstations
Rooms: 10
Tariff: per person - K18 all
 meals

Accommodation in Kaintiba
It is possible to stay at the Catholic Mission if you arrange it in advance.

ARTIFACTS
There is little art work done in Western Province now — the kundu drums of Lake Murray are very rare and the Kiwai people do not carve so much — but art is still strong in the Gulf region. Unfortunately when the missions first arrived in the Gulf area their attitude towards local culture was considerably less enlightened than it later became. Along with abandoning their spiritual beliefs and giving up head-hunting the Gulf villagers were also pressured to

halt their artistic pursuits and in some cases the missionaries actually persuaded them to burn and destroy their best work in a form of cultural arson. Old artifacts still in existence today are zealously protected.

In the Gulf region from the mouth of the Fly around to Kerema, seven distinct artistic styles have been categorised. Once upon a time the men's longhouses in the delta villages were veritable museums and although there is no "fully-furnished" spirit houses left there is still a busy trade turning out figures, bullroarers, kovave masks, headrests, skull racks (every home should have one) and gope boards.

Gope boards are elliptical in shape, rather like a shield, and incised with brightly coloured abstract patterns or stylised figures. Once upon a time warriors were entitled to have a gope board for each act of bravery or to celebrate each successful conflict. Boards were often cut from the curved sides of old canoes and a board from your vanquished enemy's own canoe had particular significance, transferring some of its previous owner's strength to the new victor.

Hohao boards are similar in their original role to gope boards but can be recognised by their squared off edges, coming to a point at the top and bottom. These were particularly prevalent around Ihu and Orokolo at the eastern end of the Gulf but greater affluence in this region has caused the skill to virtually die out. It was also in this area that the Hehevi ceremonies once took place, a cycle of rituals and dramatic rites that took a full 20 years to complete. The ceremonies have been halted for 50 years now and the huge masks which were used in dances have also disappeared.

GETTING THERE & AROUND

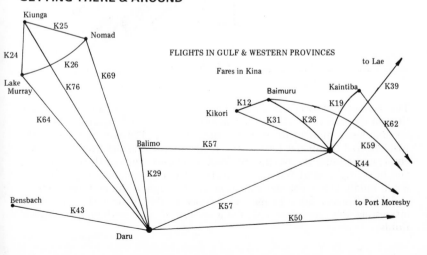

There is only one Air Niugini route into the Gulf and Western Provinces, the twice weekly flight to Daru from Port Moresby. Talair and Douglas Airways have extensive networks around the region — mainly Talair in Western and Douglas Airways in Gulf. They're heavily subsidised by the government as air travel is so important in these remote and otherwise isolated areas. Some of the main route costs are detailed on the previous page.

Otherwise getting around is a choice of coastal shipping or boats up the rivers. There are only very limited roads as of yet. Some roads are being built in the north of Western Province to link the Ok Tedi mining project with Kiunga and other stations in the area. In the Gulf there is a road between Kerema and Malalaua but from there to Bereina, where the road west from Port Moresby terminates, is a long stretch of empty and difficult terrain. There is almost a track through from Kaintiba to Menyamya in Morobe Province in the north, when a road is then built to link Menyamya and Aseki there will then be a link all the way to Lae. It is possible to travel south from Kaintiba some distance towards Kerema by motorcycle.

Northern

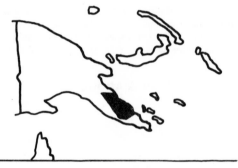

Area: 19,827 square km
Population: 74,000

The Northern Province is sandwiched between the Solomon Sea and the Central Owen Stanley Range. It is another little visited region of the country but has a number of areas of some interest. The northern end of the Kokoda trail terminates here at the village of Kokoda and from here to the coast, and around the beaches of Buna and Gona, some of the most violent and bitter fighting of WW II took place. Mt Lamington, near Popondetta, is a still mildly active volcano which, in 1951, erupted with cataclysmic force and killed nearly 3000 people. In the east of the province there are more interesting volcanoes near Tufi and a section of coast with unique, tropical fiords.

HISTORY

Early European contact with the Orakaiva people, who live inland as far as Kokoda, were relatively peaceful but when gold was discovered at Yodda and Kokoda violence soon followed. After the first altercation between the local people and miners a government station was established, but with scarcely better results since the first government officer was butchered shortly after he arrived and made peaceful, or so he thought, contacts. Eventually things quietened down and as the mines, initially one of the richest fields in Papua, were worked out, rubber and other plantations superseded them.

The war arrived in the Northern area unexpectedly and dramatically in 1942. The Allied forces were just about to open a base in the area when the Japanese suddenly landed in late July '42 and immediately began to move down to Kokoda from where they intended to climb up and over the Owen Stanley Range to take Port Moresby. This horrific campaign is covered in more detail in the introductory history section and in the section on the Kokoda Trail under Port Moresby. As General Horii withdrew up the trail, lines of defence were drawn first at Eora Creek, mid-way along the trail, then at Oivi, on the road from Kokoda to Buna. Both were taken by the Australians after drawn out and bloody fighting. Near here Horii was drowned while attempting to cross the Kumusi River.

If the fighting down and up the trail had been bitter, the final push to retake the beach-heads at Buna and Gona was nearly unbelievable. The Australian troops who had pursued the Japanese back up the trail were supplanted by American troops who came round the coast, but the Japanese held on suicidally. Although Kokoda was retaken at the beginning of January it was the end of January before Buna and Gona had fallen. The Japanese were not so much defeated as annihilated; it has been estimated that of their total force of 16,000 men only about 700 survived.

After the war, rebuilding the region was a difficult task as the damage here was especially severe. Strangled by their supply difficulties, the Japanese troops had scoured the country of food, even being reduced to eating grass and bark off trees in often vain attempts to stave off starvation. The gardens and plantations were hardly back in operation after the war when Mt Lamington's disastrous eruption totally wiped out Higatura, the district HQ, and killed nearly 3000 people. Today the new HQ town of Popondetta has been established at a safer distance from the volcano.

GEOGRAPHY

The swamps and flatlands of the coast rise slowly inland towards the Owen Stanley Range then with increasing steepness to the peaks which stand at 3500 to 4000 metres only 90 to 100 km from the sea. The only roads of any length in the district run from the coast, inland through Popondetta to Kokoda where the famous trail starts. Cape Nelson, to the east, is marked by three volcanoes and is famous for its beautiful fiords which have formed between the fingers of lava from some ancient eruptions.

POPONDETTA

The district HQ is not of particular interest except as a base to visit other parts of the Northern Province — Kokoda further inland, the war time battle sites on the coast, or nearby Mt Lamington. There is a war memorial with an interesting map of the battle sites and a memorial to the victims of Mt Lamington in the town.

Accommodation in Popondetta

There are two places to stay in Popondetta, neither particularly cheap. The *Lamington Hotel* has 18 twin rooms, some fan cooled, some air-con. Full board accommodation costs K30 single, K50 twin in the fan rooms; K35 to K60 in the air-con ones. The simpler *Popondetta Guest House* has eight rooms and, like the Lamington Hotel, has an inclusive of meals tariff — K18.50 per person — but also offers bed and breakfast for K10.50.

Lamington Hotel
Bookings: PO Box 27,
     Popondetta
Tel: 29 7152
Cables: Lamhotel
Rooms: 18 twin
Tariff: K30 to 35 sgl, K50 to
     60 twin, incl all meals

Popondetta Guest House
Bookings: PO Box 73,
     Popondetta
Tel: 29 7060
Rooms: 8
Tariff: K10.50 sgl incl breakfast, K17.50 incl all meals

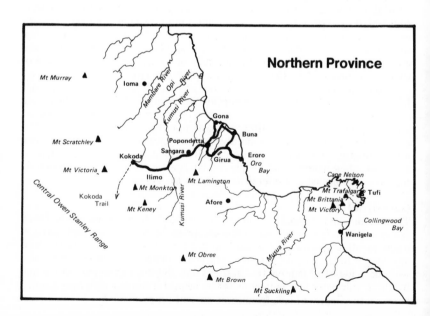

MT LAMINGTON

The 1585 metre peak of Mt Lamington is clearly visible from Popondetta but the original HQ was even closer, only 10 km from the volcano. Like many other volcanoes in PNG, Mt Lamington still shakes and puffs a little and the local residents paid no attention to a slight increase in activity in 1951. Then half of the mountain side suddenly blew out and a violent cloud of super-heated gases rushed down, incinerating all before it. The entire European population of Higatura, 35 people, died. It was later estimated that the temperature there stood at around 200°C for about a minute and a half and that the gas cloud rolled down at over 300 km per hour. The destruction was far worse than the death toll of 3000 people would indicate, as nearly 8000 were left homeless, more than one person in ten of the whole province. It took a number of years for the region to get over this catastrophe.

Mt Lamington has been fairly calm since that time and keen bushwalkers can climb it today. You start from Sasenbata Mission, a little way off the Kokoda road. Like most mountains the best time to reach the summit is in the early morning before the clouds roll in; there's a campsite on a ridge line. There is no crater atop Mt Lamington but the views are very fine. The tribal name of the mountain is Sumburipa. Take care, it's still active.

KOKODA

The road from Popondetta has brought Kokoda to within a couple of hours' drive. The Kumusi River is now crossed by a bridge near Wairopi ("wire rope" after the earlier footbridge). It was near here that the Japanese General Horii, and hundreds of other Japanese troops, died while crossing the river during the retreat from Oivi Ridge. The road climbs steeply over the ridge and then drops into the Kokoda Valley where it ends and the walking trail starts. The Owen Stanley Range rises almost sheer behind Kokoda, the old trail was at one time used by miners walking from Port Moresby across to the goldfields of Yodda, only 13 km from Kokoda.

WAR SITES

The final Japanese stand was made at Buna and Gona and there are many war relics scattered around the area, most of them considerably overgrown. At Jiropa Plantation, on the Buna road, there is a Japanese plaque commemorating their war dead. Oro Bay, south down the coast, is now the port for Popondetta but during the war was a major American base.

CAPE NELSON & TUFI

A suitably patriotic British sea captain named this scenic peninsula Cape Nelson after the legendary Captain and dubbed the three mountain peaks on the cape, Trafalgar (site of his naval victory over the French), Victory (his ship) and Britannia (she's the one who ruled the waves). The bay to the south he named Collingwood after one of Lord Nelson's captains. The cape was formed by an earlier eruption of its three volcanoes and the lava flow down into the sea created the fiords for which it is famous. Unlike the Norwegian originals, the water is always warm here and beneath the calm surface of the sheltered fiords there is beautiful coral waiting to be inspected. Tufi, the main station on the cape, has an airstrip and two guest houses.

Accommodation in Tufi
The two guest houses are both run by local clans. *Kofure Village Guest House* is one km from the airstrip and reached by outrigger canoe. The houses, with six double rooms, are built in the local style and the food is locally grown (or caught, in the case of fish). All in cost is just K12 per person, which not only includes all meals, but also fishing or diving trips — for which the region is ideal. The *Mirigina Lodge* is perched high above the fiord waters at Tufi Station and has five double rooms, which cost K17 per day including all meals. Fishing, diving and sightseeing trips can be easily arranged.

Kofure Village Guest House
Bookings: Post Office, Tufi
Rooms: 6 double
Tariff: K12 per person incl all meals

Mirigina Lodge
Bookings: Post Office, Tufi
Rooms: 5
Tariff: K17 per person incl all meals

Accommodation in Wanigela
Further south from the cape on Collingwood Bay there is a guest house at Wanigela. The *Waijuga Park Guest House* has 14 rooms with a daily cost of K25 per person including all meals. Canoe trips up the Murin River and glass bottom boat tours to the coral reefs can be arranged.

Waijuga Park
Bookings: Private Mailbag, Wanigela via Popondetta
Rooms: 14
Tariff: K25 per person incl all meals

ARTIFACTS
Tapa cloth, made by beating the bark from a paper mulberry tree until it is thin and flexible, is made in the Northern Province. Natural dyes are used to make dramatic designs on the cloth. Only in the most remote parts is tapa cloth now worn by the local people. Tapa cloth is still made at Wanigela where distinctive clay pots are also fired.

GETTING THERE & AROUND
Air Nuigini have daily connections from Port Moresby to Popondetta, the short 35 minute flight costs K19. Air Nuigini also has flights Popondetta-Lae on six days of the week for K32, but only twice are they direct when it takes just one hour and ten minutes. Talair will fly you from Popondetta to Tufi for K26, or to Wanigela for K25. From Kokoda to Port Moresby with Douglas Airways costs K22.

Manus

Area: 1943 square km
Population: 30,000

Manus is the smallest, most isolated and least visited of the provinces of Papua New Guinea. It consists of a group of islands known as the Admiralty Islands plus a scattering of low-lying atolls. Manus Island, which gives the province its name, is the largest of the Admiralty Islands. Manus is also the name of the group of people living along the southern coast and on the other Admiralty Islands.

HISTORY

Dutch explorers, who sailed through the area in 1616-17, are credited with being the first Europeans to sight Manus but it was later Spanish visitors who named many of the surrounding islands. Most of them now have new names although there are still some Spanish touches — the island where the airport is located is still called Los Negros.

Manus is a rugged, broken, relatively infertile island and with no obvious commercial gain to be had it was left pretty much alone by the colonisers. It was not until WW II that any real outside influence was introduced and when it arrived it was highly dramatic. In 1944 the American forces decided Manus would make an ideal base to counterbalance the Japanese forces at Rabaul. The Japanese strength in Manus proved more than expected but it was soon taken by the Americans and construction of a vast base was commenced. The huge naval and air base was built around Seeadler Harbour on both the main Manus Island and on Los Negros which is separated from Manus by the extremely narrow Loniu Passage.

Untold millions of dollars were lavished on the base and at times as many as 600 Allied ships were anchored in Seeadler Harbour. Then, suddenly and unexpectedly, the war ended and a year later the Americans pulled out and scrapped everything. Not surprisingly this display of profligacy had quite an impact on the local people — an impact which anthropologist Margaret Mead described in her book *New Lives for Old*.

After the war Manus more or less returned to its former easy-going ways although there are now plans to exploit the island's large timber resources. Road construction, long neglected due to the harsh terrain, is finally moving ahead although most of the roads in Manus are still a legacy of the US base.

THE MANUS PEOPLE

The Manus people have long had a reputation as one of the most progressive and flexible groups in the country. They only comprise about a quarter of the population of the province but have a considerable reputation for their ability as sailors and traders. It was this trading ability, not generally well developed amongst the many more insular Papua New Guinea peoples, that first brought them into contact with European colonists. Ever ready to make a deal, the Manus were even reputed to have sold captives from their mainland raids to cannibal tribes, although they were never cannibals themselves.

Margaret Mead first studied the Manus in her book *Growing Up in New Guinea* and came back for a second look after WW II. Persuading people to accept new ways and methods is often very difficult and has certainly been the case in many parts of New Guinea. Yet after WW II the Manus, spontaneously and independently, decided to totally revolutionise their way of life.

It was a man called Paliau who decided to turn Manus society upside down and although, at first, it was feared that his policies were largely based on cargo cult, the effect has been surprising. Old cults and rituals were thrown over, villages were rebuilt in imitation of European styles, even local schools and self-government were instituted long before the Australian administration belatedly commenced trying to persuade people they should govern themselves. Today Manus people hold positions of responsibility throughout the country, disproportionately to their small numbers.

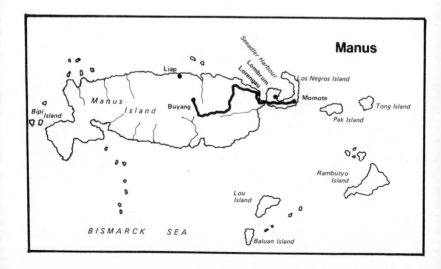

MANUS

Since roads are few there is little opportunity to explore the island except by boat or on foot. Manus is heavily timbered, with central hills rising to over 700 metres and many sharp ridges and streams. The airport is at Momote on Los Negros Island and a good road connects it with the main town, Lorengau, 27 km away on Manus. A bridge crosses the narrow Loniu Passage. There is a pleasant waterfall and fresh water pool on the Lorengau River about five km upstream from the town of Lorengau.

Manus is about 95 km long and 20 to 30 km wide, but apart from rusting remains of the US base and the rugged, but inaccessible, interior there is not much to see. Seeadler Harbour, ringed by small islets and reefs, is very beautiful quite apart from its strategic usefullness.

Of the islands around Manus, Los Negros is volcanic and rather more fertile than the main island. Lou Island, 32 km south of Los Negros, is even more so. Bipi Island, off the western end of Manus, is famed for its fine carvings.

Accommodation in Lorengau

There are a couple of places in Manus. The *Lorengau Hotel*, has just six rooms and a tariff of K17.50 per day for bed and breakfast. The licensed restaurant specialises in local sea-food. Alternatively there is the *Seeadler Lodge* where there are also six rooms and room only rates are K12 per day single. You might also try the transit lodge at Momote on Los Negros Island — phone 409 134 for details.

Lorengau Hotel
Bookings: PO Box 89, Lorengau
Tel: 40 9093
Rooms: 6 twin
Tariff: sgl - K17 b&b

Seeadler Lodge
Address: Main Rd, Lorengau
Tel: 40 9004
Rooms: 4 slg, 2 twin
Tariff: sgl - K12 room only

Getting Around

There's a bus service between Lorengau and the old US naval base at Lombrum and air base at Momote. Other than that there's not much transport because there are not many roads. The road from Lorengau goes inland as far as Buyang and will eventually continue to the north coast.

OTHER ISLANDS

The other islands in the Manus Province are principally low lying coral atolls where coconut palms are virtually the only thing that will grow and copra the only commodity. The main group, scattered hundreds of km north-west of Manus, are known as the North-Western Islands. Their people are fine canoeists and, as there are no suitable trees on their tiny islands, are said to construct their ocean going plank canoes from logs which have floated down the Sepik and out to sea.

ARTIFACTS

Carving has virtually died out in the Admiralties although the people of Bipi still do some — you can see examples in the Lorengau council office. Wooden bowls, stone spears and arrow heads from Lou Island or shields and spears decorated with shark's teeth from the North-Western Islands are other possibilities.

GETTING THERE

A problem. Unless you come on one of the irregular ships the only way in is to fly. Air Niugini fly to Manus on the Wewak-Manus-Kavieng-Rabaul route — twice a week in each direction. If you want to visit Manus you must plan your schedule carefully or be prepared to hang loose waiting for the next flight out. The airport at Momote looks just like what it is — a big runway built many years ago at vast expense and not much used since.

New Ireland

Area: 9974 square km
Population: 58,0000

New Ireland is the long, narrow island north of New Britain, it's little known and relatively unvisited, yet it has one of the longest records of contact with European civilisation in Papua New Guinea. European explorers had sailed through St George's channel, which separates New Ireland from New Britain, from the early 1600s, and St George's Bay, near the south-east tip, was a popular watering spot for early sailing ships in the region. Later, New Ireland developed lucrative copra plantations for the Germans and the first extensive road network in New Guinea was built here.

HISTORY

At the same time as they chanced upon the Admiralty Islands in 1516-17, the Dutch explorers Schouten and Le Maire "discovered" New Ireland, although they did not know it was an island. Later, in 1700, the flamboyant British buccaneer-explorer William Dampier, sailed through the Dampier Straits between New Britain and the mainland and named St George's Bay between New Ireland and New Britain — thinking they were both one island. It was nearly 70 years later again that Carteret sailed into Dampier's

St George's Bay and discovered it was really a channel and New Ireland a separate island, not just part of New Britain. The pattern of discovery moved slowly in those days.

It was 1877 when the first missionaries arrived, always an important date in New Guinea. The Reverend George Brown, stationed in the Duke of York Islands between New Britain and New Ireland, arrived at Kalili during that year and crossed over to the north-east coast and after some suitably hair raising adventures moved back to safer climes. It was not long after that the amazing Marquis de Ray saga took place near the south-east corner of the island — see the separate section on the "Marquis de Ray and Cape Breton".

Despite its inauspicious beginnings, New Ireland soon became one of the most profitable parts of the German colony of New Guinea. Under the iron-handed German administrator Baron Boluminski, a string of copra plantations were developed along the north-east coast and a road system which was long the envy of other parts of the country was constructed.

Boluminski died, of heatstroke, before the Australian takeover, and although his road (it still bears his name) was gradually extended, in other respects the island simply marked time. When WW II spread to the Pacific, New Ireland fell almost immediately and Kavieng was subsequently developed into a major Japanese base, although never a rival to Rabaul. Most of the Australians in Kavieng managed to escape but those who chose to stay behind as coastwatchers were gradually captured as the Japanese extended their control over the island.

Like Rabaul, the Japanese held the island right until the final surrender and, again like Rabaul, although the Allies made no attempt to retake New Ireland they inflicted enormous damage upon the island. Kavieng, the main Japanese base, was comprehensively flattened and the Boluminski Highway and its adjoining plantations were severely damaged since the Japanese used it to move supplies down the coast and across to Rabaul. Extensive redevelopment since the war has restored the productive copra plantations along the highway and coffee, rubber and timber industries have also developed. Kavieng is also an important fishing port and has a major, Japanese developed, tuna fishing base.

GEOGRAPHY

New Ireland is long, narrow and mountainous. For most of its length the island is only six to ten km wide with a high spine falling straight to the sea on the south-west coast and bordered by a narrow, but fertile, coastal strip on the north-east coast. It is along this strip that the efficient New Ireland copra producers are based. The highest peak in the central Schleinitz Range is just under 1500 metres. The island bulges out at the south-eastern end and here the mountains of the Hans Meyer Range and the Verron Range are somewhat higher, the tallest peak reaches 2399 metres. Despite the narrow channel that separates this part of New Ireland from New Britain there is no comparable volcanic activity in New Ireland.

New Ireland province also includes a number of offshore islands. The major island is New Hanover, also known as Lavongai, off the north-west end of New Ireland. Well offshore from the north-east coast are the islands of Tabar, Lihir, Tanga and Feni. Further off to the north-west is the large island of Mussau in the St Matthias Group and the smaller islands of Emira and Tench.

KAVIENG

A somnolent little town — the very image of a Somerset Maughan south sea island port. It's even hard to pinpoint the centre of town although it would have to be Coronation Drive which not only has the hotel and the club but also the Air Niugini office, the post office and, of course, Beeps — Burns Philp if you're new to PNG. The nicest part of Kavieng is the harbour drive, a gently curving road, shaded by huge trees and with most of Kavieng's points of historical interest dotted along it.

Harbour Drive

Starting from the Coronation Drive intersection you come to a small local market and, on your left, a gentle grassy slope leading up to the District Commissioner's residence. The slope, with a jumble of paving stones along each side, is all that is left of the imposing stairway to Boluminski's residence. The legendary German administrator's home was destroyed during WW II and the far less imposing District Commissioner's residence built on the same site. A few other stones and bits of paving can be seen on top of the ridge. Further along this waterfront ridge is a large Japanese gun still pointing, futilely, out to sea from its original mounting point.

Down at the shorefront a small, inconspicuous workshop houses another New Ireland relic — the castings to hold the stone grain grinding wheel for the Marquis de Ray's ill fated project. The wheel itself is in Rabaul but the castings are in remarkably good shape with their date of manufacture, 1852, clearly visible.

The main wharf area looms up next, then an ugly shark proof swimming enclosure. Across the road, and another hundred metres along, is the old cemetery with Boluminski's grave, marked by a plain cross, taking pride of place.

The Harbour

Kavieng has a large and very beautiful harbour and a day can profitably be spent having a look at it. The fishing enjoys a high reputation, particularly game fishing if that's your blood sport. Keep your ears open in the hotel or club and you may get a chance to invite yourself along for a fishing trip. If not, then a wander along the waterfront should turn up a *mons*, the graceful outboard powered canoes, bound somewhere or other. There are more or less fixed charges for trips out to various islands or you can arrange a charter or a "drop me off, pick me up later" trip.

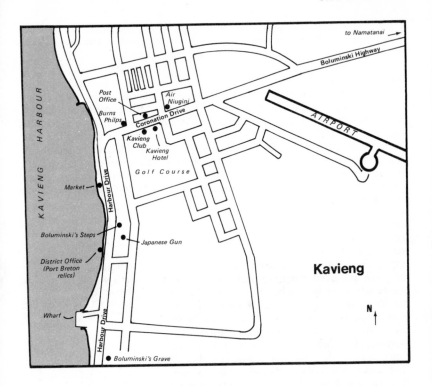

Kavieng

A good place for the latter would be the idyllic little island of Edmago. A tiny dot with palm trees, white sand beach all the way round and beautiful clear water over the coral. Finding a way in through the shallow coral to the shore is not easy. On the way out there, you'll pass the Japanese tuna processing plant on a large island. The tuna are salted or frozen for export and a large fleet of tuna boats plus their mothership patrol the waters around New Ireland. Further out is the island of New Sulaman — another popular local picnic spot where you can see copra being prepared by the handful of local families living there.

Shark Calling
New Ireland is the centre for the art of shark calling, shark callers can be found at Kontu and Tabar. Certain men have the ability to "call up" sharks. The unfortunate shark swims up to the caller's boat where they can be speared, netted or even, if they are small enough, grabbed. A variant on shark calling is the shark propellor: a noose is hung with half coconut shells which make a rattling noise which attracts the shark up through the noose.

A rope attached to the noose is connected to a wooden propellor which is spun round to tighten the noose and simultaneously pull in the rope. Good-bye shark.

Close to Kavieng

If you've got transport there are a number of points of interest within a few minutes drive of Kavieng. A couple of km out of town along the Boluminski Highway, a little pathway leads off the road to a limestone cave filled with crystal clear water. You have to know where it is to find the trail. During WW II the Japanese used this grotto as a drinking water source. At Utu village the high school has a small museum which you can look around, if you can find someone who can locate the right key to the door. There are exhibitions of Malanggan carvings, ancient stone tools and vessels and a shark catching propellor.

Accommodation in Kavieng

The *Kavieng Hotel* is another of those drowsy places out of *Tales of the South Pacific*. A large dog, draped across the doorway for most of the day, doesn't even deign to wake up as hotel guests step over him. The fan and neon light in my room must have had similar ideas since they both required a kick to wake them up. There are a variety of rooms from fan cooled single/doubles at K13/K19.50 up through air-conditioned rooms, air-conditioned with private facilities and a new motel style block where singles/doubles cost K21/K30. All rates include breakfast, lunch is K3, dinner K4.50.

Kavieng Hotel
Bookings: PO Box 4,
    Kavieng
Tel: 94 1448
Rooms: 38
Tariff: K13 to 21 sgls incl
    breakfast

The Kavieng Club is only a couple of doors down the road and it has some accommodation — self contained rooms at K8 per person, K12 with air-conditioning. The club has a dining rooms — where you can get something like steak and salad for K2, also good sandwiches. As usual they are quite happy to sign in casual visitors. The club also shows films a couple of times a week. Apart from these two places Kavieng doesn't even have a Haus Kai, although there may be plans to set one up. The Kavieng Hotel has a Friday lunchtime smorgasbord for K3, the club has a Saturday evening barbecue.

BOLUMINSKI HIGHWAY

New Ireland's autocratic administrator, Herr Boluminski, achieved one thing that was not managed on the mainland until well into the '50s. He built a long road. When WW I cut short the period of German rule the Boluminski Highway already ran 100 km out of Kavieng along the north-east coast. Under the Australians it was gradually extended and it now reaches about 80 km beyond Namatanai to Rei, before petering out into a 4-wheel drive track. There are also a number of crossings from the east to the west coast and a generally acceptable road along that coast. New Ireland is extremely well endowed with roads by Papua New Guinea standards.

Boluminski built the road by simply requiring that each village along the coast should construct and maintain their section. On his tours of inspection, Boluminski would summon the villagers to personally push his carriage over any deteriorated sections and woe betide them if repairs were not underway when he returned.

The highway is paved with koronos, crushed coral, a fine surface for an unsealed road although the glare is rather hard on the eyes in bright conditions and when it's wet it acts like grinding paste on car tyres. Almost all the way along, the coast is one continuous copra plantation — in places cocoa trees fill the gaps between the palms. The island is very narrow so the streams that run down from the central mountains are short, sharp and delightfully clear.

Libba village, just before Konos, is a good place to look for Malanggan carvings — see the separate note. Konos itself is the approximate halfway point to Namatanai and the only major village along the road. It's also the loading point for Japanese timber ships which collect logs from the project operating from a little beyond Konos all the way to Namatanai. About 30 km from Konos, near the Lemerica Plantation, a new road leads up onto the Lelet Plateau. There's an enormously deep limestone cave here, but as of yet nobody has reached its full depth. There are also bat caves near Mongop. The isolated people of the Lelet Plateau will be brought into closer contact with the people along the coast when the new road is completed.

Beyond here the road climbs a couple of times and occasionally deteriorates a little, but in general it continues to hug the coast all the way to Namatanai and beyond. Although there are many fine stretches of white sand, backed by the obligatory palm trees, the swimming is not so good on most of the coast because the water is very shallow and rocky until it suddenly drops steeply away. Pinis Passage, just on the Namatanai side of Konos, is a popular small beach.

The Marquis de Ray & Port Breton
The story of the colony of Cape Breton and the Marquis de Ray is one of the more outrageous in the European development of the Pacific. The Marquis had never set foot on New Ireland, yet on the frail basis of a ship's log he contrived to sell hundreds of hectares of land to gullible would be settlers at the equivalent of about 40c an acre. He raised no less than $60,000 (an amazing sum for 1879) on the basis of his flimsy prospectus but many of his unfortunate colonists paid with their lives as well as their savings.

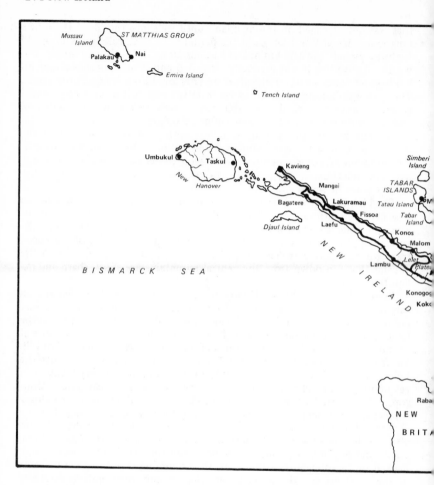

The Marquis had shown Cape Breton, near Lambon on Cape St George, as a thriving settlement with fertile soil, perpetual sunshine and friendly natives. In actual fact there had been no development at all, the settlers were dumped off into a tangled jungle. The rainfall was so heavy that even today there has been virtually no development of the area. The Reverend George Brown, an early visitor to this part of New Ireland, had found the natives very far from friendly.

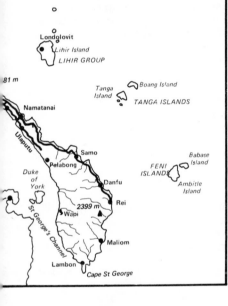

New Ireland

Malanggan Carvings

Ten years ago it was widely reported that the art of Malanggan carving had completely died out. Now there has been a modest revival although finding carvings for sale can be difficult. One carver making these interesting artifacts with their American Indian totem pole look, can be found in a coastal village about midway between Kavieng and Namatanai. An American collector prompted Hosea Linge, the son of a famous carver, to resurrect the forgotten craft. You can find him, and his carvings, at Libba, a small village about 22 km before Konos.

The Malanggan carvings were just part of a whole series of ceremonies and rituals which were centred on the north coast, east of Kavieng. The carvings would be displayed during initiation and burial rites. Only one man in a tribal group had the right to carve or display the Malanggans and it was a matter of considerable prestige.

On Masahet Island, a beautiful little isle near Lihir, with a population of less than a thousand, the Catholic mission church has Malanggan carved posts. Panamecho, a village on the west coast, has some old Malanggan carvings. Other places of interest for artifacts on New Ireland are Le Musmus on the west coast where shell money is still made as it is also on Lihir Island.

With only three weeks' supplies and such useful equipment as a grain grinding wheel for an area where grain would never grow, the settlers soon started to die like flies. It's doubtful whether malaria or starvation took the larger toll but the Marquis helped things along by sending supply ships from Australia with useful cargoes like cases of notepaper or loads of bricks. Not to mention three more shiploads of naive land-buyers from Europe.

Eventually the pitiful survivors were rescued by Thomas Farrel and his wife Emma, who later became famous as Queen Emma. Much of the equipment abandoned on the beaches of Cape Breton was used to construct her magnificent mansion near Rabaul. Although most of the rescued settlers were sent on to Australia, one 16 year old did eventually become a successful plantation holder — but on New Britain not New Ireland. The Cape Breton grain grinding wheel can still be seen in a small park off Mango Avenue in Rabaul. The crazy Marquis ended his days in a lunatic asylum in France.

NAMATANIA

A green, quiet, little town midway down the coast, Namatanai is only a 15 minute flight from Rabaul. It was an important station in German days and the Namatanai Hotel is on the site of the old German station house. You can find the grave of Scheringer, the German administrator who, like Boluminski, died in 1913, in the picturesque old graveyard down the road from the National Works compound on the other side of the airstrip.

Just before you enter the town from Kavieng, the road goes through a deep cutting, the old road winds off below it and down on the shore there is a jumble of Japanese tanks and guns which were bulldozed off after the war. From the road you can only see one rusting tank — you have to clamber down the steep cliff face to see the whole pile of them. About 20 km before Namatania, there is the mid-section of a Japanese bomber aircraft sitting by the roadside.

Accommodation in Namatanai

The *Namatania Hotel* has the easygoing atmosphere that you'd expect in some south-seas hostelry. There are just four rooms — each taking up to three people — with fans, private facilities but just cold water (no real hardship). Per person cost is K9.50 bed only. Breakfast costs K2.50, lunch or dinner costs K3.50 or you can opt for full board for K18 per day. The hotel is run by Bernie Gash, an easygoing character to match his establishment. It's right down by the waterfront, near the new wharf.

Namatanai Tavern
Bookings: Post Office, Namatanai
Tel: Namatanai 25
Rooms: 4
Tariff: K18 per person incl all meals

THE SOUTH

The southern "bulge" of the island is still relatively isolated because the roads are not so good there. The rugged mountains and heavy rainfall further complicate things. The people in the south are similar to the Tolais of East New Britain, but are less sophisticated than the other New Irelanders who have long been connected by the coast road.

NEW HANOVER

The island of New Hanover, or Lavongai, largest, after New Ireland itself, in the New Ireland Province, is a mountainous, isolated island with productive copra plantations on the volcanic soils of its coastline. The people of New Hanover are best known for their brave attempt to buy Lyndon Johnson. When the first House of Assembly elections in PNG were held, the New Hanover voters decided, quite reasonably, that if this was democracy and they could vote for whomever they chose they might as well vote for Lyndon Johnson. New Hanover went "all the way with LBJ", but when the American President showed no sign of taking up the cause for the island the islanders decided to take more direct action. They refused to pay their taxes and instead put the money into a fund to "buy" LBJ. They raised quite a large sum but even this example of Texas style capitalism failed to bring the man to New Hanover. Just another example of cargo cult.

EASTERN ISLANDS

There are four island groups strung off the north-east coast of New Ireland — Tabar, Lihir, Tanga and Feni. There are a number of airstrips on the island and it is also possible to get out to them by local shipping services; they are only 30 to 50 km offshore and clearly visisble from the coast. In particular there are ships running out from Konos to Tabar reasonably often. Tabar is thought to be the original home of the Malanggan carving and ceremonies. The islands are all quite beautiful and the island peoples are great canoeists. There is no organised accommodation on any of them so they are very much places for the adventurous travellers with open-ended schedules.

ST MATTHIAS GROUP

The island of Mussau, Emirau and Tench are some distance north-west of New Ireland; they put up determined resistance to the early European take-over. Tench was the last "uncontrolled" part of the New Ireland region. During the war there was an American base at Emirau with a larger force than the entire present day population of the group. Today they have reverted to their former isolated ways, the people build fine, large canoes which can carry 30 or more people and do not have outriggers. The people on Tench are noted for their woven mats. These islands and New Hanover make up the sub-province of Lamet — the name comes from the first letters of LAvongai (New Hanover), Mussau, Emirau and Tench.

GETTING AROUND

The Boluminski Highway runs 270 km from Kavieng to Namatanai and for about 80 km beyond Namatania is still in reasonably good shape even for conventional vehicles. There used to be a regular service between those two towns but although it has stopped there are still a fair number of PMVs zipping back and forth on weekdays. The Highway is not a bustling main artery at the best of times and on weekends it can be very quiet indeed. So be prepared for some long roadside waits if you don't get a direct ride. Straight through it takes about five or six hours but I've got no idea of the cost — I was told various figures from K2 to K20. When I travelled down the road it cost only K2 but more than half of the ride was hitched rather than PMVed.

There are four main roads crossing from the north-east to the less visited south-west. They are from Fangalawa to Panamefei/Lesmusmus, Karu to Konogogo, Bo (near Namatanai) to Labur Bay and from Bo to Ulupatur. Although some of these trans-island roads can be rough or even impassable to conventional vehicles during the wet, the longest is only 11 km. It's a narrow island! The south-west coast road is very rough for 40 km in the north and 41 km in the centre.

Talair have a reasonable selection of flights around New Ireland as well as across to New Britain. Kavieng-Namatanai costs K37, to Tasku on New Hanover for K13, to Mussau Island in the St Matthias Group for K35, Mapua on Tabar Island for K29 or Londolovit on Lihir Island for K42. From Namatanai it costs K23 to Boang on Tanga Island, K18 to Londolovit on Lihir Island.

GETTING THERE

Apart from the usual "if you're lucky" shipping services, you'll have to fly to New Ireland. There are frequent ships through Kavieng and you should have no great difficulty in finding something, going somewhere, fairly quickly. Elsewhere it's not so easy, although Rabaul looks a very short distance from New Ireland, there appears to be very few shipping services directly across — you'll usually have to go all the way to Kavieng.

Air Niugini have flights from Rabaul to Kavieng six days a week and from Wewak (via Manus) twice a week, also from Lae direct twice a week. Air Niugini fares are from Rabaul K24, from Manus K40, from Wewak K69 and from Lae K75. There is a daily flight between Namatanai and Rabaul with Talair — if you miss it there's a good chance that another Talair plane or some other charter carrier will come in during the day. The short hop takes only about 15 minutes and costs K18.

New Britain

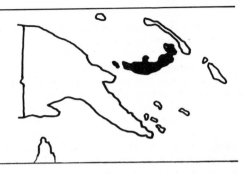

Area: 39,807 square km
Population: 193,000

The island of New Britain, largest of Papua New Guinea's offshore islands, offers a strange contrast between its two provinces. East New Britain ends in the Gazelle Peninsula, the part of PNG where contact with European civilisation has been longest, where the people are probably the most economically and culturally sophisticated, and where, due to the high fertility of the volcanic soil, despite the high population density they are also among the most affluent people in the country.

In complete contrast, the other end of the island, West New Britain, is comparatively sparsely populated, little developed and did not come into serious contact with Europeans until the 1960s. For most visitors New Britain will mean Rabaul — the beautiful harbourside city on the Gazelle Peninsula with its dramatic, sometimes too dramatic, cluster of volcanoes.

HISTORY
East New Britain's history has been far from a placid one and in terms of contact with Europeans it has been one of the longest, if not the longest, in Papua New Guinea. Early explorers from Europe spent much more time around the northern islands than they did around the mainland. William Dampier, the swashbuckling English pirate-adventurer-explorer, was the first to land in the area. He arrived here early in the year 1700 and named the island New Britain when he sailed around the east coast of New Britain and New Ireland. Although he proved New Britain was an island, separated from the New Guinea mainland by Dampier Strait, it was not until 1767 that Phillip Carteret converted Dampier's St George's Bay into St George's Channel when he sailed through it and discovered that New Ireland was actually a separate island, not part of New Britain.

A hundred years passed with only occasional contact although many whalers and other sailors passed through St George's Channel and sometimes paused to water or provision their boats. Then in the 1870s, traders started to arrive, often in search of copra, and in 1875 the legendary Methodist missionary Dr George Brown showed up and with six Fijians set up the first mission station in the Duke of York Islands, which are situated in St George's Channel.

179

Brown could hardly be faulted for lack of energy, apart from working flat out on converting the heathen he also found time to be a keen amateur vulcanologist, a linguist, a scientist, an anthropologist and did a fair bit of local exploring. His reception was not the best and only one of his original Fijian assistants survived the first turbulent years in New Britain, but Brown did, and left a respected and even loved man.

Not only the missionaries were active in the area. In 1878 a Mrs Emma Forsyth arrived here from Samoa, started a trading business at Mioko in the Duke of York Islands and took the first steps towards her remarkable fame and fortune. In 1882 Captain Simpson sailed in on HMS *Blanche*, named the harbour where the town of Rabaul now stands after himself, and the bay after his ship. Two years later the Germans, thoroughly beaten by malaria and the climate on the north New Guinea coast, moved their HQ to Kokopo on New Britain, they named it Herbertshohe.

In 1910 the Germans moved round the bay to Rabaul's present site, the name means mangrove in the local dialect for the town site was in the middle of a mangrove swamp. The Germans did not have long to enjoy what soon became a very beautiful town, for when WW I arrived Australia invaded New Britain in order to take the German radio station at Bita Paka. The first six Australians to die in the war lost their lives here, along with one German and 30 of their native soldiers. A larger contingent of Australians also died when their submarine mysteriously disappeared off the New Britain coast during the attack.

For the rest of the war things carried on much as before since Australia was in no position to take over the efficiently run and highly profitable German copra plantations. They were allowed to keep on operating under close military supervision. At the end of the war the unfortunate planters all had their plantations expropriated and were shipped back to Germany where they were compensated, as part of the war reparations agreement, in German marks which soon became totally worthless in the bout of hyper-inflation suffered by Germany in the early '20s. One doubly unfortunate individual made his way back to New Britain from Germany, started again from scratch and once more built up a thriving plantat-

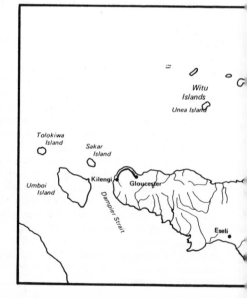

ion, but neglected to take out Australian citizenship and in WW II had it all expropriated again.

Between the wars Rabaul continued on its busy and profitable way, now as the capital of Australian New Guinea, until nature decided to shake it up a little. East New Britain is the most volcanically active area of Papua New Guinea and nowhere is this more evident than in Rabaul. Blanche Bay, Rabaul's beautiful harbour, is simply the flooded crater of an enormously large volcano — it's over three km wide. That cataclysmic eruption took place eons ago but the Rabaul area has had many more recent upheavals — as the string of volcano cones around the rim of the super-crater indicates.

Sputterings and earthquakes are an everyday occurence in East New Britain and it takes more than a little shake to upset the citizens of Rabaul. In 1971 a major quake was followed by a tidal wave that temporarily swamped the city centre, but the last disastrous upheaval took place in 1937. There was plenty of warning — minor quakes became more and more frequent and around Vulcan, a low lying island in the harbour which had appeared after an 1878 eruption, the water boiled and dead fish floated to the surface. But when the big bang happened it was loud and unexpected. Vulcan suddenly erupted, killing over 500 Tolais assembled there for a festival. All night it continued to erupt and, 27 hours later when it finally stopped, the low flat island was a massive mountain joined to the mainland.

The harbour was coated in yellow pumice stone and everything was covered in a film of ash and dust, brought down by a violent thunderstorm that

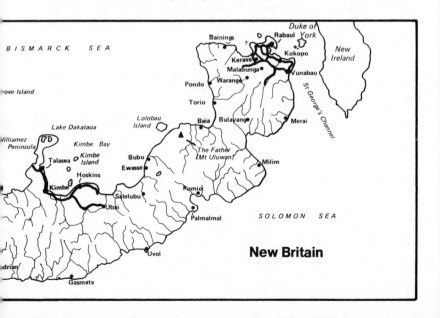

accompanied the eruptions. Nor was that all, Matupit now started to fume and continued erupting for three days. Months later, when an $80,000 clean up had restored the town, Matupit continued to rumble and cough. The frangipani earned its special place in Rabaul after that eruption for it was the first flower to bloom through the layers of dust and ash.

Government minds soon turned to thoughts of transferring the New Guinea capital to a safer site. The mainland had barely been touched when Australia took over German New Guinea but now it was much more widely explored and the goldrush in Wau and Bulolo had prompted much development. Accordingly the decision was taken to transfer the HQ to Lae, but the move had barely been commenced when WW II arrived in Rabaul. It was to have an impact even more dramatic than the volcanoes.

After the Japanese attack on Pearl Harbour it was obvious that Rabaul would soon be in danger, women and children were evacuated by the end of December 1941, but there were still about 400 Australian civilians in the town when a huge bombing raid on 22 January heralded the coming invasion. The following day the small contingent of Australian troops was completely crushed by the Japanese assault. Those who managed to escape found themselves cut off in the jungle, isolated from the New Guinea mainland where, in any case, the Japanese had already captured Lae and Salamua. In an amazing feat of endurance patrol officers based in New Britain, including the legendary J K McCarthy who retells the operation in his book *Patrol Into Yesterday*, shepherded the surviving troops along the inhospitable, roadless coast to the southern tip of the island where a flotilla of private boats performed a minor-Dunkirk and eventually rescued 400 of the 700 men who had escaped the Japanese.

The civilians left in Rabaul were not so fortunate and none of them were ever heard of again. It was later established that they were loaded on the prison ship *Montevideo Maru* and on their way to internment in Japan the ship was torpedoed by an American submarine off the Philippines, sinking with all the prisoners aboard.

The Japanese intended to use Rabaul as a major supply base for their steady march south, but the tables were soon to be turned. With their defeat at Guadalcanal in the Solomons, at Milne Bay and Buna on the New Guinea mainland, and with their naval power shattered from the Battle of the Coral Sea, they were soon not advancing anywhere and instead turned to making Rabaul an utterly impregnable fortress which they would yield to the Allied advance only at enormous cost. They dug 500 km of tunnels into the hills around Rabaul, a honeycomb of interconnecting passages used for storage, hospitals, anti-aircraft guns, bunkers, gun emplacements and barracks. At the peak of the war 97,000 Japanese troops were stationed on the Gazelle Peninsula, today the total local population is only about 60,000. They even had 800 Japanese and Korean whores. The harbour was laced with mines and the roads were camouflaged with trees. And the Allies never came.

MacArthur had learnt the lesson of Guadalcanal and Buna where the bitter fighting had led to enormous casualties on both sides. Never again did the Japanese and Allied forces meet head-on, bases like Rabaul were simply bypassed. With the Japanese air force unable to compete effectively with Allied airpower, over 20,000 tons of bombs were rained down upon the Gazelle Peninsula. The Japanese forces were kept underground and impotent. When the war ended they were still there, trapped in a bastion which may well have been invulnerable but was never put to the test.

Rabaul was utterly flattened, photographs taken just after the Japanese surrendered show Mango Avenue, the main street in Rabaul, marked only by occasional heaps of bricks. In the harbour over 40 ships lay at the bottom. It took two years just to transfer all the troops back to Japan. Meanwhile they were held in huge internment camps.

Rabaul soon bounced back although today the evidence of the war is still readily seen. The hills are riddled with tunnels although many are sealed up for safety's sake. Remnants of barges, aircraft, guns, cranes and other military equipment can be seen littered around the area. For the keen diver the harbour bottom is carpeted with sunken shipping. The transfer of the New Guinea headquarters from Rabaul to Lae, which it was feared would be disastrous to Rabaul, proved to be redundant for Papua and New Guinea were now administered as one territory and the capital was Port Moresby.

Rabaul came back into the limelight in the years leading up to self-government and then independence. The Tolai people of the Gazelle Peninsula, with their long contact with European culture, together with steady efforts by the missions, has led to their having a high general level of education. Also their land is remarkably fertile and was developed into plantations by the Germans, starting almost one hundred years ago. So together with their high level of education they are relatively well fed and wealthy; no Tolai does the boring unskilled work on a copra plantation — men from the less affluent Highlands or Sepik regions must be imported to perform this dull labour. Their bounteous peninsula is heavily populated so there are considerable land pressures and these forces are compounded by the large percentage of land which was bought from the Tolais by the Germans and is still owned by Europeans.

Land has become a major issue in East New Britain and discontent rose to a fever pitch as the concepts of self government came into existence. Many Tolais wanted all land bought from them in the German days, when they were considerably less sophisticated in their dealings with the west, to be returned to them. A political organisation, known as the Mataungan Association, sprang up with the aim of subverting the Australian managed local councils and self government programmes. The Tolais wanted self government but on their own terms, they successfully boycotted the first pre-independence elections and then demanded their own Mataungan leaders be given the reins of power. The problem did not go away with independence but does appear to have quietened down considerably today.

Queen Emma

Queen Emma was one of those larger than life people destined to become legends in their own lifetime. Born in Samoa of an American father and Samoan mother, her first husband disappeared at sea and in 1878 she teamed up with Thomas Farrell, an Australian trader, and started a trading business at Mioko on the Duke of York Islands. Emma was an astute businesswoman and she soon realised that a plantation on the rich volcanic soil of the Gazelle Peninsula would be an excellent investment.

With her brother-in-law Richard Parkinson, who conveniently happened to be a botanist, Emma soon acquired land at Ralum, near Kokopo and became the manager and owner of the first real plantation in New Guinea. When Thomas Farrell died he was succeeded by a steady stream of lovers.

By the time the Germans arrived in New Britain, Emma had extended her little empire to several other plantations, a number of ships and a whole string of trade stores. She astutely made use of her American citizenship to avoid possible German takeovers. Emma built a mansion called Gunantambu, you can still see the regal stairway to the front door today, and entertained like royalty. There was her own wharf where she met guests, accompanied by her friends and servants, dressed in the finest clothes Europe could provide — then up to the mansion to dine on imported food and champagne.

"Queen Emma" may have been a joke at first, but it was soon a name she had earned. For many years Emma was faithful to her lover Agostino Stalio, but after his death she married Paul Kolbe. He died in Monte Carlo in 1913 and Emma herself died a few days later. Her empire fell apart soon after she was gone and her fine home was destroyed during the last war.

GEOGRAPHY

New Britain is a long, narrow, mountainous country. It is nearly 600 km from end to end but at its widest point is only 80 km across. The central mountain range runs from one end of the country to the other. It is a harsh and rugged island, split by gorges and rapid rivers and blanketed in thick rainforest. The highest mountain is The Father (Mt Uluwan) an active volcano rising to nearly 2300 metres. The north-eastern end of the island terminates in the heavily populated, highly fertile and dramatically volcanic Gazelle Peninsula, with the three peaks known as The Mother, North Daughter and South Daughter.

New Britain lies across the direction of the monsoon winds so the rainy season comes at opposite times of the year on the north and south coast. From December to April the mountain barrier brings the heavy rain down on the north coast, while in June to October it is the south coast that has the rain. Rainfall varies widely around the country, at Pomio on the south coast it averages 8500 mm a year (nearly 30 foot of rain!) while in relatively dry Rabaul it is only 3000 mm annually — still 10 foot of rain a year. Pomio once had over a metre of rain in one week.

PEOPLE

Surprisingly the Tolais are not the original inhabitants of the Gazelle Peninsula. They are thought to have moved to the Duke of York Islands from New Ireland and then on to the main island where they killed (and ate!) most of the Sulka and Bainings people who once lived on the peninsula. Those who escaped, fled into the mountains behind the Gazelle. The Bainings still perform their spectacular fire dances, costumed in huge, Disney like masks. If you are lucky enough to be in Rabaul when a fire dance is on, usually at Gaulim, it is an experience not to be missed.

There are probably four or five thousand Bainings people left, mainly up in the rugged mountains behind the Gazelle. The Mokolkols, a group of nomadic bushmen who even after WW II continued to make murderous raids on peaceful coastal villages, were far fewer in number. It was not until 1950 that the government finally managed to capture a handful of these people, even though they lived within 100 km of Rabaul! After a civilising spell in the big city, the captives led government officers back to the rest of their clan — there were only 30 in all.

When the first missionaries arrived the Tolai were still a pretty wild bunch — a long way from their current status as probably the most politically and economically sophisticated people in PNG. The Tolai Duk-Duk still continue though — at one time they were a form of secret society and a force of law and order in Tolai villages. A law-breaker would find a weirdly costumed Duk-Duk at his front door — and mend his ways or else. Today their function is probably more ceremonial than official but they can still be seen, and still have a surprising amount of local power.

At one time Rabaul had a very large Chinese minority — they originally came to the area as cooks and houseboys for the German planters. Even after WW II Rabaul still had a large and busy Chinatown but many of the Chinese left at independence and today the Rabaul Chinatown is a shadow of its former importance.

RABAUL

Arching round Simpson Harbour, Rabaul vies with Madang for the title of most beautiful town in Papua New Guinea — or even the Pacific. It may not have Madang's beautiful waterways and parks but it does have the dramatic volcanoes towering over it on all sides. There is probably more to do and see around Rabaul than any other town in PNG. You can climb volcanoes, inspect war relics, dive on some of the best coral (and wrecks) in PNG and to top all that there is a better choice of hotels and restaurants than you will find in almost any other town. One word of caution for Rabaul, earth tremors are still common so don't be surprised if the grounds sometimes seems to shake beneath you.

Museum

A tiny war museum stands opposite the New Guinea Club on the corner of Central Avenue and Clarke St. The club, incidentally, was built just before the war, gutted during the bombing and subsequently rebuilt to the original plan. The museum is housed in Admiral Onishi's war time command bunk-

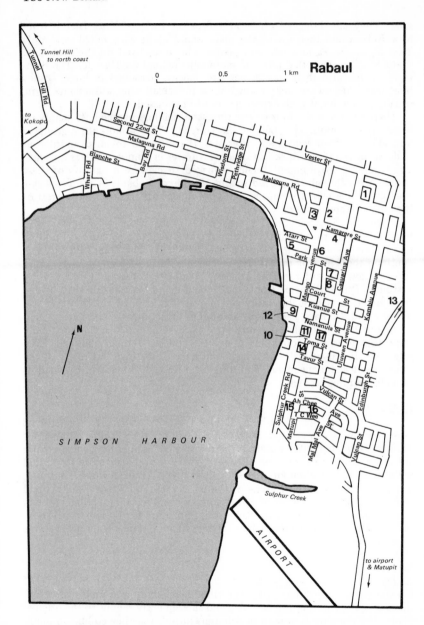

Rabaul

0   0.5   1 km

RABAUL		9	Travelodge
		10	RSL Club
1	Rabaul Market	11	Air Niugini
2	Ascot Hotel	12	Rabaul Yacht Club
3	Port Breton Wheel	13	to Orchard Park &
4	Orim's Lodge		Lookout
5	Rabaul Community Hostel	14	Kaivuna Motel
6	Cafe de Paris	15	New Guinea Shells
7	War Museum	16	Chang's Restaurant
8	New Guinea Club	17	Post Office

er. Outside there's a lightweight Japanese tank, an anti-aircraft gun and a field gun. Inside there's a miscellaneous collection of odds and ends and in two control rooms the Japanese maps can still be seen on the walls. There are some interesting photos of Allied raids on Japanese ships in the harbour. A photo looking up Mango Avenue just after the end of the war shows just how complete the destruction was.

Other WW II Relics
There are countless tunnels and caverns riddling the ground around Rabaul, many of them are closed up now but a knowledgeable local guide can still take you around some amazing complexes. One of the most interesting, but now closed, is the tunnel which used to house the Japanese phone exchange. There is an anti-aircraft gun near the Vulcanology Observatory (one of many) while on the waterfront a scuttled Japanese ship was filled with cement and became a wharf.

Around Rabaul
In the little park, towards the market end of Mango Avenue, by the town and Gazelle area maps, stands the grinding wheel from Port Breton (see New Ireland). It illustrates the complete futility of the Marquis de Ray's crazy project — nobody was going to grow grain in this climate! Across from the Rabaul Community Hostel on the waterfront is a memorial to the Rabaul prisoners on board the *Montevideo Maru*. For years there was a considerable controversy over whether or not they were ever actually despatched to Japan or simply executed in Rabaul, but it is now generally accepted that they did indeed meet their fate on that ship.

The Market
The market, or "bung", in Rabaul is the most bustling and colourful in Papua New Guinea. Like every PNG market it really comes to life on Saturdays. You'll see a wider selection of fruit and vegetables (and larger quantities) than anywhere else in PNG. Scattered amongst the food stalls are sellers of bamboo combs, wicker baskets, shells and shell jewellery.

New Guinea Shells

If you're interested in shells then head for New Guinea Shells on the corner of Ah Chee St and Mango Avenue. There is a large and varied collection of shells not only from the waters around Rabaul but also of land snails — PNG has some amazingly colourful varieties. Also look for the insects preserved in clear plastic. When I looked in there was a live *Valentia* slithering reasonably happily around a fish tank; little realising that the home on his back was worth over K1000 to a collector. Considerably more than his two *Golden Cowrie* companions which were worth only about K300 each.

Brian Parkinson, the local shell expert, stresses that there is probably no such thing as a "rare" shell — just ones that are difficult to find. The *Valentia* normally lives at depths of 200 metres or more so they are only rarely caught up in fishing nets or found when they wander up to shallower waters waters — as their *Valentia* had done. Shells are normally collected by scuba divers at night, during the day they go into hiding. Although some of the shells are sold to local collectors or visitors, in the main it's an export business to shell enthusiasts or shops abroad.

German Residency

Northing remains of the old German residency apart from the stone gateposts and the crumbling staircase. The site offers fine views as it is situated on top of a ridge overlooking Rabaul in one direction and out to the open sea in the other. Those two little cement footpaths from the car park to the two lookout points? For Missus Queen's last visit to PNG.

Orchids

The Rabaul orchid collection overlooks the town from up the hill towards the old German residency. There's also a collection of parrots and New Britain cockatoos here, a large and hungry crocodile and a couple of cassowaries.

Accommodation in Rabaul -- the top end

The number one hotel in Rabaul is the *Travelodge*, on the corner of Mango Avenue (the main street) and Namanula St — right across from the Air Niugini office. The Travelodge has 40 rooms, all air-conditioned and with private facilities. Room-only costs are K21 single, K29 double or twin, K34 family. There is also a pleasant swimming pool and the evocatively named Queen Emma's Room restaurant. Whether you stay here or not, drop in to look at the photographs of the 1971 tidal wave which temporarily inundated the Travelodge.

Vying with the Travelodge for number one

Rabaul Travelodge
Address: Mango Ave,
Bookings: PO Box 449
Tel: 92 2111
Rooms: 40 family
Tariff: sgl - K21, dbl - K29,
fmly - K34, room only

spot is the *Motel Kaivuna*, only about 100 metres away on the other side of Mango Avenue. Here there are 34 assorted rooms, all air-conditioned and with private facilities. Room only costs is K19.50 single, K26 double. There is a restaurant, swimming pool and a top floor open air bar area where counter style lunches are available.

The third top-end hotel is also on Mango Avenue but down at the other end of the road, close to the town centre. The *Hotel Ascot* has 43 rooms and room only costs are K20 single, K28 twin. Again all rooms are air-conditioned and have private facilities and there is a licensed restaurant.

Rabaul has one other rather interesting place that more or less bridges the gap between the top-end and bottom-end in Rabaul. Or rather out of Rabaul since the *Kulau Lodge* is a few km out, across Tunnel Hill on the north coast road. The Kulau Lodge is best know as a popular local eating spot (see Eating Out) but it also has five separate units, built like local Kunai huts but with all mod-cons and in a very pleasant garden setting right by the waterfront. The units cost K12 single, K22 double including breakfast. Worth trying if you don't mind taking the PMVs the 13 km out from town (40t a trip) or have a car available.

Accommodation in Rabaul — the bottom end

The Rabaul cheapie is probably one of the best bargains for the backpacker in all of PNG — the *Rabaul Community Hostel* on the corner of Atarr St and Cleland Drive. For K5 a night you get bed, breakfast and an evening meal. If you're a student you pay just K2.50 a night — the same as PNG nationals. Food is straightforward but quite OK — you've got to turn up on time if you want to be fed though. Breakfast consists of fruit (papaya usually), toast and tea from 6.45 to 7.30 am. Dinner is similarly basic, meat/potatoes/vegetables plus dessert — no shortage of quantity and it's available from 5.45 to 6.30 pm.

Motel Kaivuna
Address: Mango Ave
Bookings: PO Box 395
Cables: Kaivuna
Tel: 92 1766
Rooms: 34 assorted
Tariff: sgl - from K19.50,
dbl - from K26, rm only

Hotel Ascot
Address: Mango Ave
Bookings: PO Box 212
Cables: Hotel Ascot
Tel: 92 1999
Rooms: 26 sgl, 17 twin
Tariff: sgl - K20, twin -
K28, room only

Kulau Lodge
Bookings: PO Box 359,
Tel: 92 2667
Rooms: 5 units
Tariff: sgl - K10, dbl - K20,
fmly - K27, b&b

Rabaul Community Hostel
Address: Cleland Drive
Bookings: PO Box 409
Tel: 92 2325
Rooms: 10??
Tariff: per person - K5 incl
all meals, K2.50 - stdts

Orims Lodge
Address: Kamarere St
Bookings: PO Box 1208
Tel: 92 2077
Rooms: 4 twin, 3 fmly
Tariff: from K8 per person
bed only to K15 incl
all meals

The rooms, singles or doubles, although there are larger rooms for long term local residents, are spartan but reasonably comfortable. Their only drawback is that, in Chinese hotel style, the walls don't reach the floor or ceiling so noise tends to travel. There's an additional, PNG style drawback that although the place is new, modern and generally well equipped it is already showing the results of shoddy maintenance and half-hearted cleaning.

The only other place of anything like reasonable cost is *Orim's Lodge* on Kamarere St, where there are seven, straightforwards, fan-cooled rooms. Per person costs is K8 bed only, K10 including breakfast, K12.50 including dinner or K15 with all meals. There is a pleasant, large lounge-dining area.

Eating Out in Rabaul

Rabaul has an excellent choice of places to eat at. If Chinese is your style then head to Ah Chee Avenue in Rabaul's now depleted Chinatown. The atmosphere may have been considerably dampened down by the departure of so many Chinese but there are still a couple of places worth trying. The *Slamat Makan* is supposedly a Chinese Club but anyone is welcome in the restaurant. Good food, plain surroundings and service which is dependably slow — come with plenty of time. *Changs* is very similarly priced (K3.50 is about average for a main dish) and has slightly flashier, more restaurant like, surroundings plus snappier service. Again the food is very good but the quantities are probably a little smaller — if you've brought a big appetite with you.

Right in the middle of town the *Cafe de Paris* (quite a name for Rabaul) is a pleasantly relaxed and quite reasonably priced restaurant. Excellent selection of hamburgers (even a Bombay curry-burger!) and good desserts. Main dishes are around K3 to K4. Across the road, and a little further along Mango Avenue, the *Kai Kitchen* is a shiny, new take-away place — has a touch of the Kentucky Frieds about it but the food is good, better than the vast majority of PNG take-aways. The *Gazelle Cafe*, round beside the market, is more the usual local Kai Haus style.

At lunchtime or in the early evening you can get the usual excellent value meals at the various clubs around Rabaul — out of town guests always welcome. The big three are the RSL (corner of Kaunua St and Casuarina Avenue) with its Rendezvous Restaurant, the New Guinea Club (across from the Museum) and the Rabaul Yacht Club (Mango Avenue near the Kaivuna and Travelodge. There is also the *Steak House* round the harbour on Pethridge St.

For a flash night out Rabaul residents tend to head across to the *Kulau Lodge*, to dine romantically on the waterside. It's about 13 km out of town and you can count on at least K10 a head to eat here. Equally popular and somewhat lower priced is the Kulau Lodge's excellent Sunday smorgasbord. It costs K4.50 and there's an enormous variety of delicious food served on the long table in the airy dining-bar area.

The top-end hotels/motels all have their own licensed restaurants serving

pretty much the sort of food you'd expect them to serve. Good value counter style food at lunchtimes. Shoestring backpackers will find the food in
the Community Hostel is quite adequate, edible and filling. And cheap!

Handicrafts
There are no local artifacts of note around Rabaul although shell necklaces
and bracelets are popular in the market place. The carvings you will see are
modernistic or else local interpretations of other New Guinea styles — leaping dolphins, prancing sea horses or some highly painted, vaguely Sepik-ish
masks. A popular selling point is around the Travelodge Motel in the evenings. Hidden away in their bags, waiting to be whipped out at the slightest
sign of interest, are the Rabaul speciality — wooden salt and pepper shakers
in the shape of male genitals.

ROADS OUT OF RABAUL
Three roads lead out of Rabaul, connecting to the excellent bitumen road
network around the Gazelle Peninsula. The roads are another legacy of the
orderly German days for they laid them out to connect their productive
plantations. One road leads out south-east by the airstrip (and the city
dump) to Matupit Island from where you can get canoes across to Matupit
Volcano. The road to the north coast exits Rabaul via Tunnel Hill — during
the German days it actually did go through the hill in a tunnel but it was
later opened out to a cutting. The third road continues to skirt the coast
round Blanche Bay to Kokopo and beyond. Other roads turn inland from
the Kokopo Road, including the Burma Road which climbs up and over the
original huge crater rim on its way to Coastwatcher's Lookout and further
inland.

Matupit
There's a standard and a non-standard way of climbing to the crater of
Matupit — the volcano that deluged Rabaul with dust in 1937. Whichever
route you take, try to do it early in the day when it's cooler and possibly
clearer. First take a PMV to Matupit village which is just a little beyond the
airport, it's a 20t ride from Rabaul. Matupit is an island, but only barely,
since a bridge connects it with the mainland. As soon as you hop off the
PMV you'll be pounced on by someone willing to paddle you across to the
base of the cone. It costs a kina each way to scoot around Matupit Harbour
in an outrigger canoe.

You're dropped off on the beach from where a clear path runs up to the
crater, or more correctly craters since Matupit has a number of them. It's
less than a half hour's steady (and hot and sweaty) climb to the crater rim.
There's a firmly anchored rope leading down to the bottom of the crater
should you want to inspect Matupit from within as well as without. It's
still mildly active with foul, sulphur smelling smoke billowing out at various
places.

You can follow the crater (or craters) rim around in either direction although you can't do a complete circuit since there's a great gash in the rim around the back. It's worth clambering around clockwise towards the highest point for although Matupit is not the highest cone around the harbour the view from up there is very fine indeed. It's one of those places where you wish you had a camera that could take 360° pictures.

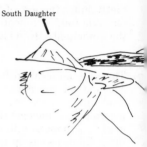

South Daughter

view from the top of Matupit volcano

When you've finished looking around you can stroll back down to your canoe or try the alternate descent by following the crater rim right round to the back of the cone and beating your way down through the bush to the coconut plantations and on to the Praed Point road where you can grab a PMV. The path is much steeper and less clearly defined than on the harbour side route. I got down by going round anti-clockwise then slithering down a steep trail — hard work. I wouldn't recommend trying to ascend that way although a PMV driver could probably point out the best starting points.

Aircraft Wreckage

Beside the Rabaul runway there's quite a mass of Japanese aircraft wreckage scattered amongst the palm trees. Just past where the road curves off from beside the strip towards Matupit village, a dirt road runs off to the right. You're unlikely to have to guide yourself as the local kids have a thriving business showing visitors to the remains. Careful you don't end up with too many guides — even at 10t a time they soon mount up!

There are two main chunks of wreckage. First you'll come to the fuselage mid-section and part of the wings of a bomber, then a little further along the much more complete wreckage of a Betty bomber — the tail section lies upside down behind it. The rising sun is still clearly visible underneath the wing. Various bits of engines, nacelles and undercarriage lie scattered around. As well as lots of Japanese aircraft wreckage the plantation also has lots of mosquitoes so come prepared or get bitten. By the bridge to Matupit village there's the much more recent wreckage of an American registered light aircraft which unfortunately managed to land amongst the palm trees instead of on the runway in 1977.

Praed Point

If you turned left off the Matupit Road, just after passing the airport, a dirt road will take you through coconut plantations, passing between Matupit and South Daughter, through Talwat village to Praed Point. There are a couple of coastal guns at Praed Point, when the Japanese invaded they were virtually the only defense Rabaul had — and were not used. On the other side of the road, as you skirt round Matupit, there is a small, peaceful Japanese war memorial. There are quite frequent PMVs along this road.

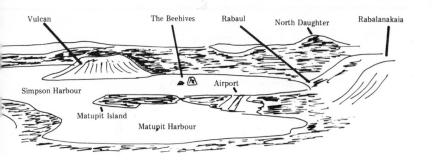

Vulcan — The Beehives — Rabaul — North Daughter — Rabalanakaia — Simpson Harbour — Airport — Matupit Island — Matupit Harbour

Vulcanology Observatory
The road to the Vulcanology Observatory turns off the Tunnel Hill road and climbs up to the top of the old crater rim, overlooking Rabaul. It is the main vulcanological station in volcanic PNG. You must phone ahead if you want to look around.

Keravat
A little beyond the Kulau Lodge on the north coast road, Keravat is a major lowland agricultural experimental station where research is carried out on coconuts, oil palms, cocoa, coffee and fruit trees. There is also a forestry department set up here.

The Beehives
The cluster of rocky peaks rising out of the centre of Simpson Harbour are said to be the hard core of the original old volcano. You can visit them by boat but the diving around them is not terribly good.

Barges
A few km out of Rabaul, on the Kokopo road, a very inconspicuous sign points towards the Japanese barge tunnel. A long passage cut into the hill houses a number of Japanese barges used, some say, to carry supplies around the coast at night. Others say they were just held in readiness for emergency use and were never actually operated. Either way they would have been winched down to the sea on a long track as the tunnel is a considerable height above sea level. There's a 20t admission charge but I wish they would charge another 20t and put some lights in or offer a portable light for hire — the tunnel is said to contain five barges, lined up nose to tail, but it fades into darkness beyond the second barge and the back three are totally invisible. The first one is badly rusted and the second little better, but the back three are said to be in reasonable condition. Parallel tunnels were used to house supplies and as offices. A little further around the bay is the wreckage of a huge crane which the Japanese towed here from Singapore. It was bombed as soon as it arrived and never actually used.

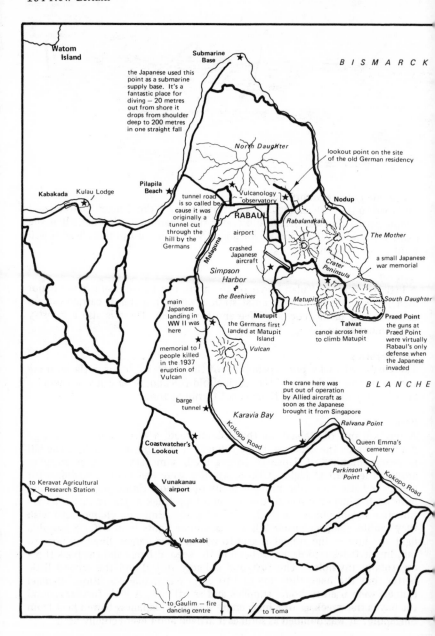

Watom Island

Submarine Base

BISMARCK

the Japanese used this point as a submarine supply base. It's a fantastic place for diving — 20 metres out from shore it drops from shoulder deep to 200 metres in one straight fall

North Daughter

lookout point on the site of the old German residency

Kabakada

Kulau Lodge

Pilapila Beach

tunnel road is so called because it was originally a tunnel cut through the hill by the Germans

Vulcanology observatory

Nodup

RABAUL

Rabalanakaia

The Mother

airport

crashed Japanese aircraft

a small Japanese war memorial

Malaguna

Simpson Harbor

Crater Peninsula

the Beehives

Matupit

South Daughter

main Japanese landing in WW II was here

Matupit

the Germans first landed at Matupit Island

Talwat

canoe across here to climb Matupit

Praed Point

the guns at Praed Point were virtually Rabaul's only defense when the Japanese invaded

memorial to people killed in the 1937 eruption of Vulcan

Vulcan

the crane here was put out of operation by Allied aircraft as soon as the Japanese brought it from Singapore

BLANCHE

barge tunnel

Karavia Bay

Ralvana Point

Kokopo Road

Queen Emma's cemetery

Coastwatcher's Lookout

Parkinson Point

Kokopo Road

to Keravat Agricultural Research Station

Vunakanau airport

Vunakabi

to Gaulim — fire dancing centre

to Toma

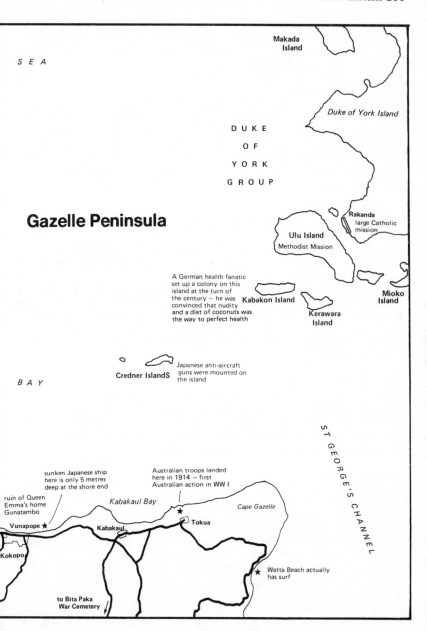

SEA

Makada
Island

Duke of York Island

D U K E

O F

Y O R K

G R O U P

Gazelle Peninsula

Rakanda
large Catholic
mission

Ulu Island
Methodist Mission

A German health fanatic
set up a colony on this
island at the turn of
the century — he was
convinced that nudity
and a diet of coconuts was
the way to perfect health

Kabakon Island

Mioko
Island

Kerawara
Island

Japanese anti-aircraft
guns were mounted on
the island

Credner IslandS

B A Y

S
T
G
E
O
R
G
E
'
S

C
H
A
N
N
E
L

sunken Japanese ship
here is only 5 metres
deep at the shore end

Australian troops landed
here in 1914 — first
Australian action in WW I

ruin of Queen
Emma's home
Gunatambo

Kabakaul Bay

Cape Gazelle

Vunapope ★

Kabakaul

Tokua

Kokopo

Watta Beach actually
has surf

to Bita Paka
War Cemetery

Queen Emma Relics
Very few traces of Queen Emma remain in the Rabaul area. Her stately residence, Gunantambu near Kokopo, was destroyed during the war — all you can find today is the impressive staircase which led from the Kokopo waterfront up to the house. The view she must have enjoyed is still magnificent, it's by the Ralum Club.

Her cemetery is a couple of km back towards Rabaul and has been allowed to become totally overgrown. It overlooks the Rabaul-Kokopo road and although the steps are easily negotiable you would have to know where they are to find them as there is no sign. All that remains of Queen Emma's grave is a cement slab with a hole in the centre — her ashes were stolen a few years after she died. The gravestone of her brother and of her lover Agostino Stalio, are in much better shape; the latter with a romantic inscription:

Oh for the touch of a vanished hand
and the sound of a voice which is still

About 1½ km north of here is her brother-in-law, Richard Parkinson's, cemetery, which is even more overgrown. It's called Kuradui after his plantation, but only the tombstone of Otto Parkinson, a suicide in the early 1900s, remains standing. Richard Parkinson is nowhere near as well known as his flamboyant sister, but he wrote some of the earliest works on New Guinea island anthropology and natural history, a book titled *Thirty Years in the South Seas* and was an enthusiastic botanist who planted many trees in the Rabaul-Kokopo area. His matmat, the local word for cemetery, is near Parkinson Point.

Coastwatcher's Lookout
Coastwatcher's lookout is just off the Vuruga road, which turns away from the coast a couple of km out of Rabaul towards Kokopo. It offers one of the best views in the area — you look out over Vulcan, the harbour and to the volcanoes beyond Matupit Island. There's a very tatty and badly preserved Zero fighter rotting away on a stand here.

Beaches & Diving
There is not much in the way of good swimming or diving in the harbour itself unless you're a keen wreck explorer and want to get down to some of the Japanese ships on the bottom. Otherwise the best swimming places are on the north coast or further round Blanche Bay. Pilapila, just across Tunnel Hill, is a popular beach spot and close to town. Submarine Base is an incredible place for scuba diving — the coral shelves gently away from the beach until about 20 metres from the shore, where you are hardly out of your depth, it suddenly drops straight down to 200 or more metres! Swimming over this incredible drop feels like leaping off a skyscraper, but not falling — or at least I imagine it might. Plenty of colourful coral and fishes, the Japanese used to provision submarines here during the war. At Takubar,

just beyond Vunapope, there is a Japanese ship which sunk right up against the shore — at one end it reaches to about five metres from the surface while at the other end it goes down quite a depth. There are several places in town where you can rent scuba diving gear or have air bottles refilled. Some of the best beaches are round the corner from Cape Gazelle, quite a drive from Rabaul.

Vunapope
Just beyond the town of Kokopo, Vunapope is the Catholic Mission centre and one of the largest mission establishments in PNG. Vunapope is pronounced as if it ended in a 'y' and means "place of the Catholics". The Catholics arrived in New Britain in 1881, only a few years after the pioneering Methodists, and at first established themselves at Nodup, on the north coast across from Rabaul. They soon moved round to Vunapope near Queen Emma's plantations.

Bita Paka
Bita Paka War Cemetery is several km inland, the turnoff is a little beyond Vunapope. The graves of over 1000 Allied war dead from the New Britain area are lined up here, including many Indians who came to the Rabaul area as prisoners-of-war captured in Singapore. There are also memorials to the six Australian soldiers killed in the capture of the German WW I radio station at Bita Paka, to the crew of the Australian submarine that disappeared off the New Britain coast in the same operation, and to the civilians who went down with the *Montevideo Maru*.

Getting around the Gazelle
The Gazelle is the one place in New Britain with a good network of roads and transport facilities. Lots of PMVs run back, forth and around with fares starting from the usual 20t. There are also plenty of taxis and Air Niugini has a free bus service for their flights. Avis/Nationwide rent Geminis in Rabaul — K29 per day with unlimited kms. Blue Star Hirecars, office next to the ANZ bank on Mango Avenue (tel 92 2063, 92 1951) have a variety of cars starting from K14 a day plus 10t a km for a Mazda 1300.

DUKE OF YORK ISLANDS
The Duke of York group is about 30 km east of Rabaul, approximately midway between New Britain and New Ireland. Duke of York Island is the largest in the group but there are also a cluster of smaller islands. This was the site for the first mission station in the area, the place where Queen Emma started her remarkable career, and is also blessed with some beautiful beaches and scenery. It's relatively easy to get there by small ships from Rabaul and there are also flights across.

Port Hunter, at the northern tip of the main island, was the landing point for the Rev Brown in 1875 and the site of his first mission. You can still see the crumbling chimney of his house, overlooking the entrance to Port Hunter's circular bay. Near the beach is the cemetery where most of his assistants ended up.

Mioko, where Emma and Thomas Farrell established their first trading station, is a small island off the other end of Duke of York Island. Mioko Harbour is a large stretch of sheltered water between Mioko and Duke of York. Kabakon, closest of the group to Rabaul, has a rather curious history — a German health fanatic named Engelhardt established a nudist colony here in 1903. He was soon dubbed Mr Kulau (Mr Coconut) by the locals for not only did he consider nudism was the path to perfect health but he supplemented it with a diet of nothing but coconuts. At one time he had 30 or more followers on the island, but coconuts must get boring, even with nude bodies added, and he died alone just before WW I.

WEST NEW BRITAIN
Surprisingly, considering the high level of development and many places of interest in East New Britain, the rest of the island is relatively untouched and little developed. The places there are to see are mainly around the Williamez Peninsula where the roads of West New Britain are concentrated. Almost all of the rest of the island — away from the Gazelle Peninsula in East New Britain and the Williamez Peninsula plus the stretch of coast from there through Hoskins — is huge tracts of virgin rainforest.

TALASEA & THE WILLIAMEZ PENINSULA
The pretty little town of Talasea looks across the bay with its many islands from Williamez Peninsula. The peninsula is an active volcanic region, there are even bubbling mud holes in Talasea. Lake Dakataua at the end of the projection, was formed in a colossal eruption in 1884. On Pangula Island, across from Talasea, there is a whole collection of thermal performers (geysers and fumaroles) in the Valley of Wabua. The name means "Valley of Hot Water" and is only a short walk from the shore.

KIMBE
Situated about 40 km from Talasea and the same distance from Hoskins, Kimbe is the provincial HQ and the major centre for oil palm production in West New Britain. Oil palms are a much more efficient producer of oil than coconuts but require a much larger investment for processing. There is a large project underway along this fertile coastal strip of West New Britain to successfully exploit oil palms.

Accommodation in Kimbe
The new *Palm Lodge Motel* has 35 rooms which cost K27 single, K50 double, K54 twin — including all meals. There is also a tavern and a

Palm Lodge Motel
Bookings: PO Box 32,
Kimbe
Tel: 93 5001

club in Kimbe. You can arrange visits from the hotel to nearby hot springs or to inspect oil palm production.

Rooms: 35 assorted
Tariff: K27 sgl, K50 dbl incl all meals.

HOSKINS
The coastal road from Talasea runs through Kimbe to Hoskins where the main airport in West New Britain is located. The small town is a major logging and oil palm production centre. There are some hot springs near Hoskins.

Accommodation in Hoskins
The *Hoskins Hotel* has nine twin rooms which cost K16 single, K20 twin for bed and breakfast. Rooms are fan-cooled, there is a licensed restaurant and also, of course, the Hoskins Club.

Hoskins Hotel
Bookings: c/o Post Office, Hoskins
Tel: VHF 93 0145
Rooms: 9 twins
Tariff: K16 sgl, K20 twin, bed & breakfast

OTHER
Mt Langila, on Cape Gloucester at the south-western end of the island, is still active and hiccups and rumbles every few months. Tribes inland from Talasea used to bind their babies' heads to make them narrow and elongated. Other tribes near Kandrian used Malay-style blowguns to hunt birds and fruit bats. The wooden "darts" are shot through a long bamboo tube. Pomio has been noted for its cargo cult style belief in their land being turned into some sort of earthly paradise. The Kimbe islanders, off the Williamez Peninsula, are expert sailors and canoe builders who live on the islands but tend gardens on the mainland. The Witu Islands, west of the Williamez Peninsula, are about 80 km off the coast and are of volcanic origin. Unea has a peak 738 metres high while Garove, the largest island, has a beautiful bay formed when the sea broke into its extinct crater. During the first ten years of this century a smallpox epidemic virtually wiped out the people on these fertile and quite heavily populated islands.

GETTING THERE & GETTING AROUND
Air Niugini fly to Rabaul in East New Britain and to Hoskins in West New Britain. Rabaul will take F-28s but improvements must first be made to the airport -- the approach to Rabaul's runway is highly spectacular since Matupit Volcano is in a direct line from the end of the runway. Aircraft have to make a sharp turn as they approach to land and this is not acceptable practice with the F-28 jets! Buying land to improve the runway approach has been difficult due to the land shortage in the area and the resulting reluctance to sell.

There are two flights Rabaul-Port Moresby on most days of the week, 2 hours 15 minutes flight time at a cost of K86. There are also flights to Lae (K59), Kavieng (K24) on to Wewak (K90), Kieta (K49) and Hoskins (K30).

From Hoskins there are direct flights to Rabaul and to Lae — Hoskins-Lae costs K36, Hoskins-Port Moresby K74.

Talair has flights to and from a number of centres around New Britain. There are also quite a few connections from Rabaul to New Ireland and its associated islands — Rabaul-Namatanai costs K18, it's an up-then-down again flight. Costs from Hoskins include Cape Gloucester (K40), Gasmata (K22), Kandrian (K28), Open Bay (K38), Finschhafen (in Morobe Province) (K59).

Rabaul is also a good place to look for boats to ports all over PNG. There are many local shipping services and even a couple of regular ones. Some possibilities:

Rabaul-Kimbe-Lae operated by Coastal Shipping, using the barge *Huris*. Weekly departures on Tuesday at 2 pm, gets to Lae midnight Thursday, departs midnight Friday and gets to Rabaul at 2 pm on Sunday. Cost is K25 deck, K36 cabin, including all meals.

Rabaul-Kimbe-Madang once a month departures on the *Simbang*. Cost is K38, company is Lutheran Shipping whose agent is Rabtrad NG.

Rabaul-Kieta check with Burns Philp Coastal Shipping and Kayel Shipping Company, cost is K12 to K16 deck class, there may be a cabin class.

Rabaul-Kavieng — irregular departures.

dukduk

North Solomons

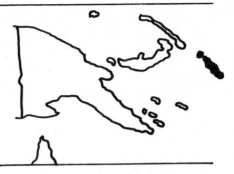

Area: 10,620 square km
Population: 110,000 (Buka 20,000)

The islands that comprise the North Solomons — Buka, Bougainville and a scattering of smaller islands — are not related geographically or ethnically to the other islands of Papua New Guinea. They are closely related to the neighbouring, independent Solomon Islands group — just as the name suggests. It's another piece of colonial manipulation that led to its inclusion in PNG. The major island, Bougainville, is green, rugged, little developed and yet provides a very considerable portion of PNG's gross national product due to the massive open cut copper mine at Panguna.

HISTORY

Bougainville acquired its very French name from the explorer Louis Antoine de Bougainville who sailed up the east coast in 1768. Near the narrow passage which separates Bougainville from Buka he came across natives paddling long, artistically carved canoes. They greeted him with cries of "Buka, Buka" which de Bougainville promptly named their island. Actually "buka" simply means "who" or "what" — a very reasonable question to ask! Of course de Bougainville was not the first European to drop by, Torres had also noted the place over a century earlier in 1606.

It was a hundred years later that the first attempt at establishing permanent contact took place when Catholic missionaries tried to set up a station at Kieta. On their first attempt they were firmly driven away but on their second try they were more successful. Later the Germans set up copra plantations on the fertile volcanic soil of Bougainville's coast but the Bougainvilleans had a reputation for being "difficult" and although the country was widely explored by the later Australian administration, at the start of WW II the only development was still on the coast. Until 1898, Bougainville and Buka were still considered as politically part of the Solomons group, which was a British possession, but at that time they were traded off with Germany — the Germans added them to their New Guinea colony and in return the British had their ascendancy over Vavau in Tonga and the other islands in the Solomons confirmed.

In mid 1942 the Japanese arrived, swiftly defeated the Australians, and were still holding most of the island when the war ended. Buka in the north became an important air base and Shortland Island to the south of Bougainville, part of the Solomons group, was a major naval base. In the attack on Guadalcanal their ships moved down the "slot", the channel of water between the two groups of the Solomons. Buin was an equally important base for ground troops.

Bougainville was another place where the coastwatchers scored some notable successes, particularly during the battle for Guadalcanal. Jack Read, a District Officer, and Paul Mason, a plantation owner, retreated into the jungle after the Japanese occupation. Read watched over Buka Passage, near his former station, while Mason set himself up near Buin in the south. Bomber aircraft bound from Rabaul passed over Buka and Buin while the fighters were based right at Buka. The coastwatchers were thus able to give the Allied forces a two-hour warning of an impending air strike. The result to Japanese air-power was devastating for: "The coastwatchers saved Guadalcanal and Guadalcanal saved the Pacific". Paul Mason and Jack Read both, miraculously, survived the war despite determined efforts by the Japanese to track them down.

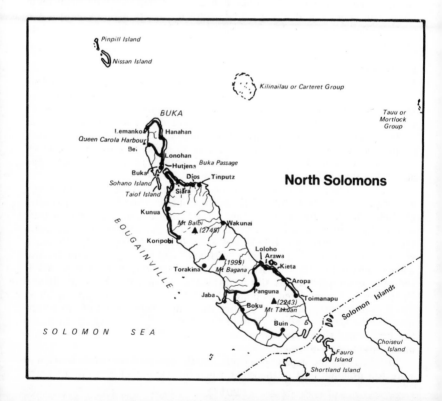

In November 1943, American troops captured the west coast port of Torokina and in 1944 Australian forces started to fight their way south towards Buin. Fortunately, the war ended before they came to grips with the main Japanese concentration. Nevertheless the cost of the war in Bougainville was staggering. Of 80,000 Japanese troops only 23,000 were finally taken prisoner at the end of the war. 20,000 are thought to have been killed in action and the remaining 37,000 died in the jungles of disease and starvation.

After the war Bougainville went back to its sleepy copra plantation style of life. The district HQ was transferred from Kieta to Sohano in Buka Passage but found its way back to Kieta in 1960. Then in 1964 the copper discovery at Panguna revolutionised Bougainville and formed the basis for PNG's remarkably healthy economy. Over K400 million was invested in the development of the mine and its ancillaries and the district HQ has been transferred from Kieta to Arawa, the main dormitory town for the mine.

The Panguna mine has had some interesting political as well as economic effects. In the lead up to Independence, Bougainville was a strong part of the push for an independent grouping of the Bismarck archipelago islands. That plan quickly faded but around Independence time strong Bougainville secessionist movements sprang up and for a time it seemed like they just might pull it off. But, their "difficult" reputation notwithstanding, the Bougainvilleans have now taken their place in Papua New Guinea although it is probably no coincidence that the North Solomons Province was the first to have its own local provincial government.

GEOGRAPHY

Bougainville is about 200 km long and 60 to 100 km wide and covered in wild, generally impenetrable jungle. There are two major mountain ranges — in the south the Crown Prince Range and in the north the higher Emperor Range. The highest mountain is Mt Balbi at 2745 metres; Balbi is an active volcano like its smaller and more spirited cousin Mt Bagana, and is visible from both coasts. The coastal areas are extremely fertile and most of the population is concentrated there.

Buka, in the north, is separated from Bougainville by a channel only 300 metres wide and a km long. Tidal currents rush through the passage at up to eight knots. In the south Buka is hilly, reaching 400 metres at its highest point. Buka is generally low-lying, apart from this southern hill region, and very wet — annual rainfall is over 600 cms (about 20 feet). There are many coral islands off its south and west coast.

PEOPLE

The people of Bougainville and Buka are often collectively referred to as Bukas, the early German colonisers favoured them due to their energy and abilities. The Bougainville people are instantly recognisable anywhere in PNG due to their extremely dark skins, said to be the blackest in the world. Today their relative affluence has, like the Tolai of East New Britain, led to a reluctance to perform the dull work on copra plantations and copralabourers are imported from other parts of the country.

Fishing
People on the islands north-west of Buka Passage still occasionally fish by the unique kite and spider web method. A woven palm leaf kite is towed behind a canoe and a lure, made of a wad of spider webs, is skillfully bounced along the surface of the sea. Garfish, leaping at the lure, would get their teeth entangled in the web and were then hauled in.

KIETA

Kieta, and nearby Arawa, are really just adjuncts to the Panguna mine today. Kieta is still a quiet little town since its tightly constrained situation led to the decision to build a complete new town on a former plantation up the coast. Arawa is 10 km north from Kieta and the airport, situated right on the coast, is 26 km south. Aropa Plantation, further south again, is an important experimental station where rubber and cocoa are also developed. North of Kieta, Ronovana Village is a beautiful picnic spot and used to be renowned for its carvings.

Accommodation in Kieta — The Top End

Kieta/Arawa is a bit of a disaster area for accommodation of any type. There are just two hotels — both of the PNG-expensive variety and catering for the Panguna mine people who can presumably afford it. The cheaper, marginally, is the *Hotel Kieta* in Kieta where singles cost K20, doubles K30. Rooms are air-con, self-contained, with fridges and tea/coffee making facilities. There's a bar, video TV lounge and restaurant with fairly terrible food from K5 a dish.

Hotel Kieta
Bookings: PO Box 31, Kieta
Tel: 95 6277
Rooms: 27 twin
Tariff: K20 sgl, K30 dbl

Davara Motel
Bookings: PO Box 241,
  Toniva Beach, Kieta
Tel: 95 6175
Cables: Davara
Rooms: 46
Tariff: K26 sgl, K36 dbl

The *Davara Motel* is 5 km closer to the airport at Toniva Beach — it boasts a swimming pool (the beach is unattractive) and the rooms also have piped in music. Singles here cost K26, doubles K36 and the restaurant is also more expensive — main dishes from K6 and up.

Between Kieta and Arawa there's a turnoff to the *Kobum Hotel*, a pleasant restaurant close to the beach. Arawa has a number of Haus Kai places and the big supermarket has a good takeaway food section.

Accommodation in Kieta — the Bottom End

Very chancy — right at the point, just the airport side of the Kieta docks, is the Rigu Catholic Boys School and right beside it is St Michael's mission. The mission has rooms with cooking facilities for just K2 a night — but they are almost always full. There's also a guest house at the school but that too is "always" full. So you've got to be lucky.

BOUGAINVILLE COPPER — PANGUNA

High in the centre of Bougainville is one of the world's major man-made holes in the ground — Bougainville Copper's gigantic open cut mine at Panguna. Back in 1964 a geological expedition walked into this area and ascertained that there were possibly very large copper deposits. By 1967 the investigations were sufficiently advanced for an access road to be cut from Kobuna on the coast up to Panguna. Progress from that point was rapid — in 1969 construction of the mining project started, advance sales of the copper production were made, the temporary road was upgraded and port facilities constructed at Arawa. At its peak period, before the mine started commercial operation in 1972, 10,000 people were employed in construction and preparation.

Today 4,000 people work for Bougainville Copper of whom approximately one in four are expatriates. Some of the workers live in the Panguna "company town", but in addition a full sized satellite town has sprung up on the coast at Arawa and has become the North Solomon's government centre. The mine is a mainstay of the PNG economy with annual sales of around K200 million.

The mine is a huge circular depression where gigantic mechanical shovels tear great hunks of ore and waste up and drop it into collosal dump trucks — each with a capacity of 155 tons! Each year 70 million tons may be moved, approximately half of which is waste and the balance is processed to produce about 200,000 tons of concentrate. The copper comprises less than 1% of the original ore and as the mine is dug deeper the concentration of copper is gradually falling. The crude ore is first crushed then fed to the ball mills where it is ground, with progressively smaller steel balls, then passed on to the separator where it is chemically treated until the copper concentrate is about 30% copper and is pumped as a liquid slurry down a 25 km pipeline to the coast. There it is dried out and loaded by conveyor onto ships for export. Japan takes about 50% of the annual production with Germany and Spain as the 2nd and 3rd biggest customers.

Although the percentage of gold and silver in the ore is extremely small — less than a gm per tonne for gold, about 2 gm per tonne for silver — they make up a considerable part of the mine's earnings. The gold value is 30 to 40% of the annual total.

If you want to visit the mine 'phone 95 8022 and ask for public relations on extension 591. There are tours each morning and afternoon and they last about two hours. If you're unlucky, like me, you may find that the regular tour guide has disappeared — after ten minutes reading a Bougainville Copper annual report I could have told my "guide" more about the mine than he could tell me. If my pidgin were better that is. You've got to get up to Panguna from Kieta (39 km) or Arawa (29 km) but that's no problem. There are frequent PMV buses from Kieta to Arawa for 50t from where there are free company buses running up and down for each shift change. Or you can very easily hitch a ride up as there's a constant flow of vehicles. The road turns in from the coast a little beyond Arawa and climbs gently until about 12 km from Panguna where it starts climbing steeply and spectacularly with frequent hairpin bends. Stunning views on the way down. The road is paved all the way and is in great condition.

BUIN & ADMIRAL YAMAMOTO
Right in the south of the island, Buin is extremely wet during the November to April wet season. It is here that the finely made Buka baskets are woven — not, as the name might suggest, at Buka Island in the north. During the war, Buin was the site of a very large Japanese naval base from which ships made their dangerous runs down "the slot" to Guadalcanal. The area is packed with rusting relics of the war.

One of the most historically interesting wrecks is the aircraft of Admiral Isoroku Yamamoto — the architect of the attack on Pearl Harbour. On 18 April '43 he left in a Betty bomber, little realising that the Japanese naval code had been broken and that the Americans would be waiting for him near Buin. As his aircraft approached Buin the US P-38s pounced and scored an enormous psychological victory over the Japanese. The wreckage still lies in the jungle, only a few km off the Buin-Kangu Hill road.

In 1968, only 400 metres from the same road, an American Corsair fighter was discovered, its pilot still in the cockpit, where it had crashed in November '43. There are probably countless other similar wrecks scattered around the country — some of much more recent arrival.

BUKA PASSAGE
The narrow channel that separates Bougainville from Buka is steeped in history and legends and packed with beautiful islands. It's also thick with fish just waiting to be hauled out. Sohano Island, in the centre of the passage, was the district HQ from just after the war until 1960. There is a guest house on the island today. Nearby Tchibo Rock features in many colourful local legends. Saposa is a popular local picnic spot and an old meeting ground on the island is marked by traditionally carved posts.

BUKA
A crushed coral road runs up the east coast of Buka Island, connecting the

copra plantations. Construction of the road caused some local strife between the Local Government Council and the locally organised Hahalis Welfare Society centred around Hanahan. Both of them insisted that road construction was their prerogative and members of the society refused to pay the head tax. Even more colourful was their Hahalis baby farm in the '60s which had a certain flavour of organised prostitution about it. Read John Ryan's *The Hot Land* for the full story.

Hutjena, in the south-east, is the main town and site for the Buka airstrip. Queen Carola Harbour, on the west coast, is the main port in Buka.

Accommodation in Buka
The *Buka Luman Guest House* costs K20 a night including all meals and has a licensed restaurant. It's on Sohano Island in Buka Passage and reached by the ferry from Buka.

Buka Luman Soho Guest House
Bookings: PO Box 251, Buka Passage
Tel: 96 6057
Rooms: 4
Tariff: per person — K20 all meals

OUTER ISLANDS
There are a scattering of islands far away from Bougainville and Buka which, nevertheless, come under North Solomons jurisdiction. Some are as easily accessible from New Ireland as from the North Solomons.

Nuguria (Fead) Group
The 50 odd islands in the group have a total area of only five square km and a population of not much over 200 Polynesians. They are about 200 km east of New Ireland and a similar distance north of Buka.

Nukumanu (Tasman) Islands
Nukumanu is the largest island in the group with an area of less than three square km. They lie about 400 km north-east of Bougainville and much closer to the extensive Ontong Java Atoll south in the Solomon Islands. Population is about 300, pure Polynesians.

Kilinailau (Carteret) Group
Only 70 km north-east of Buka they comprise six islands on a 16 km circular atoll. The population of about 900 are Buka people who appear to have supplanted earlier Polynesian inhabitants.

Tau (Mortlock) Group
Situated 195 km north-east of Bougainville the ring shaped reef has about 20 islands, virtually mid-way on a line drawn from the Carteret to the Tasman Islands. The population of around 600 is predominantly Polynesian.

Nissan Islands
The Nissan Islands, an atoll about 16 km by 8 km, lie approximately 70 km

north-west of Buka. Nissan is the large elliptical shaped island with the smaller ones situated within its curve. The population of the low-lying group is about 3200 and Pinpill Island, a little further north, is included in the group. The textbook perfect atoll was totally evacuated during the war while a large American airbase was operated here. After the war vast quantities of supplies were dumped and thousands of drums of fuel were sold off at only 3c a gallon. There was no shortage of war surplus material in New Guinea.

ARTIFACTS

Brian Darcey's shop at Toniva Beach, just across from the Davara Motel, has a very good selection of artifacts from all over Papua New Guinea including some you may not see in other PNG artifact stores. The people running it seem very knowledgeable and have selected good items. It's especially interesting for the lesser known "island" art items from Bougainville, such as bows and arrows. Apart from the Buka baskets, you generally don't see very much from Bougainville.

Other interesting items include shell money from Malaita; fish, sharks and dolphins from the Solomons with bits of mother of pearl inlaid; and some beautiful work in mottled ebony from the Woodlark Islands. The Woodlark carvings are similar to the Trobriands but more intricately carved and better finished. Ebony bowls and flat "plaques" of fish or sea horses are popular subjects. The only catch is the prices here are on the steep side — if you're after something straightforward such as a Sepik mask you'll be paying well over the odds.

Buka baskets are made from jungle vine, the variation in colour is made by scraping the skin off the vine. They're amongst the best made baskets in the Pacific but with prices up towards K20 they're strictly tourist items now — rarely used for food holders as they were originally intended. The old carved wooden figures are now rarely made on Bougainville.

GETTING AROUND

Bougainville and Buka have sketchy road networks. On Buka there is an 84 km road up the east coast from Buka Passage to Kessa Point (Lemankoa) and another road across the island from Lonohan to Bei via Gagan River. From Kieta the coast road runs south via Aropa where the airport is situated to Toimanapu and this road will soon extend south to Buin.

Northwards the road from Kieta goes through Arawa to Loloho and turns inward to Panguna then drops down to Jaba on the other coast. It's an excellent road up to the Panguna mine with some spectacular views down to the east coast just before you reach the top of the range before Panguna. Beyond Panguna the road is nowhere near as good but before reaching Jaba on the west coast an intersection branches off south to Boku and Buin. In the north of Bougainville there is a road up the west coast from Koripobi and on the east coast from Dios.

Between Kieta and Arawa there are frequent PMVs and also south from Kieta. Between Arawa and the mine at Panguna there is a shuttle bus service at shift change times. It's easy to get a ride up there at any time since there is a constant flow of vehicles back and forth. Beyond Panguna it's rougher going, there are rivers to be forded which can be difficult after rain. Count on about K5 for a truck ride Kieta-Buin.

Bougair have an extensive network of flights around the North Solomons. It costs K14 to fly Kieta-Buin, K19 for Kieta-Buka. From Buka out to Nissan Island costs K25.

GETTING THERE
Air Niugini have at least one flight a day to or from Port Moresby, fare is K106 for the 1 hour 35 minute flight by F28. Flights to Rabaul, by F27, are also at least daily, cost K49 and take 1 hour 20 minutes direct or 1 hour 50 minutes via Buka. Buka-Rabaul costs K35.

There are reasonably frequent ships between Kieta and Rabaul, usual cost is K12 to K16 for deck class.

The Back Door from the North Solomons
Thanks to Ruediger Kurth for this information: You can fly with Air Niugini between Kieta and Honiara, the capital of the Solomons, for K44 and also between Moresby and Honiara for K122. The third level carrier Solair also island hops through the Solomons to Kieta if you want to keep closer to the surface, but if you've got time on your hands you can work your way along "the slot" from Honiara to Buin. One warning — this will certainly work out more expensive than just jumping on a plane.

Once a week there's a boat service from Honiara to Munda on New Georgia Island or to nearby Gizo Island, the Western Solomon's administrative capital. Fare is A$11 to A$14 depending which ship is operating the route. Coral Seas on Commonwealth St in Honiara are the operators of this service.

The extremely tatty *Saratoga* also operates this route and on to Shortland Island just south of Buin. It's so run down you may feel you're taking your life in your hands. In Munda you can stay at *Agnes Wigley's Rest House* for A$5 a night or look for her brother who also lets out rooms. Both are near the airport. It costs about A$40 to fly Munda-Kieta, again this will work out cheaper than continuing overland, but we're not doing this to save money are we? So take a boat, only about A$3, to Gizo and stay at the Council Rest House (only 50c a night) or the Government Rest House for A$3. There is also a shabby and over-priced hotel here.

Once a week the council boat *Lanalau* makes the day long trip from here to Koravou on Shortland Island. It costs A$7 and Koravou is the last place to collect a Solomons' exit stamp on your passport. There are closer islands to Bougainville but they do not have police posts. There is an extremely spartan, but free, rest house here. You have to get a canoe ride from here to

Buin and Friday afternoon or Saturday morning is your best bet as many people go across then to the Saturday market. As a passenger it will cost you A$3 to A$5, on other days if you decided to charter a canoe from the council you'd be up for about A$20 including fuel. The trip takes about 1½ rather wet hours.

Buin village is a few km inland from the coast, try the Chinese trade-store owner who may be going "to town". You've got one other problem in Buin — it's not a recognised entry point to PNG but if your passport and visa are in order and you present yourself to the "skuriti" you'll probably be waved through and told to get your passport stamped when you get to Kieta. You can change money at the Chinese shops in Buin.

Milne Bay

Area: 20,254 square km
Population: 128,500

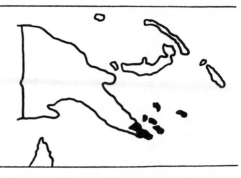

At the eastern end of Papua New Guinea, the Owen Stanley Range plunges into the sea and a scatter of islands dot the ocean for hundreds of km further out. This is the start of the Pacific proper — tiny atoll islands, coral reefs, waving palms and white beaches. Yet here there is one big difference to the better known areas of the Pacific — no visitors. When they say that the Trobriand Islands are the only place to have developed a tourist industry they should add that in a busy week there may be 20 visitors!

HISTORY
The islands of the Milne Bay Province have been well known to Pacific explorers for centuries and many of the islands still bear names related to those early explorers. The Louisiade Archipelago, for example, was named after Louis Vaez de Torres, who sailed through them way back in 1606. In 1793 Bruny D'Entrecasteaux donated his difficult name to the island group further north and west.

In 1873, Captain John Moresby, having a nose around New Guinea, discovered the deep inlet which he named Milne Bay after Alexander Milne, then the current Lord of the Admiralty. Moresby had earlier landed on Samarai Island and named it Dinner Island after his most recent meal; it must have been a memorable one. He also paused long enough to run up the flag and claim the whole area for Queen Victoria. Unfortunately the good Queen was not too keen on finding further places where the sun never set and, like other keen extenders of the Empire, his claim was repudiated.

Even before this time there had been attempts at permanent European settlements; a mission had been set up on Woodlark Island way back in 1847 but the islanders were extremely unenthusiastic about Christianity and the missionaries who survived their lack of enthusiasm soon departed. After Moresby's visit, traders and other missionaries followed and a thriving trade developed in pearl shells and bêche-de-mer, the large sea slugs which are a Chinese delicacy. The Milne Bay area also suffered from blackbirding, the forcible collection of "voluntary" labour for Queensland plantations.

In 1888, gold was discovered on Misima Island and the miners soon flooded in and, as in other parts of PNG, soon died like flies from the effects of disease, malnutrition and unfriendly natives. Misima was a non-starter in the gold stakes but a later find on Woodlark Island eventually produced nearly $1½ million of gold at a time when the price was much lower than it is today. With all this passing trade, plus a major missionary station, the island of Samarai had established itself as the major port and outpost in the region, a position it was to hold until after WW II.

Soon after the war spread to the Pacific, the Milne Bay area was to serve as the stage for the turning point conflict between Japanese and Allied forces. In the Battle of the Coral Sea, the Japanese rush south was abruptly halted. Although this was one of the classic naval battles the Japanese and American warships never came within 300 km of each other, the fighting was entirely conducted by aircraft. Some of the most violent dogfights took place high above Misima Island in the Louisiades. American losses were severe, but the Japanese fleet was crippled and never again played an effective role in the Pacific.

Despite this setback the Japanese were still intent upon the capture of Papua New Guinea and in July '42 they landed at Buna and Gona in the Northern Province and pressed south down the Kokoda Trail towards Moresby. In August they made a second landing in Milne Bay, in an attempt to take the eastern end of the island. Again, as in the Coral Sea conflict, the Allies had advance warning and a strong Australian force was waiting for them. Worse, for the Japanese, they had landed at Ahioma, too far round the bay, and had to slog through terrible swamps to meet the Australians and attempt to take the airstrip. This blunder contributed to their total defeat, the first time in the war that a Japanese amphibious assault had been repelled. Active fighting did not again encroach on the Milne Bay area, but Milne Bay itself became a huge US naval base through which hundreds of thousands of servicemen passed.

GEOGRAPHY

The mainland part of the province is extremely mountainous, for the eastern end of the Owen Stanley Range marches almost to the end of the island

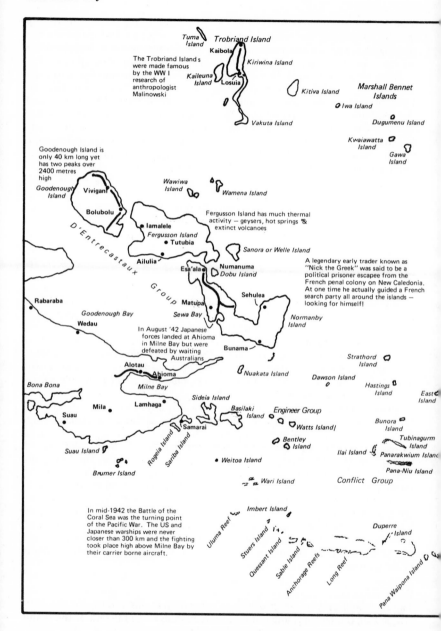

Tuma Island
Trobriand Island
Kaibola
Kiriwina Island

The Trobriand Islands were made famous by the WW I research of anthropologist Malinowski

Kaileuna Island
Losuia

Kitiva Island

Marshall Bennet Islands

Iwa Island

Dugumenu Island

Vakuta Island

Kwaiawatta Island

Gawa Island

Goodenough Island is only 40 km long yet has two peaks over 2400 metres high

Goodenough Island

Vivigani

Wawiwa Island

Wamena Island

Bolubolu

Iamalele

Fergusson Island has much thermal activity — geysers, hot springs & extinct volcanoes

Fergusson Island
Tutubia

Ailulia

Sanora or Welle Island

Esa'ala
Numanuma
Dobu Island

A legendary early trader known as "Nick the Greek" was said to be a political prisoner escapee from the French penal colony on New Caledonia. At one time he actually guided a French search party all around the islands — looking for himself!

Rabaraba

Goodenough Bay

Wedau

Matupa

Sehulea

Sewa Bay

In August '42 Japanese forces landed at Ahioma in Milne Bay but were defeated by waiting Australians

Normanby Island

Bunama

Alotau
Ahioma

Nuakata Island

Strathord Island

Dawson Island

Bona Bona

Milne Bay

Mila

Lamhaga

Sideia Island

Hastings Island

East Island

Suau

Samarai

Basilaki Island

Engineer Group

Watts Island

Bunora Island

Tubinagurm Island

Bentley Island

Ilai Island

Panarakwium Island

Suau Island

Rogeia Island
Sariba Island

Weitoa Island

Pana-Niu Island

Brumer Island

Wari Island

Conflict Group

In mid-1942 the Battle of the Coral Sea was the turning point of the Pacific War. The US and Japanese warships were never closer than 300 km and the fighting took place high above Milne Bay by their carrier borne aircraft.

Imbert Island

Uluma Reef

Stuers Island

Duperre Island

Quessant Island

Sable Island

Anchorage Reefs

Long Reef

Pana Waipona Island

Milne Bay

Woodlark Island had the first goldrush in Papua New Guinea towards the end of the last century — over $1,400,000 of gold was found

Madua Island

Kaurai
Kulumanadu
Woodlark Island

Guasopa

Cannac Island
Wabomat Island
Laughlan Group

Alcester Island

There are 160 named islands in the Milne Bay area , plus over 600 islets, atolls and reefs. 20,000 square km of land in 250,000 square km of water

During the 1880s and 1890s, "Blackbirding" was the scourge of the Milne Bay area and other parts of Papua New Guinea. Unscrupulous labour "recruiters" would forcibly carry off "voluntary" workers to conditions of near slavery in Queensland, Australia.

600 km off the eastern end of the PNG mainland only one 200 metre sandbar stands above water at high tide on the Pocklington Reef. In 1978 a $40 million Cannabis seizure in Australia led to a search for more on the hulls of wrecked ships on the reef

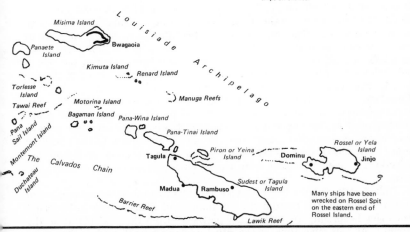

Misima Island
Louisiade
Panaete Island
Bwagaoia
Kimuta Island
Renard Island
Archipelago
Torlesse Island
Tawai Reef
Motorina Island
Manuga Reefs
Pana Sail Island
Bagaman Island
Pana-Wina Island
Montemont Island
Pana-Tinai Island
The
Calvados Chain
Tagula
Piron or Yeina Island
Dominu
Rossel or Yela Island
Jinjo
Duchateau Island
Madua
Rambuso
Sudest or Tagula Island
Barrier Reef
Lawik Reef

Many ships have been wrecked on Rossel Spit on the eastern end of Rossel Island.

before plunging straight to the sea. It is the islands that are of greatest interest in Milne Bay and there are plenty of them — 160 named islands plus more than 600 islets and atolls and untold numbers of reefs waiting to trap the unwary sailor. The islands are enormously varied, from tiny dots barely breaking the surface of the sea to larger islands such as Fergusson and Goodenough in the D'Entrecasteaux Group. The highest mountain on Goodenough rises to over 2400 metres and there are so many other lesser peaks that for its size this is one of the most mountainous places on earth. By contrast the Trobriand Islands are virtually flat with hardly anything that could be called a hill on the whole island group.

The Milne Bay Islands are divided into seven main groups — Trobriands, Woodlark, Laughlan, Louisiade Archipelago, the Conflict Group, the Samarai Group and the D'Entrecasteaux Group.

THE MAINLAND
The district headquarters was transferred from Samarai Island to Alotau on the mainland in 1968 — principally because access to Samarai is only possible by sea and the island was already crowded to its limits. Any further expansion had to be on the mainland. Alotau is a new township, on the site of the fighting for Milne Bay and many reminders of that brief but bitter struggle can still be seen. The Alotau airport is at Gurney, 15 km away. There will eventually be a road linking Alotau with Rabaraba on the north coast, via Dogura, an Anglican mission centre since 1891. Across Milne Bay from Alotau is Discovery Bay, where Captain Moresby spent several days during his 1873 visit. The mysterious "moonstones" in the hills behind this bay are though to have some pre-historic significance.

Kula Ring
Despite modern technology, the trading of the Kula Ring has still not completely died out although the sea voyages in outrigger canoes are unlikely to be as lengthy as in "the time before". This traditional, ritual, exchange of goods served to bind islands together in much the same way that yams formed a link between villages and clans. Two articles are traded in the ring — red shell money necklaces and decorated armlets made from cone shells.

The ring extends right around Milne Bay, including the Trobriands, Woodlark, Misima, the D'Entrecasteaux Group and around Samarai. The exchange between islands on the "ring" are purely ritual, since the goods rarely go out of the ring and are always eventually traded on to the next island in the circuit. Eventually they would get right back to their starting point, although this would take many years. The ring goods go in opposite directions — shell necklaces were traded clockwise, armlets counter-clockwise.

Today traders on the ring are more likely to make their voyages on board modern ships but the custom still continues and villagers from every island still offer hospitality to their "ring partners" from the next island on the circuit. At the same time as the ritual exchanges were made, other more mundane items were also traded — pottery, food, baskets — but not with your "ring partner".

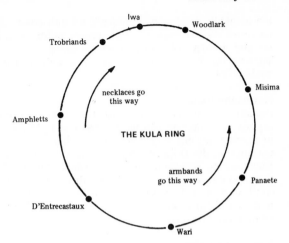

THE KULA RING

necklaces go this way

armbands go this way

Iwa · Woodlark · Trobriands · Misima · Amphletts · Panaete · D'Entrecastaux · Wari

Accommodation in Alotau

The 11 room *Masurina Lodge* charges K11 per person room only, K14 for bed & breakfast or K22 with all meals. Diving trips can be organised by the lodge or tours to nearby village, out to Samarai Island or to the local pearl farm.

Masurina Lodge
Address: PO Box 5, Alotau
Tel: 527
Rooms: 6 sgl, 5 dbl or twin
Tariff: per person — K22
all meals, K11 bed only

THE D'ENTRECASTEAUX GROUP

The three comparatively large islands of the D'Entrecasteaux Group are separated from the north coast of the mainland only by a narrow strait. They are extremely mountainous and flying on the Air Niugini flight between Alotau and Kiriwina in the Trobriands you pass directly over them.

Goodenough Island

Furthest north-west of the group, Goodenough is amazingly mountainous with a high central range that has two peaks topping 2400 metres. Quite something for an island only about 40 km long from end to end. There are fertile coastal plains flanking the mountain range and a road runs around the north-east coast through Vivigani, the main station and site of the major airstrip in the group. In the centre of the island there is a large stone, covered in mysterious black and white paintings, which is said to have power over the yam crops and is regarded with fearful wonder by the islanders.

Fergusson Island

Fergusson is the central island in the group and the largest in size. Although it is mountainous, it pales in comparison to nearby Goodenough. The highest mountain here is only 2073 metres with two other lower ranges from which flow the island's many rivers and streams. Fergusson's large population is mainly concentrated along the south coast. Fergusson is notable for its active thermal region — hot springs, bubbling mud pools, spouting geysers and extinct volcanoes. Thermal springs can be found at Deidei and at Iamalele on the west coast. There is a Methodist mission at Salamo on the south coast.

Normanby Island
Separated from Fergusson by the narrow and spectacular Dobu Passage, the highest mountain on Normanby is a mere 1158 metres. There are a number of mission stations dotted around the island, Esa'ala is the district HQ at the entrance to the Dobu Passage. Actually in the passage is tiny, fertile Dobu Island where the Methodists established their first Milne Bay area mission, the mountains rise sheer on both sides of the strait. In the middle of the south-west coast is Sewa Bay, used by Allied warships during WW II and a port of call for small inter-island ships today. There are strange, unexplained rock carvings around the bay.

Amphlett Islands
The tiny Amphlett Islands are scattered to the north of the main D'Entrecasteaux Group. The people here are part of the Kula Ring trading cycle and they make some extremely fine and very fragile pottery.

THE TROBRIAND ISLANDS
The Trobriand Islands lie to the north of the D'Entrecasteaux Group and are the most accessible and interesting islands in the Milne Bay area. They take their name from Denis de Trobriand, an officer on D'Entrecasteaux's expedition. They are the only island in the province which Air Niugini fly to, although the airstrip at Vivigani on Goodenough is also able to take F-27s. The Trobriands are coral islands and very low-lying, in complete contrast to their southern neighbours. Largest of the group is Kiriwina, where the HQ is Lousia.

The Trobriands were made famous after WW I by the work of German anthropologist Bronislaw Malinowski. One of the stories about Herr Malinowski is that at the start of the war he was offered a choice of internment in Australia or banishment to the remote Trobriands. He sensibly chose the latter and his studies of the islanders, their intricate trading rituals, their yam cults and, to many people most interesting of all, their active sexual practises, led to his classic series of books — *Argonauts of the South Pacific, Coral Gardens and their Magic* and *The Sexual Life of Savages*.

The Trobriand islanders have strong Polynesian characteristics, many of them are very handsome people and unlike almost any other part of Papua New Guinea they have developed hereditary chieftans who continue their local aristocracy to this day. The soil of the Trobriands is very fertile and great care is lavished on the gardens, particularly the yam gardens which have great importance to the Trobriands. The villages are all laid out in a similar pattern — which you can see most clearly from the air as you fly in

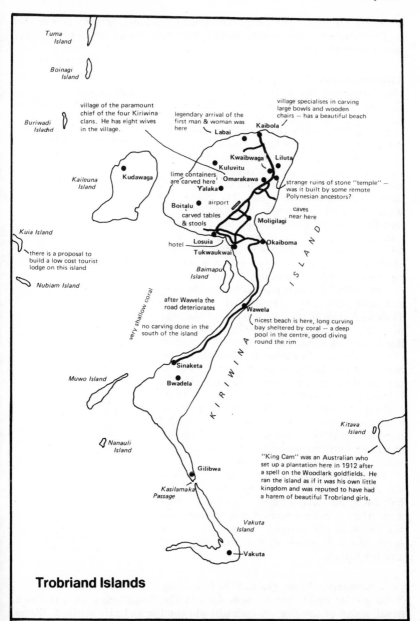

Tuma Island

Boinagi Island

Buriwadi Island

village of the paramount chief of the four Kiriwina clans. He has eight wives in the village.

legendary arrival of the first man & woman was here

village specialises in carving large bowls and wooden chairs — has a beautiful beach

Labai

Kaibola

Kaileuna Island

Kudawaga

Kwaibwaga

Liluta

Kuluvitu

lime containers are carved here

Omarakawa

Yalaka

strange ruins of stone "temple" — was it built by some remote Polynesian ancestors?

Boitalu

airport

carved tables & stools

Moligilagi

caves near here

Kuia Island

hotel

Losuia

Tukwaukwai

Okaiboma

I S L A N D

there is a proposal to build a low cost tourist lodge on this island

Baimapu Island

Nubiam Island

very shallow coral

after Wawela the road deteriorates

Wawela

no carving done in the south of the island

nicest beach is here, long curving bay sheltered by coral — a deep pool in the centre, good diving round the rim

K I R I W I N A

Sinaketa

Muwo Island

Bwadela

Kitava Island

Nanauli Island

Gilibwa

"King Cam" was an Australian who set up a plantation here in 1912 after a spell on the Woodlark goldfields. He ran the island as if it was his own little kingdom and was reputed to have had a harem of beautiful Trobriand girls.

Kasilamaka Passage

Vakuta Island

Vakuta

Trobriand Islands

or out of Kiriwina. The village yam houses form an inner ring, surrounded by the villagers' outer sleeping houses, the whole lot encircled by a ring of trees and vegetation.

Accommodation in the Trobriands

The *Kiriwina Lodge* is the only real hotel on Kiriwina Island, atlhough there is talk about staying in villages or building some new, cheaper lodges. Meanwhile the Kiriwina Lodge is on the coast, a km or so from Losuia, the main town. The lodge has five double or twin rooms along a verandah, two self contained doubles and a new block of four twins sharing central toilet and shower facilities. The rooms are straightforward, without air-conditioning or fans (which is no problem since the Trobriands seem to be generally cool and breezy). Costs are K25 single, K40 double including all meals. Meals are filling and the bar will stay open at night longer than you can stay awake.

Kiriwina Lodge
Bookings: PO Box 2, Losuia
Rooms: 14
Tariff: K23 sgl, K38 to K42 twin, incl all meals

The lodge has a fair reputation for the sassy girls who work there — appropriately attired in Trobriand grass skirts (tasol) much of the time of course. Its biggest drawback, from the visitor's point of view, is its location. It's right on the waterfront with a green and pleasant garden running down to the water, but on the side of the island where the water is shallow and mainly swampy. Good beaches are a long way away, not within walking distance at all. So it may be a pleasant place to laze around in but you'll need wheels if you want to get around and see things or find the sea and sand which tropical islands are supposed to be all about.

Tours to the beaches and other attractions are arranged in the lodge's minibus — K5 for half day tours, K10 all day. You'll often have a bit of local culture when a dance is put on at the lodge in the evening. Barbecues on the lawn and Polynesian style mumu feasts are another feature.

Local Customs — Yams, Sex and the Kula Ring

Yams are far more than a staple food in the Trobriands — they're also a ritual, a sign of prestige, an indicator of expertise and a tie between villages and clans. The quality and size of the yams you grow is a matter of considerable importance. Many hours can be spent on discussions of your ability as a yam cultivator and to be known as a *Tokwaibagula*, a "good gardener", is a mark of high ability and prestige.

The yam cult reaches its high point at the harvest time — usually July or August. The yams are first dug up in the gardens and before transporting them back to the village they must be displayed, studied and admired in the gardens. At the appropriate time the yams are carried by the men back to the village with the women guarding the procession. This is a time of sexual freedom for the normally faithful wives and any man from another village who foolishly wanders too close can be attacked, robbed, beaten and even gang-raped! Sounds unlikely, but Malinowski said they managed it.

yam house

In the villages the yams are again displayed, in circular piles before the next stage takes place — the filling of the yam houses. Again there are extended rituals to be observed and it is here that the tie between villages takes place. Each man has a yam house for each of his wives and it is his brother-in-law's responsibility (in other words his wife's clan's) to fill his yam house. The chief's yam house is always the first to be filled. So yams are not merely a food — they're also part of a complicated annual ritual and an important and ongoing connection between villages.

Sex

For married women the yam harvesting time is an occasion for unusual sexual promiscuity — an activity the Trobriand islanders have plenty of experience of in their younger years. The place must be a Christian missionary's nightmare because promiscuity is not just condoned it's actually encouraged. A women is expected to have as many partners as possible from puberty until marriage — when she settles down with the partner finally chosen as compatible. It is said that despite all this activitiy few children are born to women without permanent partners although that seems scarcely believable — and there are plenty of kids in all the Trobriand villages.

Malinowski's weighty tome on their sexual habits, with its detailed analysis of Trobriand customs (which led to it being dubbed the "Island of Love") — their free and easy manners, their good looks and the standard Trobriand women's wear of a short grass skirt plus, perhaps, a flower in the hair, led to the general idea that the Trobriands were some sort of sexual paradise. It's hardly that for a visitor since freedom of choice is the basis of Trobriand life and why choose some ugly, pale *dim dim* (local language for a whitey). It's worth remembering too, if you want to do things the local way, that there are only two "approved" positions for intercourse in the Trobriands. A side by side position is used where space is limited — as in the bachelors' house — but in the preferred position the male squats on his heels and the female lies on her back and spreads her legs over his hips. This is said to give both partners the maximum freedom of movement. The western missionary position is reckoned to be far too restrictive on the women.

Male islanders leave home when they reach puberty and move into the village *bukumatula* or bachelor house. Here they are free to bring their partners back at any time although preference is usually given to places with a little more privacy — like a quiet garden.

Artifacts in the Trobriands
By far the best known artifacts in the Milne Bay area, although not the only ones, are the Trobriand carvings. Like other parts of PNG, certain villages tend to specialise in certain styles and types of carvings. In general they're more highly polished and have a more modern appearance than PNG art in general. Curiously it is only in the north of Kiriwina that the people carve.

Some of the specialities include bowls — popular for use as salad or fruit bowls. They often have decorative rims or flat surrounds carved like fish or turtles — with shells for eyes. Prices range from K3 for a small one up to K15 or even more for large ones; much more away from the Trobriands. Carved statues are usually delicate and elongated with curiously convoluted figures — a woman with a tree kangaroo perched on her head and a crocodile balanced on its tail behind her, for example. The walking sticks, which are particularly well finished, are simply a development of these carvings. There are also some squat little carvings — particularly of coupling pigs. Occasionally they do some finely carved erotic scenes, but these are rarely seen.

Then there are stools — solid circular ones with carved figures holding up the seats. They cost from only about K8 in the Trobriands but are rather heavy for carrying away. Three legged tables are also popular. Lime spatulas, carved gourds for use as lime containers, and wooden chains are other items you may see. Unfortunately the ebony wood which some of the finest Trobriand work was carved from is now very rare. Nor did I see any of the beautifully carved ebony Afro-combs while I was in the Trobriands.

Traditionally some of the best carving went into the magnificent canoe prows, particularly those used for the Kula ring trading ceremonies. This *Massim* style of carving can also be seen on important yam house frontages.

On the non-carving side you can get shells and shell money although the latter is likely to be very expensive. Beware of plastic "shell" money. The colourful grass skirts also make interesting buys.

Some Interesting Things to Say

My surname, in the Trobriands language, has a rather unfortunate translation. To an islander I'm Tony Cunt! Once they'd got over the sheer amazement that anybody could be so dumb as to call himself Wheeler (or Wila) the girls at the Kiriwina Lodge took great pleasure in calling me Wila as frequently as possible. Amy in particular. Just so you have your sexual terminology all lined up OK before you get there, remember that it is:

female:	her wila	male:	his kwila
	my wiga		my kwiga
	your wim		your kwim

If you'd like something nice to whisper in your girl friend's ear try, "yoku tage kuwoli nunum; kwunpisiga" or when things get a bit heaver try "wim, kasesam!" Or for female readers if you want to insult your man just shout out "kaykukupi kwim". I've always had this urge to write an R-rated travel guide. You can further enhance your questionable Trobriand phrase store at festivals during the yam harvesting season when islanders sing songs of amazing vulgarity known as *mweki mweki*.

WOODLARK ISLAND

The people of Woodlark Island are Melanesians similar to the people on the eastern end of the mainland. Their island is a continuous series of hills and valleys and lightly populated. Woodlark was the site for the biggest goldrush in the country until the later discovery of gold at Edie Creek near Wau. A form of "greenstone", similar although inferior to the greenstone or jade of New Zealand, was also found here and made into axes and ceremonial stones.

Today the people are renowned for their beautiful wood carvings made of mottled ebony. Since there is less demand for their work than that of the more touristed Trobriands, due to their isolation, the carvings tend to be extremely well done. Kulumadau is the main centre although there is now an airstrip at Guasopa. Woodlark is east of the Trobriands and north of the Louisiade Islands. It takes its name from the Sydney ship *Woodlark* which passed by in 1836 although the real name is Murua. The Laughlan Group is a handful of tiny islands and islets 64 km east of Woodlark and conveniently considered with it.

LOUISIADE ARCHIPELAGO

The Louisiade Archipelago received its name after Louis Torre's 1606 visit but it was probably known to Chinese and Malay sailors much earlier as there are distinct traces of Asian mixture. The name was originally applied to the whole string of islands including the group now known as the D'Entrecasteaux.

Sudest or Tagula Island
Largest island in the archipelago, Sudest had a small goldrush at about the same time as Woodlark. It consists of a similar series of valleys and hills. highest of which is Mt Rattlesnake at 915 metres.

Rossel Island
Most westerly of the islands — if you discount uninhabited Pocklington Reef — Rossel's rugged coastline ends at Rossel Spit which has had more than its fair share of shipwrecks.

Misima
Mountainous Misima Island is the most important in the group with the district HQ at Bwagaoia. Mt Oiatau at 1037 metres is the highest peak on the island. Misima too had its gold days although this took place between the wars, much later than on the other islands of Milne Bay. During the brief span when Papua was a British colony rather than an Australian one, the people of Misima were thought of as the most "dangerous and difficult" in the country. Today Misima has about half of the total population of the archipelago.

Calvados Chain & Conflict Group
The long chain of islets and reefs between Sudest and the mainland make navigation through the Milne Bay area an exacting and often dangerous operation. None of the islands are of any great size. To the west they terminate with the three islands of the Engineer Group.

Accommodation in the Louisiades
The *Bwagaoia Guest House* in Misima has three rooms with beds for eight people. Cost is K15 a night including all meals.

SAMARAI
The tiny island of Samarai, it is only 24 hectares in area, was long the provincial HQ and is still the commercial centre and main port despite its governmental role being taken over by Alotau on the mainland. Samarai is only 5 km from the mainland and fairly easily reached by launch from Alotau — which is some distance around the coast on Milne Bay. The launch meets every Air Niugini flight and takes about four hours for the crossing. There are also regular shipping services from Port Moresby which is 400 km to the west.

Samarai lies on China Strait, so named by Captain Moresby because he considered it would be the most direct route from the east coast of Australia to China. It was one of the most attractive settlements in the Pacific and despite being totally burnt out in 1942 by Japanese air raids it is still an interesting little place. A road encircles the island but you can stroll right round it in 20 minutes!

There are a number of nearby islands you can conveniently visit from Samarai. The Kwato Mission is on a small island only 20 minutes out by boat. It was one of the earliest mission establishments in Papua and functions as a busy boat building centre. At tiny Pearl Island, squeezed between the mainland and Sariba Island, there is, as you might expect, a pearl farm where cultured pearls are produced. Deka Deka, another tiny islet, is a popular beach and picnic spot as is nearby Logea Island. The small cluster of the Wari Islands, 45 km from Samarai, is another boat building centre and the people there are also fine potters.

Accommodation in Samarai

The *Samarai Guest House* charges K20 per person all inclusive. They can arrange trips to nearby islands.

Samarai Guest House
Bookings: PO Box 29,
   Samarai
Tel: Samarai 258
Rooms: 2 twin
Tariff: K20 per person incl
   all meals

CLIMATE

The weather in Milne Bay is very unpredictable, as I discovered when I was there! Rainstorms can be sudden, unexpected and heavy, while high winds can quickly make the sea very rough. November to January generally has the best and most consistent weather while March to June can generally be counted on to be less windy.

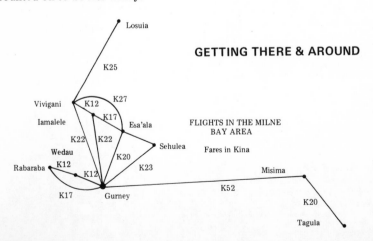

GETTING THERE & AROUND

FLIGHTS IN THE MILNE BAY AREA

Fares in Kina

There are Air Niugini connections from Port Moresby to Gurney (the airport for Alotau) five times a week and to Losuia, in the Trobriands, twice a week. Air fares are Port Moresby-Gurney K41, Port Moresby-Losuia K51 and Gurney-Losuia K28.

Talair have a network of flights around many of the 21 airstrips in the Milne Bay Province. The chart on the previous page details some of the connections.

Of course the ideal way to explore Milne Bay would be by sea and there are plenty of ships moving around the islands. It's just a matter of patience, waiting for one to come by. Samarai is the major port in Milne Bay Province.